Paths To Victory

Ex Líbrís

Paths To Victory

A History and Tour Guide of the Stone's River, Chickamauga, Chattanooga, Knoxville, and Nashville Campaigns

JIM MILES

RUTLEDGE HILL PRESS
Nashville, Tennessee

Published in Nashville, Tennessee, by Rutledge Hill Press, Inc., 513 Third Avenue South, Nashville, Tennessee 37210.

Typography by Bailey Typography, Inc.
Design by Harriette Bateman, Studio Six.
Drawings by Tonya Pitkin Presley, Studio III Productions.

Unless noted differently, photographs are by the author.

Library of Congress Cataloging-in-Publication Data

Miles, Jim.
    Paths to victory : a history and tour guide of the Stone's River, Chickamauga, Chattanooga, Knoxville, and Nashville Campaigns / Jim Miles.
        p.   cm.
    Includes bibliographical references and index.
    ISBN 1-55853-126-2
    1. Tennessee—History—Civil War, 1861-1865—Battlefields—Guide-books.   2. United States—History—Civil War, 1861-1865—Battlefields—Guide-books.   3. Historic sites—Tennessee—Guide-books.   4. Tennessee—Description and travel—1981- —Guide-books.
5. Alabama—Description and travel—1981- —Guide-books.
6. Georgia—Description and travel—1981- —Guide-books.
7. Automobile travel—Tennessee—Guide-books.   8. Automobile travel—Alabama—Guide-books.   9. Automobile travel—Georgia—Guide-books.
I. Title.
E470.5.M55   1991
973.7'3—dc20   91-29167
                                                                                        CIP

Printed in the United States of America
1 2 3 4 5 6 7 8—98 97 96 95 94 93 92 91

Dedicated with great affection

*to my distinguished colleagues
        at Peach County High School
and to the many students
        it has been my honor to teach.*

Introduction

Control of the Confederate Heartland—Kentucky, Tennessee, and the northern parts of Mississippi, Alabama, and Georgia—was so important that many of the war's bloodiest battles were fought on its soil.

The year 1862 had been eventful for the western theater of the Civil War. Union general U. S. Grant's twin victories at Forts Henry and Donelson had shattered the initial Confederate line in the West. The Cumberland River came immediately under Union domination, and with it the vital manufacturing center of Nashville. Control of the lower Tennessee River opened an invasion route through Tennessee into the Deep South states. These triumphs also flanked a strong Confederate position at Columbus, Kentucky, on the Mississippi River, which soon led to the capitulation of Memphis and Federal control of this mighty waterway all the way to Vicksburg.

In April the carnage of Shiloh, which dwarfed any previous American battle, left West Tennessee in Northern hands. The battle allowed Grant to concentrate on the reduction of Vicksburg, which would split the Confederacy, and Federal general Don Carlos Buell was free to proceed east to capture Chattanooga and open Georgia to invasion.

The summer invasion of Kentucky by Confederate generals Braxton Bragg and Kirby Smith was a desperate attempt to save Chattanooga, liberate Tennessee and Kentucky, destroy Buell, and draw Grant back into Tennessee for a great western showdown. Due to the ineptitude of the Southern leaders, the bungled campaign led to the confused, inconclusive battle of Perryville. The Confederates retreated to Knoxville, then moved by rail to Chattanooga and north to Murfreesboro. Buell was relieved of command because of his reluctance to pursue the Confederates, and William Rosecrans assumed control of the Union army in Nashville.

Much of the Confederate West had been conquered, leaving large cities, industrial regions, rich agricultural land, vital river and railroad transportation lines, and a considerable population under Federal control. While seriously impaired, Southern resources in the Heartland still constituted a dangerous threat to the Union. The coming years would be crucial in deciding who would control the region.

The end of 1862 found Federal and Confederate forces engaged in the savage battle of Stone's River, fighting for control of Middle Tennessee. Spring and summer 1863 saw a brilliant campaign of maneuver by Rosecrans that resulted in the seizure of Chattanooga and threatened Georgia. The eventful autumn witnessed brutal fighting along the "Stream of Death" at Chickamauga, a battle second only to Gettysburg in intensity and casualties. Soundly defeated and under siege at Chattanooga, the Union army was massively reinforced from Virginia and Mississippi in the greatest logistical accomplishment of American arms to that time. A masterful strategy, culminated by unparalleled Federal valor, routed the besiegers and allowed the Atlanta campaign to be launched in spring 1864.

The Heartland seemed to be securely under Union control; but during the following fall—after Atlanta had been captured—Confederate general John B. Hood led the Confederates in a final attempt to regain Tennessee. The resulting battles at Franklin and Nashville resulted in the destruction of Confederate forces in the West.

While Union gains in Virginia had been slim during four years of war, Federal armies in the West captured the South's territory, resources, and population. When Lee was finally cornered at Appomattox, the Confederacy was an empty, shrunken shell, the result of the western campaigns.

The Union conquest of the Heartland signaled the demise not only of the Confederate West, but of the Confederacy itself.

Contents

Tips for Enjoying the Tour Guide

This driving tour to historic sites in Tennessee, Alabama, and Georgia has been exhaustively researched, but readers need to bear in mind that highways and streets are occasionally altered and the names and designated numbers of roads are often changed. That is why we have included written directions, mileage, and maps. These should enable you to circumvent any changes that might be made to the tour route in coming years. Also, remember that odometers can vary considerably. Our 2.1 might be your 2.2, so please take this into account. When in doubt about your location, don't hesitate to ask local residents for directions. While preparing this guide, we were frequently "misplaced."

For safety's sake, it is obviously best to drive the tours with a companion. While one drives, the other can read and direct. It is also advisable to read the touring information before beginning the tours. Familiarizing yourself with the tour will enable you to choose beforehand the sites you would like to visit.

Traffic in parts of metropolitan Nashville, Chattanooga, and Knoxville can be fast and hazardous, so please be cautious in stopping to view a historic site and in reentering traffic flow.

By all means, be respectful of private property. Do not trespass on land or call on the residents of a private historic home. It is extremely difficult to live in or on a part of history, and there are too many vandals and arsonists around for residents to be tolerant toward uninvited visitors. Fortunately, many historic homes are open as part of community tours around Christmas and during the spring. Check calendars of events for specific dates.

Paths To Victory

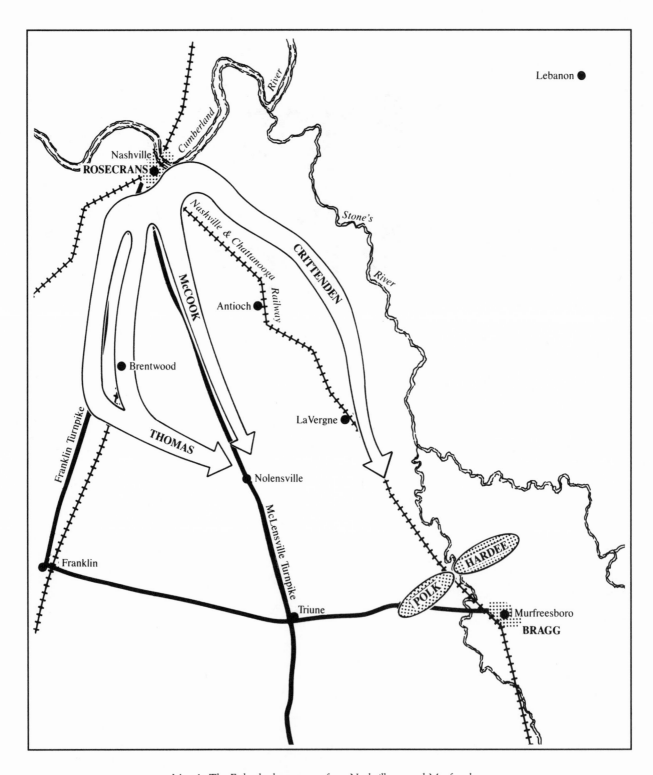

Map 1: The Federal advancement from Nashville toward Murfreesboro.

The Battle of Stone's River

I nstead of pursuing Confederate general Braxton Bragg following the battle of Perryville, Union general Don Carlos Buell insisted on returning to Nashville, from which he planned a march to northern Alabama to resume his attack against Chattanooga from the west. After General-in-Chief Henry W. Halleck rejected that strategy, Buell was ordered to clear the Confederates out of Kentucky and East Tennessee. When Buell refused to follow instructions, President Lincoln replaced him on October 23, 1863, with William S. Rosecrans, a methodical man.

Rosecrans joined his new command in Nashville and slowly built up a base of supplies. By early December Halleck issued the first of many threats to relieve Rosecrans for his time-consuming efforts to ready the army.

Also on October 23, Bragg reached Knoxville after a two hundred-mile retreat. He had only half an army left, and those soldiers were hungry, ragged, and plagued by disease. William Hardee, Leonidas Polk, Edmund Kirby Smith, and other Confederate generals condemned Bragg's leadership, and the Southern public clamored for his dismissal. After a conference with Confederate president Jefferson Davis in Richmond, Bragg returned to Tennessee with plans to move his army to Murfreesboro and attack Nashville. However, the army was in too wretched shape for any action. Over 15,000 of his 27,000 men were sick in hospitals. The rest were malnourished and suffering from exposure as snow covered the ground. Despite the poor condition of the men, in early November the army moved south by rail from Knoxville to Chattanooga, then north to Tullahoma and Murfreesboro, thirty miles south of Nashville. In camp at Murfreesboro, Confederate discipline deteriorated, resulting in drunkenness and brawls.

On November 24 Jefferson Davis appointed General Joseph E. Johnston commander of the western theatre. He also made Kirby Smith subordinate to Bragg and renamed the army. History will long remember the exploits of the Army of Tennessee. Davis rejected Johnston's first piece of military advice, which was to abandon Vicksburg and concentrate Southern forces in Tennessee to decisively defeat Rosecrans and disrupt the Federal transportation system. Without supplies, Grant would be forced to retreat from Mississippi, and the Confederates could turn on his weakened army. Not only did Davis reject this plan, he asked Bragg to send reinforcements to

The Murder Attempt Against Braxton Bragg

In October 1847 Braxton Bragg was charged with keeping order in the American military camp outside Monterey, Mexico, where his discipline was felt by some soldiers to be too severe. "I am somewhat obnoxious to a few," he wrote. One night a soldier placed an eight-inch shell under Bragg's bed and laid a train of powder outside the tent. According to a press account at the time, the "explosion was terrific, but fortunately the captain received no injury. Two of the missiles went through his bed without touching him."

Bragg believed a private who had joined the army to escape prosecution for crimes in Ohio planted the bomb. As he wrote, however, the "reasons that satisfy me might not convince a court, and therefore I do not charge him with it."

Several years later Lieutenant George H. Derby arrested a deserter who confessed to the attempted murder. ∎

Federal troops defend a Cumberland River ford near Gallatin, Tennessee, against Confederate cavalry on November 21, 1862. [BATTLES AND LEADERS]

Braxton Bragg's First Crisis

On October 22, 1862, Edmund Kirby Smith sent a letter to Jefferson Davis that disparaged Bragg's leadership in Kentucky. Bragg initially blamed the failure of the invasion on the people of Kentucky, then turned his wrath on Leonidas Polk. Bragg was angry that Polk's campaign report had criticized him. In part, Polk charged that Bragg knew that Don Carlos Buell's entire army was on the field at Perryville, but Bragg continued the attack even after Polk had warned him of the consequences of such an action. William J. Hardee supported Polk's version of events, claiming that Polk had saved the army from destruction. Eleven of Bragg's generals wrote Richmond to call their leader a failure.

In late October Bragg was summoned to Richmond to discuss the problems in his command. As he left, Polk arrived in the capital to condemn Bragg and urge his removal and replacement with Joseph Johnston. Kirby Smith followed Polk to Richmond and also requested Johnston.

Jefferson Davis ended this controversy by retaining his old friend Bragg, a decision that led to the bungled battle of Stone's River. ■

Vicksburg. Johnston refused the request, but when Davis visited Murfreesboro on December 10, he bluntly ordered Johnston to dispatch 9,000 men, a quarter of Bragg's strength, to the besieged Mississippi city. Rosecrans now had three times the strength of Bragg for any military activity he planned.

The only bright spot for the Confederates was the havoc the cavalry under Nathan Bedford Forrest and John Hunt Morgan was wreaking on the railroads that brought vital supplies to Nashville. While they destroyed miles of rail, numerous bridges, engines, and cars, Confederate general Joseph Wheeler kept an eye on Union troop movements.

On December 26 Rosecrans finally advanced his force, which also had a new name. Now called the Army of the Cumberland, it would seize and defend Tennessee and strike deep into Georgia before the Civil War ended. Rosecrans's three corps were led by Thomas L. Crittenden, Alexander McCook, and George H. Thomas. Because of the cavalry raids against his supply lines, Rosecrans brought only 44,000 of 82,000 available men. The rest were needed to guard the railroads.

Bragg spread out the Army of Tennessee in a thirty-two-mile-long line to cover all possible approaches from Nashville. Hardee held the left at Triune, fourteen miles west of Murfreesboro on the McClensville Pike; Polk covered the Confederate center at Murfreesboro; and a division of Hardee's troops held the right at Readyville, twelve miles to the east.

On December 26 Crittenden, on the Union left, led the advance south on the Nashville Pike; McCook was in the center, marching on the Nolensville Pike toward Triune, where he would turn east to Murfreesboro; and on the right Thomas was approaching Brentwood on the Franklin Pike, where he would turn east to cross behind McCook and continue on to Murfreesboro.

When McCook encountered stout resistance from Wheeler's cavalry, Thomas went to his aid. Crittenden was slowed by rebel troopers near La-Vergne. Rosecrans's army slowed as it deployed to deal with the cavalry, giving Bragg time to consolidate his army into a compact line across the roads that led to Murfreesboro. Polk guarded the Franklin, Nashville, and Wilkinson pikes, while Hardee covered the Lebanon and Jefferson pikes.

Because the Union cavalry was vainly trying to corner Morgan and For-rest, Rosecrans had no idea where the Confederate position was. On December 29 Crittenden ran into the entire Confederate army drawn up along Stone's River. While Rosecrans spent the day aligning his troops, Wheeler cut a swath through the Federal rear, capturing 1,000 prisoners, destroying

At Stone's River, Union troops advance to bolster the Federal right at Nashville Pike. [Battles and Leaders]

450 supply wagons, and burning goods worth $1 million, mainly ammunition and medical supplies, which resulted in serious shortages in the Union army.

Crittenden held the Union left at Stone's River, facing Hardee, who had swung around Polk, with Thomas in the center and McCook on the right, opposite Polk. The two Confederate wings were separated by Stone's River, a shallow but still dangerous obstacle to coordination.

Because Rosecrans failed to issue written instructions, his plan of attack was vague. On the morning of December 31 he wanted Crittenden to attack the Confederate right, with Thomas in support and McCook holding the right to prevent Polk from reinforcing Hardee. His idea was to swing behind Bragg's right to catch the Confederates in a pincers, cutting off their route of retreat to Murfreesboro and destroying the army. McCook was ordered to build hundreds of campfires on the right to deceive Bragg into thinking the Union attack would fall there.

Ironically, the ruse worked, which led Bragg to develop a battle plan identical to Rosecrans's. During the night, Hardee was ordered to cross Stone's

(Continued on page 20)

The Army of Tennessee and Vicksburg

By the fall of 1862, U. S. Grant was hammering away at Vicksburg, and William Rosecrans was preparing for a move against Chattanooga. The South had 50,000 men to counter Rosecrans's 95,000, and there were a mere 30,000 men available to protect the Mississippi River against Grant's 130,000. These odds convinced Jefferson Davis to appoint a regional commander who would supervise the activities of four widely scattered departments. Despite a history of conflicts between the men, Davis chose Joseph Johnston to command the Confederate West. Unfortunately, Johnston had little real power. For instance, the department commanders often reported directly to Richmond, leaving Johnston ignorant of important developments. A more crippling problem was Davis's penchant for meddling in western affairs.

The two main Confederate armies in the West, the Army of Tennessee under Braxton Bragg and John C. Pemberton's Mississippi force, were separated by several hundred miles. Johnston pointed out that Robert E. Lee's army was closer to him than he was to Pemberton. He proposed shifting forces as needed between Virginia (where Lee consistently fought to retain every soldier he had) and Tennessee, with Pemberton receiving reinforcements from west of the Mississippi. Davis disagreed. Johnston also believed that he should concentrate against Rosecrans or Grant, but not try to split his forces to fight both. He felt Tennessee was the more important. Davis again disagreed, ordering that every inch of the Confederacy be defended.

On December 15, 1862, Davis ordered Bragg to send a division—one-fourth of his strength—to Mississippi. The soldiers departed on December 18, and a week later Rosecrans advanced to battle at Stone's River. The loss of that division may have saved Rosecrans's army from destruction. Following the savage fighting near Murfreesboro, Rosecrans had twice Bragg's numbers, and even with the reinforcements, Grant and William Sherman had double Pemberton's strength.

Johnston next urged Davis to temporarily abandon Mississippi and concentrate in Tennessee. He again pointed out the geography of the Confederacy and urged that Bragg be reinforced from Virginia. Davis refused, and Johnston warned that he might be forced to abandon Middle Tennessee. When the Vicksburg crisis worsened, Johnston, left ignorant of the situation in Mississippi, urged Pemberton to concentrate against Grant, while Richmond instructed him to split his forces to defend Vicksburg and Port Hudson.

In May Johnston was directed to send an additional 3,000 of Bragg's men to Mississippi. Orders for 6,000 additional infantry and 2,500 cavalry for Mississippi quickly followed. In the six months since Stone's River, Rosecrans had been heavily reinforced. When the Army of the Cumberland drove Bragg out of Tennessee, Ambrose Burnside and the Army of the Ohio entered East Tennessee to capture Knoxville. Davis had confidently assured Johnston that the Federals could not attack simultaneously in Mississippi, Middle Tennessee, and East Tennessee, but they did.

Johnston took command of a small army in Mississippi, hoping to join forces with Pemberton; but that general had allowed himself to be trapped inside Vicksburg. Johnston's presence did nothing but hurt Bragg, who was down to 30,000 men by June. Rosecrans's advance shattered Bragg and threw him back into Georgia. Vicksburg and Chattanooga were lost, with Georgia soon following. This mismanagement by President Davis lost the West, and, ultimately, the Confederacy. ∎

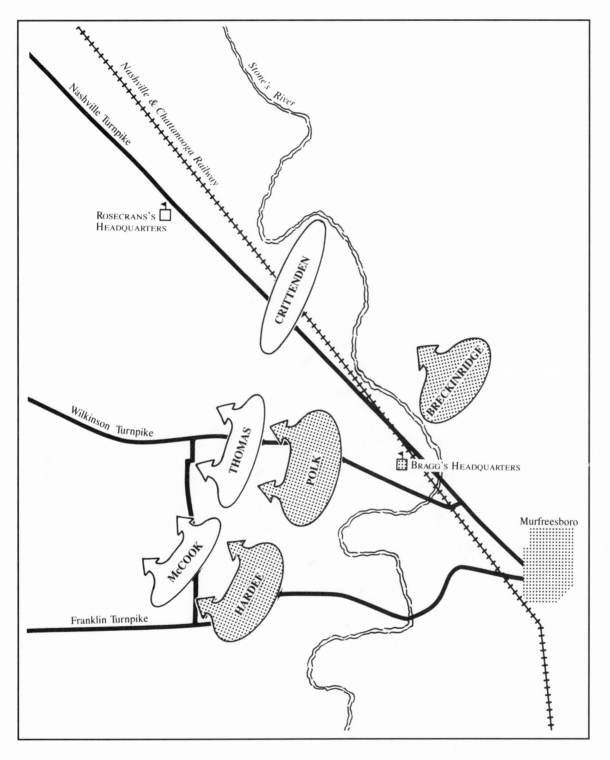

Map 2: Stone's River, the morning of December 31.

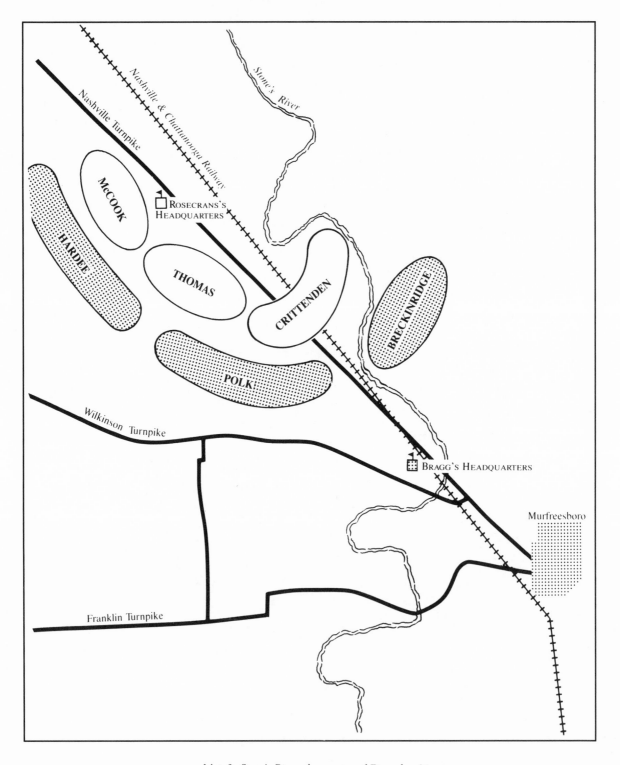

Map 3: Stone's River, the evening of December 31.

Union general William Rosecrans's troops being attacked by Bragg at Stone's River on January 2, 1862. [HARPER'S WEEKLY]

The Third Western Leader ■ Philip Henry Sheridan

Sheridan, born in New York in 1831, was raised in Ohio. He was an alternate selection to West Point, admitted when another candidate failed the entrance exam. Sheridan, who was supposed to be in the class of 1852, graduated a year late because of a suspension resulting from a fight with another cadet, William R. Terrill, later a Union general killed at Perryville. He spent eight years as a second lieutenant and was only promoted upon the resignation of higher ranking officers. His lackluster peacetime career has been likened to that of U. S. Grant and William Sherman. Like those fellow Westerners, Sheridan only blossomed during the war.

Sheridan was assigned administrative duties through the campaign against Corinth. He made colonel in May 1862 and was promoted to brigadier general in September. His brigade fought stubbornly at Perryville and Stone's River. After becoming a major general, he led a division at Chickamauga under Alexander McCook, where he lost 1,500 of 4,000 soldiers. His was part of the force that charged impulsively up Missionary Ridge, an exploit which garnered the attention of Grant, who soon picked Sheridan to lead his cavalry in the Army of the Potomac.

Sheridan inspired the eastern cavalry, so long in the shadow of flamboyant Confederate trooper J. E. B. Stuart. Sheridan's cavaliers killed Stuart at Yellow Tavern, then brought Grant and Sherman's style of total war to the Shenandoah Valley. He defeated Jubal Early at Winchester and Fisher's Hill, then rallied his routed force and smashed the Confederates at Cedar Creek, for which the U.S. Congress expressed its gratitude. Sheridan systematically destroyed the Shenandoah Valley, then joined Grant at Petersburg. After Robert E. Lee's line was shattered, Sheridan defeated the fleeing Confederates at Five Forks and Sayler's Creek, then cut off their escape route at Appomattox to force the surrender.

After the Civil War, Sheridan helped remove Emperor Maximillian from Mexico. He so severely enforced Reconstruction laws in the Fifth Military District, which consisted of Louisiana and Texas, that he was removed after six months. His service was rewarded with the rank of lieutenant general, and he retired in 1883 as a full general and commander of the army. Sheridan was instrumental in establishing Yellowstone National Park before his death in 1888. ■

River and pass behind Polk to extend the Confederate left, while a division under Breckinridge remained to face Crittenden on the right. Hardee would launch an assault in the morning against the Union right, then Polk would attack. Bragg hoped to cut off the Federal escape route to Nashville, then batter Rosecrans against the river.

In the cold darkness, bands took turns playing Confederate and Federal tunes. Then all combined for the sentimental "Home, Sweet Home," before the troops settled down for the night.

Had both armies jumped off at the same time, history might have recorded an interesting "revolving door" battle, but the Confederates struck first. Two of Hardee's brigades overlapped the Federal flank, and 2,000 Confederate cavalrymen ranged to the left of them as they attacked through a chill morning dawn. At 6:00 A.M. seven Confederate brigades, 11,000 Rebels arrayed in a line six deep, smashed into two of McCook's brigades. The Northern brigades were destroyed, with most of their artillery captured, and the Confederate cavalry threatened the Union rear. The surviving

The General Who Fought with Everyone ■ Braxton Bragg

The combative Bragg was born in Warrenton, North Carolina, in 1817, and graduated from West Point in 1837. He fought the Seminole Indians in Florida, then participated as an artillery officer in the Mexican War, where he became a minor celebrity when General Zachary Taylor, during the heat of a hard-fought battle, said, "A little more grape [shot], Captain Bragg."

Bragg left the army in 1856 to become a Louisiana cotton planter. He entered Confederate service as a brigadier in March 1861, in command of the Gulf Coast from Pensacola to Mobile. Because of Bragg's stern discipline, his soldiers soon gained a reputation for order and drill.

When Confederate forces were concentrated at Corinth, Bragg, now a major general, brought his garrisons to Mississippi. He led a corps at Shiloh, was promoted to full general after Albert Sidney Johnston's death, and replaced Beauregard as leader of the Army of the Mississippi (soon to be the Army of Tennessee) when Corinth was evacuated.

Bragg performed an admirable logistical feat by quickly transporting his army from Mississippi to Chattanooga, then, working with Kirby Smith in Knoxville, threw the North into an uproar by boldly invading Kentucky in the summer–fall of 1862. These brilliant accomplishments were negated by the failure of the two generals to cooperate in Kentucky. After the battle of Perryville, Bragg abandoned the state and started a long retreat to Knoxville.

Bragg survived the first disputes with his generals over conduct of the Perryville campaign, then shifted his army to Murfreesboro to block the Federals in Nashville. He savagely attacked Rosecrans at Stone's River on New Year's Eve 1862, but was incapable of completing the victory. Bragg withdrew to the Duck River and weathered a second round of controversy regarding his competency.

In the summer of 1863, Rosecrans outflanked a bewildered Bragg and forced the Confederates out of Tennessee without fighting a battle. At Chickamauga Bragg turned

and furiously assaulted Rosecrans. After half the Union army was destroyed on the second day of battle, Bragg refused to pursue, a decision which may have doomed the Confederate West. He besieged Chattanooga while somehow managing to withstand a third crisis concerning his leadership.

After U. S. Grant, George Thomas, and William Sherman shattered the Army of Tennessee at Missionary Ridge, Bragg finally resigned, but he was summoned to Richmond to serve Jefferson Davis, an old and incredibly tolerant friend, as chief military adviser. Bragg helped undermine the position of his successor, Joseph Johnston, then was unable to control the actions of John Hood as he invaded Tennessee and destroyed the army. Bragg ended the war serving under Joseph Johnston in North Carolina.

Recognized as an effective trainer of soldiers, Bragg was able to devise sound battle plans and set them in motion, but he proved unable to make crucial decisions once combat was joined. He frequently is-

sued confusing orders, then blamed subordinates when his instructions were not properly carried out. Bragg's abusive personality caused his officers to revolt against his authority, and the ranks had no love or respect for their commander.

Following the Civil War, Bragg became the chief engineer for the state of Alabama. In 1876 he collapsed and died on a street in Galveston, Texas. Braxton Bragg, one of the most important and controversial figures of the Confederacy, is buried in Mobile. ■

[GEORGE COOK PHOTOGRAPH]

From this position above Stone's River, fifty-one Union cannon shattered John C. Breckinridge's attack on January 2, 1863.

A Rosecrans Story

William Rosecrans was a devout Catholic, but he also cursed with all the eloquence of the proverbial sailor. A Reverend Dr. Morris was visiting with Rosecrans in camp when an officer arrived to announce the capture of a spy. Rosecrans, angry and excited over this event, began to swear profusely. Suddenly, remembering that the good Reverend was present, Rosecrans apologized and explained, "Gentlemen, I sometimes *swear,* but I never *blaspheme!*" ■

The Fighting Bishop ■ Leonidas K. Polk

Polk was born into a prosperous North Carolina family in 1806. He had intended to follow a military career, but only six months after graduation from West Point in 1827, he resigned his commission to enter the ministry. Polk was soon an Episcopal priest and served throughout the South and Southwest, becoming the bishop of Louisiana in 1841, and helping to found the University of the South (Sewanee) in 1861. His duties brought him into contact with Jefferson Davis, who had been one year behind Polk at West Point, and the two men became fast friends.

When the Civil War started, Davis offered Polk the rank of major general and a post in the West, commanding Department No. 2, which stretched along the Mississippi River region from Paducah to the Red River. The bishop accepted the position, then concentrated all his resources to protect the Mississippi, ignoring the possibility of being flanked via the Tennessee and Cumberland rivers. Polk fought in all the major battles of the Army of the Mississippi (later the Army of Tennessee): Shiloh, Perryville, Stone's River, Chickamauga, and the Atlanta campaign. While his courage was never questioned, his military aptitude was frequently disparaged. His failure to launch a coordinated attack at Stone's River may have cost the Confederacy a complete victory. After failing to attack at Chickamauga, Braxton Bragg threatened to dismiss Polk from command and court-martial him, but Davis's patronage saved his career, and, ironically, sealed his doom. Polk was dispatched to Mississippi during the siege of Chattanooga, but returned in time for the Atlanta campaign.

In June 1864, while observing Union movements from Pine Mountain in the company of Joseph Johnston and William Hardee, Sherman took personal umbrage at their activity and had a battery of cannon fire on the distant figures. The portly, dignified churchman refused to hasten to safety, and a shell passed through his chest, killing him instantly.

Polk remained buried in Augusta, Georgia, until 1945, when he was reinterred at Christ Church Cathedral in New Orleans.

Polk had been a stubborn, and sometimes even childish, general, but he had been greatly loved by the troops. He had imparted a sense of decency and morality to the soldiers, and even the leaders of the army had been favorably affected by his presence. While Polk's loss was less than "irreparable" to the cause, as Davis lamented, it seemed a symbol of declining Confederate fortunes. ■

[LIBRARY OF CONGRESS]

Federals were routed for three miles before the Rebel advance slowed in the confusion of battle. At 7:00 A.M., Polk launched a piecemeal attack that was repulsed, and a perfect opportunity to roll up the Union right flank was squandered. Fighting raged across harvested fields of corn and cotton and among dense stands of cedar trees broken by outcroppings of stone.

As Rosecrans prepared to strike from his left at 7:00 A.M., he received word of the battle on his right and dispatched reserve reinforcements that arrived in time to blunt a second furious attack. Rebels fell in heaps to artillery fire and massed musketry. The Confederates rallied and launched a third assault with a fury that collapsed more of the Federal flank. After two

Stone's River Stories

J. T. McBride was a Confederate soldier captured in a skirmish shortly before William J. Hardee's corps smashed into the Union right. Watching his captors fleeing for safety, a disgusted McBride shouted, "What yer running fer? Why don't yer stand and fight like men?"

"For God's sake, Joe," a fellow prisoner admonished McBride, "don't try to rally the Yankees! Keep 'em on the run! Do anything to continue their demoralization and let's make our escape!"

■ ■ ■ ■ ■

The Confederates flushed wildlife before their wild charge. One soldier, spotting a rabbit bounding away, cried, "Go it, Molly Cottontail, go it! I'd run too if I didn't have a reputation to sustain."

■ ■ ■ ■ ■

During the initial attacks, skirmishers from Company A of the Tenth South Carolina were surprised by Union cavalry, who captured their commander, Lieutenant C. Carroll White, and several other men. The remainder of the company hesitated to fire with their comrades in the midst of the enemy, but White shouted, "Don't mind us. Commence firing!" The Confederate prisoners dived for the ground as a volley claimed several Union troopers. White and the other captives jumped up to disarm the survivors, who were now the prisoners.

When Braxton Bragg heard of this exploit, he promoted White to captain on the spot.

■ ■ ■ ■ ■

After Confederate general Benjamin F. Cheatham charged forward shouting, "Come on, boys, and follow me!" a wounded soldier was heard to say, "Well, General, if you are determined to die, I'll die with you."

■ ■ ■ ■ ■

It was said that one Confederate regiment, whose rifles had been redistributed when the men were quarantined because of smallpox, charged the Union line weaponless and scattered the enemy. The soldiers picked up muskets discarded by the Federals and continued into the fray.

■ ■ ■ ■ ■

Behind the battle lines, a Tennessean found a wounded Union soldier who requested water. The Federal identified his outfit when the Confederate asked, then added, "A damned good regiment, too. If we had many such, you wouldn't have been here."

This statement angered the Rebel, who replied, "Well, you are here, and you want a drink of water. I won't give you a drop, for I have no doubt that when you are home, you live near a running creek or a big spring and, damn you, that's where you ought to be now!"

■ ■ ■ ■ ■

After surveying his desperate

situation, Rosecrans ordered General Thomas J. Wood's division to cancel the planned attack and reinforce the Union right. Riding away, Wood turned to Rosecrans and quipped, "We'll all meet at the hatter's, as one coon said to another when the dogs were after them!"

■ ■ ■ ■ ■

Rosecrans did not have a sense of humor on this grim day. When he found General Phillip Sheridan, who was trying to rally his division, which had sustained massive casualties and was running low on ammunition, cursing mightily, Rosecrans admonished him, "Watch your language. Remember, the first bullet may send you to eternity."

"I can't help it," Sheridan answered. "Unless I swear like hell, the men won't take me seriously."

■ ■ ■ ■ ■

After ordering the brigade of Colonel Samuel W. Price to hold a vital ford across Stone's River, Rosecrans asked him, "Will you hold this ford?"

"I will try, sir," Price answered.

Rosecrans was not reassured by that response, so he asked again.

"I will die right here," Price replied.

Rosecrans, still not satisfied, repeated the question a third time.

"Yes, sir," Price answered.

"That will do," Rosecrans barked and rode away.

■ ■ ■ ■ ■

At the end of the bloody day, Braxton Brag wired Richmond, "God has granted us a Happy New Year."

■ ■ ■ ■ ■

The topic at Rosecrans' headquarters that night was whether to retreat or remain on the field. Thomas, exhausted, fell asleep during the conference but roused himself whenever the word *retreat* was spoken to growl, "This army does not retreat. I know of no better place to die than right here."

■ ■ ■ ■ ■

When John C. Breckinridge executed Bragg's suicidal charge on January 2, the Eighteenth Tennessee had just received a new flag, sewn by Murfreesboro resident Miss Mat Watkins, which contained a piece of Mrs. Mary Breckinridge's wedding dress, a custom common during the Civil War. Three men carrying the flag on December 31 had been shot, and now six additional color bearers went down amid the deadly Union fire. When the fourth fell, Captain Nat Gooch ordered a man to pick it up off the ground. The captain was rudely told to "pick it up yourself." He did and was wounded shortly thereafter. Ironically, Logue Nelson, a Murfreesboro resident, brought the flag off the field to safety. ■

Union general William S. Rosecrans, who commanded the Army of the Ohio after Buell, survived the Confederate onslaught at Stone's River. He flanked the Confederates out of Tennessee but lost the battle of Chickamauga and his command. [HARPER'S WEEKLY]

of McCook's divisions had been mauled, the attackers turned on the third Union division, led by Philip Sheridan, and forced it to withdraw.

The Confederate success was bought at a staggering price. By 10:00 A.M., Hardee had lost one-third of his soldiers; Polk's casualties were 30 percent. Hardee pleaded with Bragg for reinforcements but, when none were forthcoming, he sent his weary men to attack Sheridan's new position. Although Sheridan's line had been extended by reinforcements, the Federals had to retreat once more when their ammunition was exhausted.

By 11:00 A.M. the broken Union line had been reformed along the path of the Nashville Pike and the deep cut of the railroad. The two angles of the line met at a strong salient consisting of four acres of woods called the Round Forest. When Polk struck this position and was thrown back, Rosecrans was finally convinced to cancel his offensive. He reinforced the Round Forest with Crittenden's troops, which had been scheduled to hit the Con-

A Union brigade advances toward Stone's River during the afternoon of January 2, 1863.
[BATTLES AND LEADERS]

Old Reliable ▪ William J. Hardee

Hardee was born near Savannah, Georgia, in 1815, and was part of the West Point class of 1838. He fought Indians on the frontier, was brevetted twice in Mexico, and became commandant of cadets at West Point. While at the military academy he wrote *Rifle and Light Infantry Tactics,* popularly known as *Hardee's Tactics,* which was adopted for use in the classrooms of West Point and in armies around the world. With the outbreak of the war, many officers in blue and gray used the manual to train hundreds of thousands of civilian soldiers.

Hardee resigned from the army in January 1861 after his native state seceded and became a brigadier, soon to rise to major general, in Confederate service. He raised a brigade in Arkansas, directed the garrison at Bowling Green, Kentucky, for

disastrous defeats suffered by the Confederates around Atlanta. After the city was surrendered, Hardee demanded a transfer. When Hood marched away to Tennessee, Hardee was assigned to protect Georgia against Sherman's legions. He assembled a scratch force of 10,000 men in Savannah but was unable to impede the Federal advance. When Sherman's 60,000 hardened veterans invested the city at Christmas 1864, Hardee slipped across the Savannah River in an audacious move that caught Sherman completely by surprise.

Hardee ended the Civil War in the same capacity as he started the Atlanta campaign. When Johnston was brought back to command the pitiful remnants of the Army of Tennessee, he rushed to oppose Sherman in

Albert Sidney Johnston, and headed a corps in the Army of the Mississippi (Army of Tennessee) for most of the war. Hardee led a wing of Bragg's army into Kentucky and commanded the corps which smashed into Union forces in the initial moments of both Shiloh and Stone's River.

Hardee earned the sobriquet Old Reliable for his steady leadership in many battles of the Civil War. With the departure of Braxton Bragg after Chickamauga, Hardee refused command of the army, preferring to serve under Joseph Johnston.

Following Johnston's departure during the Atlanta campaign, Hardee was angry that the army was given to John B. Hood, a junior officer with no command experience. Hood blamed Hardee for the series of

North Carolina, where Hardee once again came under his command. He fought in one of the last battles of the war, Bentonville, and surrendered with Johnston in April 1865.

Hardee settled in Alabama as a planter until his death in 1873. He is buried in Selma. ▪

[HARPER'S WEEKLY]

The carriages of cannon were shattered amid the trees on rock shelves that characterized the Stone's River landscape.

Braxton Bragg ■ A Slave Driver, Literally

Following the Mexican War, Bragg left the military, married, and bought a 1,600-acre sugar plantation near Thibodaux, Louisiana, for $152,000. The estate, which he named *Bivouac*, included buildings, animals, implements, and 105 slaves. Bragg was no stranger to slavery. His father had owned them, and he had always had servants. It was his personal belief that he was not responsible for the institution, and that the practice was legal and necessary for southern agriculture. Bragg found his need for slaves "just and necessary" and actually liked the plantation system, which he compared to a "small military establishment."

Bragg's subsequent well-known reputation for discipline was definitely at work here, as he wrote: "Where do you find the fewest mutinies, revolts, and rebellions? In the disciplined commands." He also noted that humanity "is the same all over the world. Give us all disciplined masters, managers, and assistants, and we shall never hear of insurrection." The result of disciplined slaves was "better health, more labor and less exertions, and infinitely less punishment, more comfort, and happiness to the laborer, and profit and pleasure to the master."

Bragg was not a cruel master, and it was probable that he drove himself hardest of all. He took no holiday for five years in his strenuous attempts to make the plantation turn a profit. ■

federate right. Bragg also shifted his few remaining units, Breckinridge's four brigades, from the right. A final Confederate attack at 4:00 P.M. was shattered by fifty cannon that Rosecrans had massed behind the forest.

During the terrible night that followed, the exhausted armies remained in position where the fighting had ceased. Wounded men were frozen to the ground by their own blood. Attempts at building campfires drew enemy fire, and many men had no rations to eat.

Bragg fell asleep thinking he had won the battle, but dawn told another story. The Confederate commander was severely disappointed to find that Rosecrans had not retreated to Nashville. While the Federals regrouped and Bragg waited for them to withdraw, New Year's Day 1863 passed without a renewal of battle. On January 2 Bragg was further distressed to find the Union army still on the field. To hasten Rosecrans's departure, Bragg decided to seize a hill east of Stone's River that would endanger the Union left flank. Reconnaissance found a Union division, supported by considerable artillery, occupying the position. Bragg was surprised to find the hill so strongly defended. Undeterred, he summoned Breckinridge and ordered the former U.S. vice president to take the objective and force a Federal retreat. Breckinridge pointed out that such an attack would be suicidal, but Bragg insisted.

When Bragg evacuated Murfreesboro following the battle of Stone's River, he left these chimneys as the only evidence of the extensive Confederate camp. [HARPER'S WEEKLY]

Yet Another Bragg Story

On the retreat from Murfreesboro, Braxton Bragg came upon a dirty, unshaven, barefooted man riding a decrepit mule. "Who are you?" Bragg inquired.

"Nobody," was the reply.

"Where did you come from?" Bragg continued.

"Nowhere," was the laconic answer.

"Where are you going?"

"I don't know," the man drawled.

Angered by this ridiculous exchange, Bragg demanded, "Then where do you belong?"

"Don't belong anywhere," the man replied in the same tone of voice.

"Don't you belong to Bragg's army?" Bragg persisted.

"Bragg's army! Bragg's army!" the man shouted. "Why, he's got no army! One-half of it he shot in Kentucky, and the other half has been whipped to death at Murfreesboro!"

Bragg rode silently away. ■

At 4:00 P.M., 4,500 Kentuckians charged bravely across 600 yards of open land and crashed into the Union line. The Yankees were routed but, instead of consolidating their gain, the Rebels impulsively pursued them, directly into the fire of fifty-eight cannon that spewed out one hundred deadly rounds a minute. The Federals splashed across the river in a counterattack that scattered the Confederate force. The position was recaptured, and Bragg had gained nothing.

Braxton Bragg in Mexico

During the Mexican War, young Lieutenant Bragg was given command of a light battery. General Zachary Taylor recorded that Bragg was "eminently qualified" for the position, which consisted of four guns, six horse teams, and twelve soldiers per piece. In February 1847 Taylor launched a reckless offensive with five thousand inexperienced men. Finding a Mexican force approaching, he established a defensive position near the town of Buena Vista on February 23. The Mexicans immediately launched a day-long attack.

Taylor's left, held by poorly prepared militia, soon fled the field. The charging Mexicans were stopped by Bragg, who had two cannon and a regiment of reinforcements, and driven back to their original line. Bragg had just replenished his ammunition when the Mexicans struck the left flank again, overrunning the regiment of one Colonel Jefferson Davis. Bragg quickly had his guns in action, and the determined enemy was turned back again.

The Mexicans next struck the American center, causing the infantry to flee and gunners to abandon their artillery. Bragg's two cannon, standing alone and stuffed with grapeshot, forced the Mexicans to withdraw for a third time. Each piece had fired 250 rounds.

"Captain Bragg," Taylor said, "saved the day."

Newspapers spread the legend that at a critical point during the battle, General Taylor had shouted, "A little more grape, Captain Bragg!" or "Double shot your guns and give 'em hell!" The latter was probably more authentic, considering Taylor's temperament. One participant claimed that when Bragg asked for infantry support, Taylor had replied, "There is none. Stand to your guns and give them hell," but yet another reported Taylor and Bragg were not close enough to speak during the battle. Bragg maintained that Taylor had simply said, "Give them hell!" ■

On January 3 the armies again faced each other without fighting. Seeing that Rosecrans had received reinforcements during the day and realizing that his army was in no shape to meet a massive Union attack, Bragg started his wagon train south. That night Polk retreated to Shelbyville as Hardee made his way to Tullahoma. Over 1,700 Southern wounded were left for capture in Murfreesboro.

In Tullahoma, Bragg's generals expressed such bitter displeasure with their leader that Jefferson Davis sent Joseph Johnston to examine the situation. Davis ultimately instructed Johnston to take charge of the army, but the general had not recovered from wounds suffered at Fair Oaks, Virginia, nearly two years earlier. Johnston declined the command, and Bragg remained in control of the Army of Tennessee.

Stone's River had been a bloody standoff. Of 41,000 Union troops engaged, 9,500 (23 percent) became casualties. Bragg lost 9,200 of 35,000 men, 27 percent of his strength. Instead of recapturing Nashville, Bragg had weakened his army so seriously that he would remain on the defensive for most of 1863. Chattanooga was again endangered. ■

Sam Davis's Last Letter Home

Dear Mother,
Oh how painful it is to write to you. I have got to die tomorrow morning—to be hung by the Federals. Mother do not grieve for me. I must bid you good-bye forever more—Mother. I do not hate to die. Give my love to all.
    Your Dear son,
    Sam ■

Murfreesboro, Tennessee, under Union rule following the Battle of Stone's River. [HARPER'S WEEKLY]

A DRIVING TOUR
■ Stone's River ■

The intention was to start this tour in Nashville and drive south to Stone's River, near Murfreesboro, but the area between is highly urbanized and not conducive to historic meditation. So we will begin at the Sam Davis Home in Smyrna, which is south of Nashville and north of Murfreesboro in northern Rutherford County.

From the south, exit from Interstate 24 onto Nissan Boulevard and turn east toward Smyrna. After crossing the Old Nashville Pike and U.S. 41, the sprawling Nissan plant will be to the right. Continue on Nissan Boulevard, and after 4.7 turn left at the intersection onto Sam Davis Road. The Sam Davis Home is on the right after .4.

From the north, exit Interstate 24 on Sam Ridley Parkway, which becomes Nissan Boulevard, and drive east. After 5.9 turn right onto Sam Davis Road to the house.

This two-story farmhouse, built in 1810, was later bought by Charles and Jean Davis. They grew cotton,

This 1810 farmhouse was the home of Sam Davis, the celebrated "boy hero of the Confederacy."

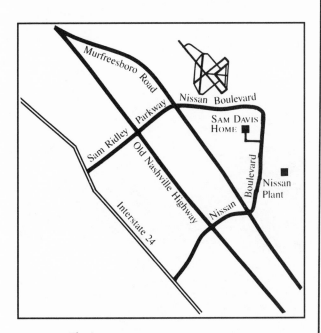

Map 4: The Smyrna area.

wheat, and tobacco on a 168-acre farm. Their oldest child was a son, Sam, who enlisted in the Rutherford Rifles, Company I, First Regiment Tennessee Volunteers, at age nineteen. He received two wounds at Shiloh and a third at Perryville. In November 1863 Davis was on a mission behind enemy lines. A scout, he had received detailed information about Federal deployments in Tennessee from his captain and was taking them to Bragg, who was besieging Chattanooga, when a patrol of Iowa cavalry captured him near Pulaski in southern Tennessee.

Davis was wearing his Confederate uniform beneath a Federal overcoat, which had been dyed black with walnut dye. Federal general G. M. Dodge believed Davis was a spy because his uniform was concealed and there was classified information secreted in his boot. The young man was found guilty of espionage and sentenced to die. Dodge offered Davis his freedom if he would divulge the source of the secret information. Davis refused, and on November 21, 1863, the twenty-one-year-old rode to the gallows perched on the coffin in which he would be buried. Before being hanged, Davis announced to his execu-

The family of Sam Davis returned his body from Pulaski and buried it in the family cemetery behind their home.

tioners, "If I had a thousand lives to live I would give them all gladly rather than betray a friend." After Davis was hanged, his body was returned to Smyrna.

Sam Davis has been called the "Nathan Hale of the Confederacy." Believing that his execution was illegal, Tennesseans consider Davis a hero. A bronze statue of the soldier stands in front of the capitol in Nashville; a stone likeness is at the courthouse in Pulaski; the site of the execution is marked; and Davis's boyhood home has been preserved near Smyrna. The house has been restored to its original condition and furnished with many of the Davis family's belongings, including china, furniture, and carpets. On the grounds are a detached kitchen, smokehouse, overseer's office, several log slave cabins, a three-hole privy (presumably people were more sociable back then), a garden, and the family cemetery where Sam Davis is buried beneath a monument that honors his sacrifice. An interesting museum with displays, artifacts, and a video illustrates the life and death of Davis.

To the west, along U.S. 31A–41A, between Nolensville and Triune, a route taken by one of Buell's corps on the advance to Stone's River, is the site where DeWitt S. Jake, a member of Coleman's Confederate scouts, was captured by the 115th Ohio Cavalry on August 29, 1864. Jake managed to swallow his dispatches, but the Federals beat and tortured him for information. Then he was dragged to death behind a galloping horse. He is buried in a family cemetery nearby.

From the Sam Davis Home, turn left onto Sam Davis Road, and at .4 turn left onto Nissan Boulevard. After 2.9 turn left, and at .2 turn left again onto the Old Nashville Pike. At 6 miles a stack of cannonballs to the right indicates the position of Rosecrans's headquarters during the battle. After .6 turn right into the Stone's River National Battlefield Park.

Considering the number of men involved in this battle—45,000 for the Union, 35,000 for the Confederacy—the casualty figures—9,500 Federal, 9,200 Confederate—and the intensity of the combat, this is a small park. Its 350 acres incorporate only parts of the major fields of battle.

Begin your exploration of the Stone's River battlefield at the Visitors Center. Displays and an audio-visual program explain the action. An encampment of reenactors are present each July, and living history demonstrations are held throughout the summer. If you wish, pick up a self-guided driving tour and a tour tape that direct visitors to nine major stops in the park.

At tour *Stop One* is the recreated Chicago Board of Trade Battery, so called because the Board of Trade financed the six-gun battery. Here at 10:00 A.M. on December 31, 1862, retreating Union forces passed through the battery, closely followed by screaming Confederate infantry who emerged from a stand of

Confederates charging out of the mists of dawn fought in open fields amid thick stands of cedar trees at Stone's River.

cedars. When the Rebels entered the clearing, this Union battery stopped the charge with loads of canisters. Another Federal battery was deployed beside these guns to help beat back a second attack.

Stop Two describes the fight for the cedars, which also occurred at 10:00 A.M. By this time Bragg's offensive had been so successful that Rosecrans was forced to cancel his planned assault. The Union commander dispatched reinforcements to this spot where, aided by artillery at the Nashville Pike, the Confederate attack was stemmed. A trail leads into a dense cedar forest.

Stop Three tells the story of the action of Water's Alabama Battery at 12:30 P.M. These Southern guns attempted to closely follow the infantry to provide support, but the dense cedar woods and rugged landscape, broken by outcroppings of limestone, prevented them from helping the foot soldiers, who were repulsed. A trail illustrates the difficulties posed for

fighting among the thick cedars and rough outcrops of stone.

Sheridan's stand (at a spot known as the Slaughter Pen) is described at *Stop Four.* At 10:00 A.M. the troops of Generals Philip H. Sheridan and George H. Thomas repulsed several strong Confederate attacks. The Southerners brought up their artillery and shelled the Federals from a range of only two hundred yards. Additional assaults were also thrown back, with both armies suffering heavy casualties. Sheridan was finally forced to retreat, but he had bought time for Rosecrans to form a second line along the Nashville Pike. A short walk leads through the forest and past shelves of rock where the Federals lost fourteen cannon.

Stop Five illustrates the Confederate high tide, from 12:00 noon until 4:00 P.M. When Crittenden's men were attacked late in the afternoon, they broke the Rebel charge with murderous fire from behind a rail fence, but a second assault an hour later forced the Federals to retire. The fighting was so fierce that as the Confederates advanced, they plucked cotton from the fields to stuff into their ears to protect them against the thunderous sounds of battle.

The Confederate advance had taken time and a huge toll in Southern lives. *Stop Six* explains Rosecrans's second line, which the attacking Confederates reached at 5:00 P.M. The position stretched from the Round Forest to the Nashville Pike. Unable to penetrate this position, the Confederates withdrew into the forest.

The Stone's River National Cemetery is *Stop Seven.* Between 12:00 noon and 4:00 P.M., artillery was emplaced from Stop One on the right, across this slope, to the Round Forest at Stop Eight on the left, to anchor the infantry manning Rosecrans's second line on the Nashville Pike, which is the road to the front.

When the battle ended, the dead were quickly buried on the field. In June 1865 this national cemetery was established for the reburial of the Federal dead. Of 6,100 Union dead, 2,562 are unknown. The cemetery also includes the dead from Franklin and Hoover's Gap, when Rosecrans broke Bragg's Duck River line in the summer of 1863. The grounds were landscaped in 1892. The Confederate dead were either buried in mass graves on the battlefield, sent home for burial, or interred in Murfreesboro.

Stop Eight tells the story of the struggle for the Round Forest, from 9:00 A.M. until 4:00 P.M. Of the original Union line, only this part held throughout the battle. Federal soldiers beat back many determined attacks, including one which advanced to within

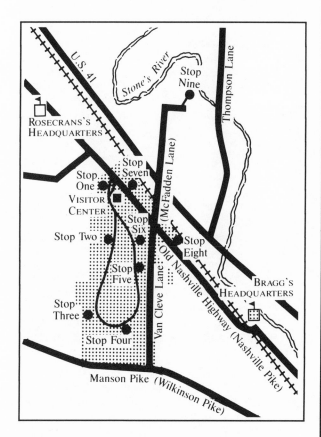

Map 5: Stone's River Battlefield.

More than six thousand Federals killed in battles in Middle Tennessee rest in the Stone's River National Cemetery.

150 yards of the position. This four-acre wood, known locally as the Round Forest, was dubbed "Hell's Half-Acre," by the soldiers who fought here. Late in the day it became the battered apex of Rosecrans's line as rows of cannon positioned behind the forest shattered the final Confederate charges that advanced across an open cotton field.

Surrounded by a stone fence, the monument here was built by Colonel William B. Hazen's brigade in 1863 to honor comrades who died in the battle. It is the oldest Civil War memorial in the nation. The inscription reads, "Their Faces Toward Heaven, Their Feet Toward the Foe."

Stop Nine is situated across U.S. 41. Before leaving this part of the park, you might wish to visit the site of Bragg's headquarters during the battle, which is marked by a stack of cannonballs at .8 south of Stop Eight on the Old Nashville Pike. After another .8 south, on the right southern bank of Stone's River, is Redoubt Brannon, part of an extensive system of fortifications built by Rosecrans to protect Murfreesboro, which had grown into an important supply point.

The exhausted armies faced each other on New Year's Day 1863 without combat, but on the following afternoon Bragg decided to attack Rosecrans's left. Stop Nine tells of Breckinridge's attack, from 4:00 P.M. until 6:00 P.M. on January 2. At this spot on McFadden's Ford, Federal soldiers watched as the Rebels scattered a division on the opposite side of the river. When the impetuous Confederates charged across the river, twelve Union batteries consisting of

fifty-one guns posted on a hill above the bank poured shot, shell, and canisters into the attackers, who lost 1,800 men in half an hour. Note the artillery monument here.

Bragg began his retreat the next day, withdrawing forty miles south to Tullahoma. Stone's River was the first in a series of battles that led the Union army to Chattanooga, Atlanta, and through the heart of Georgia to the Atlantic Ocean.

Many important sites are not included in this small park. For a complete tour of each location involved in the battle, consult Volume VI, Issue 3, of *Blue and Gray* magazine.

Stone's River, near the spot where Federals forded it to counterattack on January 2, 1863.

From Stop Nine return to U.S. 41 and carefully turn left toward Murfreesboro. After 2.8 turn right onto TN 96–Old Fort Parkway. At .5 turn right, and after .1 turn right at the sign for the golf course. Continue straight at the stop sign, and pull over after .3 into the rough parking area to the right. A slight trail leads into the woods and to an extensive earthen fort.

The Federals constructed an immense facility here, Fortress Rosecrans, the largest fortification built by the Union army, to defend Murfreesboro, which was the primary supply base for operations against Chattanooga and, later, Sherman's drive on Atlanta. The complex consisted of nine outer fortifications and four

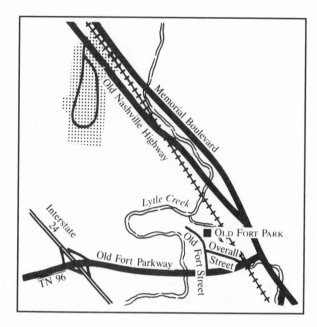

Map 6: *The Old Stone Fort area.*

inner positions. The remains of the largest work are here on the grounds of the Old Fort Park, which is a community recreation area and eighteen-hole golf course. Unfortunately, the earthworks, hidden beneath trees and brush, are undeveloped.

These overgrown remains of Fortress Rosecrans, the largest fortification built by the North during the Civil War, protected an enormous supply base.

Return to U.S. 41 and turn right. After .4 turn right on Front Street for .1 to Cannonsburgh, beside the offices of the chamber of commerce.

Cannonsburgh, the original name of Murfreesboro, is a recreated community of the late nineteenth and early twentieth centuries. It was started as a Bicentennial project in 1974, when buildings from across the South were gathered to recreate the residential, public, and commercial parts of a town from 110 years ago.

At the entrance is the first iron bridge built in the county. A tollgate represents the turnpikes that radiated in all directions from old Murfreesboro. The city's central location made it a logical choice for Tennessee's capital, which remained here for several years. The pikes, owned by families who maintained a portion of the road, were paid "pikeage" by travelers for use of the route.

In the village is a scaled down overshot waterwheel that powers a gristmill, equipped with 150-year-old machinery from Alabama; a one-room schoolhouse, built with logs from an old corncrib; a telephone exchange building; a two-part log home connected by a dogtrot dating from the mid-1800s; a small log courthouse; an ash hopper (water was added once a year to

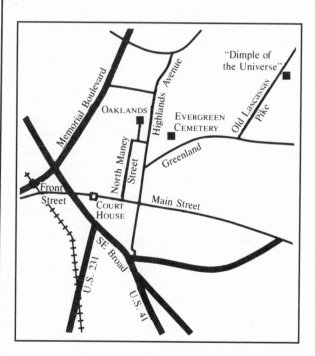

Map 7: *The Murfreesboro area.*

leach lye from the ashes, and when animal fats were added the concoction was boiled to produce soap); a recreated flatboat of a type that was built on rivers and creeks to move produce and goods to market, then was broken up and sold for timber; the Leeman House, a two-story 1820s log home with 1870s additions (girls slept upstairs front, boys upstairs back, with no connecting entrance) and authentic furnishings; a small country church (men on one side, women on the other), which was served by a circuit-riding preacher who appeared only once a month, converted from an old school; a collection of farm implements (1850–1950), mostly steam, gas, and diesel tractors from the 1920s to the present; a horse-drawn, steam-operated fire engine used by the city of Murfreesboro until 1920; a country doctor's museum; a general store; a blacksmith shop; a two thousand-gallon red cedar bucket, reportedly the largest in the world, made in Murfreesboro in 1885 and displayed around the globe; and a water-drilling rig (1885). Hand-dug and drilled wells are situated on the property.

There is also a 1906 cotton gin. Cotton was the chief cash crop of this region. In an 1870s cotton warehouse is a museum with exhibits that illustrate the life of southern communities from 1776 until 1876. An early-twentieth-century warehouse contains a diorama of the battle of Stone's River, created by the Rutherford Historical Society.

Return to U.S. 41 and turn left. After .1 turn right onto East Main Street. At .2 the Rutherford County Courthouse is directly ahead.

Murfreesboro, established in 1811, served as the capital of Tennessee from 1819 until 1826. This building (1859) is one of six antebellum courthouses still operating in Tennessee. On the grounds is a Confederate monument that honors Southerners who fell in area battles, and a plaque commemorates a brilliant raid by Nathan Bedford Forrest in July 1862. In 1946 a monument here was dedicated to the memory of General Griffith Rutherford, a hero of the American Revolution, for whom the county is named.

On July 13, 1862, Forrest divided his force to attack several camps of the occupying Federal troops. Through fierce fighting and subterfuge, Forrest captured 1,200 Union soldiers, killed nineteen, and wounded twenty more. The Confederates destroyed half a million dollars' worth of supplies and captured sixty wagons, four cannon, 300 mules, and 175 horses.

After Bragg retreated through Cumberland Gap to Knoxville in October 1862, he sent his army by rail south to Chattanooga, then north to Murfreesboro to block any Federal advance from Nashville, where the Union army returned after the battle of Perryville. When Rosecrans marched south, Bragg moved to block him at Stone's River.

In late December 1862, Confederate cavalryman Joseph Wheeler rode around Rosecrans's army, a less-publicized accomplishment than J.E.B. Stuart's raid around George McClellan earlier that year. At 1:00 P.M. on December 30 at nearby LaVergne, Wheeler destroyed 300 wagons in a Union supply train and captured 700 prisoners. Later in the day at Nolensville, Wheeler torched a second train of 150 ammunition wagons. He kept a number of ambulances for Confederate use and took an additional 200 prisoners. Wheeler camped that night near Arrington, and at 10:00 A.M. on the following morning fell upon a twenty-wagon procession at the junction of TN 102 and the Old Jefferson Pike in Rutherford County. He burned the wagons, rounded up fifty more prisoners, and returned to camp.

Murfreesboro changed hands several times during the Civil War. When Bragg evacuated the city after Stone's River, many buildings were crowded with Confederate wounded, who were abandoned to imprisonment.

The site of John Hunt Morgan's marriage, which occurred December 14, 1862, is on East Main Street. The bride was seventeen-year-old Martha Reed. The ceremony was conducted by General Polk, with Colonel Basil Duke the best man and Generals Bragg, Hardee, Breckinridge, and B. F. Cheatham serving as groomsmen.

Drive halfway around the courthouse, remaining on East Main Street. After .4 turn left onto North Maney. Continue straight at the stop sign at Roberts Street, and after .7 is Oaklands.

This mansion dates back to 1815, when it was a simple two-story house. Additions in the 1820s converted it into a comfortable brick home, and major changes in 1850 added four rooms, a large hall, and a monumental circular staircase. The exterior received an Italianate façade. Dr. James Maney owned a 1,500-acre plantation worked by 100 slaves, and his home was utilized by both Confederate and Federal forces. It was the scene of skirmishes between Forrest and the Federal occupation troops, and here Union colonel W. W. Duffield surrendered Murfreesboro to Forrest.

Oaklands, in Murfreesboro, hosted Jefferson Davis in December 1862 while he inspected the Army of Tennessee.

At Christmas 1862 Jefferson Davis and his aide, Colonel George W. C. Lee, one of Robert E. Lee's sons, were guests in the home while conferring with Bragg and inspecting the Army of Tennessee. Other distinguished guests of Dr. Maney included John Bell, Leonidas Polk, and Matthew Fontaine Maury, the pioneer oceanographer who developed mines for the Confederacy.

Oaklands has been restored to its antebellum splendor with period furnishings. On the grounds are ancient oaks and the Oaklands Medical Museum.

Return to Roberts Street and turn left. After .1 turn right onto Highland for .3, then turn left onto Greenland. Turn left into the second entrance to Evergreen Cemetery, and a Confederate section is on the left.

This plot contains 2,000 soldiers who died of illness before Stone's River or were killed during the battle. A monument honoring the men was dedicated May 12, 1915.

Return to Greenland and turn left. After .9 turn left onto Old Lascassas Pike, and at .4 to the right is a stone pillar with a plaque that marks the geographic center of Tennessee, determined in 1834. Residents of the area call this the "Dimple of the Universe."

At 501 North Maple Street is the Children's Discovery House Museum, which has hands-on science, nature, and art exhibits. ■

This monument honors the Confederate dead in Murfreesboro who died of illness in camp or in battle at Stone's River.

The Road to Chickamauga

For six months following Stone's River, Rosecrans remained at Murfreesboro while Bragg established a line along the Duck River with headquarters at Tullahoma. The opposing armies were thirty miles apart, and both were supplied by the Nashville & Chattanooga Railroad. Rosecrans planned and prepared his forces, but Bragg frittered away the time. This inactivity led Bragg's generals to hold him in greater contempt than before.

While Rosecrans ignored pressure from above to advance, 15,000 Confederate cavalry under Forrest, Wheeler, Morgan, and Earl Van Dorn broke large sections of the Louisville & Nashville Railroad, burned bridges and depots, and destroyed tunnels. In spite of this damage, Rosecrans slowly managed to build up his supplies and mounts, and accumulated 70,000 men, including 12,000 cavalry, for an offensive. Another 22,500 men would be left to protect Union supply lines. Bragg counted 40,000 troops, of which 8,000 were cavalry.

General-in-Chief Halleck wired Rosecrans that officials in Washington were watching his inactivity with "great dissatisfaction." They feared that Bragg would reinforce Vicksburg if Rosecrans did not act soon. Union soldiers spent this time drilling endlessly; they built substantial log cabins and even planted trees on company streets. The hungry Confederates drilled and hunted for food. On June 24, with Halleck again threatening his removal, Rosecrans finally advanced.

Between Murfreesboro and Tullahoma is a large ridge pierced by four passes. From west to east they are Guy's Gap, Bell Buckle Gap, Liberty Gap, and Hoover's Gap. Polk, with the greater part of the Confederate force, covered Guy's and Bell Buckle gaps from Shelbyville. At Wartrace Hardee defended Liberty Gap. Hoover's Gap was considered unsuitable for use by a large army and was patrolled only by cavalry.

Rosecrans advanced against each gap and around both sides of the ridge. Bragg, who thought the true Union effort would come from the west, aimed at Shelbyville through Bell Buckle Gap where the terrain was more accommodating. Rosecrans's actual plan was for Thomas to capture Hoover's Gap. From there he would brush aside Wheeler's cavalry and advance to Manchester, which was ten miles from Tullahoma. This move would outflank

A Story of Thomas

During the long lull between Stone's River and Rosecrans's push to Chickamauga, General George Thomas received a man who requested leave. Such matters were usually handled by subordinate officers, but Thomas was so loved by his soldiers that they casually approached him. Asked the reason for the furlough, the man answered, "I ain't seen my old woman, General, for four months."

"And I have not seen mine for two years," Thomas replied. "If a general can submit to such privation, surely a private can."

"Don't know about that, General," the soldier responded. "You see, me and my wife ain't made that way." ■

An Incident on the Retreat From Duck River

As the Confederate army labored over the Cumberland Plateau on their retreat to Chattanooga from the Duck River line, Nathan Bedford Forrest's fierce troopers protected the rear. They were withdrawing from Cowan, Tennessee, when a large Union cavalry force attacked. As the Confederates retired through the streets, a feisty Rebel woman left her house to scream abuse at the soldiers. When Forrest rode by, the woman pointed at him and shouted, "You great big cowardly rascal, why don't you turn and fight like a man instead of running like a cur? I wish old Forrest was here; he'd make you fight." Forrest laughed, but later said it was preferable to charge a battery of Union artillery than to face that woman. ∎

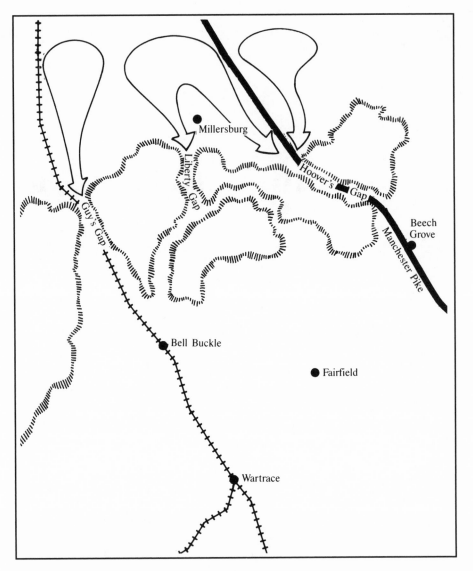

Map 8: The Federal route through the Highland Rim gaps.

Hardee and sever the Confederate route of retreat. McCook stormed Liberty Gap to hold Hardee in place as Union general Gordon Granger led a small reserve corps around the western edge of the ridge and through Guy's Gap to freeze Polk at Shelbyville. Crittenden feinted around the eastern slope toward Bradyville, then followed Thomas through Hoover's Gap. The Federals successfully seized the gaps and drove off several determined Confederate counterattacks.

Seventeen straight days of heavy rains that accompanied Rosecrans's advance slowed the maneuvering of both armies. A Confederate officer

After Stone's River, Confederates established a defensive line along the Duck River.

commented that he thought Tullahoma came from the Latin words *tulla* meaning "mud," and *homa*, meaning "more mud."

Despite the adverse weather, Thomas was approaching Manchester by June 26. Bragg, completely baffled by Rosecrans's brilliant maneuvering, had almost been cut off from his escape route. With Bragg's characteristic indecision precluding a counterattack, he ordered the army to concentrate at Tullahoma. Thomas occupied Manchester on June 27, and Rosecrans' entire force arrived three days later. Rather than attack Bragg's works around Tullahoma, Rosecrans again swept to the southeast through Hills-

Braxton Bragg's Second Crisis

In early 1863 Braxton Bragg suffered physical and nervous breakdowns. Newspapers had savaged his leadership at Stone's River, and in January Bragg counterattacked. He read the negative editorials to his staff and announced that if he had lost the confidence of his generals, he would resign. Bragg was obviously stupid, as well as incompetent, because his officers told him he should resign. He did not take their advice, but on the following day he circulated a letter to his corps and divisional leaders, asking if

it was true that he had advised retreat after Stone's River. His generals all agreed that they had urged the retreat, but Bragg repeated the claim that he would leave the Army of Tennessee if he had lost their confidence. Most reaffirmed their belief that Bragg should resign.

Jefferson Davis was disturbed by this controversy, which he felt showed poor judgment on Bragg's part. Davis sent Joseph Johnston to investigate the situation, with authorization to relieve Bragg if he

thought it necessary. However, because Johnston would take the command, he hesitated to relieve Bragg since it would look as if he were advancing his own interests.

Bragg informed Johnston that the controversy in his army was instigated by a few malcontents. Unfortunately, Johnston saw Bragg's army at its best, in camp and drilling, and he praised the condition of the Army of Tennessee. Feeling vindicated, Bragg moved against several generals, relieving them of command or ar-

resting them. They were either court-martialed or transported out of the Tennessee theater.

When problems continued, Davis sent Johnston back to take command from Bragg. Johnston, finding Bragg worried about his wife, who was thought to be dying, delayed relieving the general. By the time Mrs. Bragg recovered, Johnston found himself incapacitated by the severe wounds he had suffered a year earlier at Fair Oaks. As a result, Bragg survived to bungle the battle of Chickamauga. ■

Two Confederate spies are executed in Franklin, Tennessee, by the Union Army of the Cumberland on June 3, 1863. [HARPER'S WEEKLY]

boro and Pelham to threaten the railroad at Decherd and Cowan, twenty miles in Bragg's rear. Bragg retreated to establish a line along the Elk River near Decherd on July 1, but he soon continued south to Cowan and sent his army across the Cumberland Plateau. The Rebels crossed the Tennessee River at Bridgeport, Alabama, and marched east to Chattanooga, which they had left one year earlier on the march to Perryville.

Rosecrans paused to rest and resupply his command when he reached Tullahoma on July 3. His nearly bloodless displacement (Federal casualties totaled only 570; Confederate losses were nearly 2,000) of Bragg went unnoticed due to two momentous events: the titanic battle of Gettysburg and the opening of the Mississippi River following the surrender of Vicksburg. Secretary of War Edwin Stanton urged Rosecrans to continue the campaign, and on August 4, after six weeks of inaction, Halleck bluntly ordered Rosecrans to continue the pursuit of Bragg.

Chattanooga was not an easy target. To the north and east is a large, rugged mountain called Walden's Ridge, and to the west is the narrow valley of the Tennessee River, both easily defended. After an extensive scrutiny of his maps, Rosecrans selected an audacious strategy. He would sweep far to the southwest of Chattanooga and march on the city from the south through several narrow valleys that approach Chattanooga through Georgia. The valleys were shielded by four mountains: Raccoon, Lookout, Missionary Ridge, and Pigeon. If Bragg could be caught by surprise, he would have to give up Chattanooga. The Confederates might retreat all the way to Atlanta before making a stand.

Rosecrans began the move on August 16. On the left, Crittenden crossed the Tennessee River at Shellmound, Tennessee, to approach Chattanooga; in the center, Thomas crossed the river at Bridgeport, Alabama, twenty-seven miles from Chattanooga, to traverse Lookout Mountain at Steven's Gap and march through Trenton and LaFayette, Georgia; far out on the right, McCook bridged the Tennessee at Caperton's Ferry, Alabama, climbed rugged Lookout Mountain at Winston's Gap, and marched toward Alpine, Georgia. Nine thousand cavalry cleared the path for 50,000 soldiers and 200 cannon as the Federals advanced along a fifty-mile-wide front.

To screen his true movements and divert Bragg's attention, Rosecrans sent three brigades to creep quietly over Walden's Ridge. On August 21 they shelled Chattanooga from the north side of the Tennessee River. Their skillful maneuvering over the next three weeks convinced Bragg that Rosecrans was massing his army to the north and building pontoons for a crossing.

Mary Walker ■ Medal of Honor Winner

When the Civil War started, Mary Walker, a graduate of the Syracuse Medical College, volunteered to serve the Union as a nurse. In Washington, D.C., she met General George Thomas, who advised her to obtain further training. Perhaps Thomas thought that was the last he would see of Walker; but after a year at the Hygeio–Therapeutic Center in New York, she caught up with the general in Chattanooga, just before Chickamauga.

True to his word, Thomas gave Walker the commission of assistant surgeon. Following Chickamauga, the Union hospital system was overwhelmed by 10,000 casualties. Walker worked thirty-six hours in one stretch. She was captured while attending wounded Confederates on the field and sent to Libby Prison in Richmond.

For her unselfish service, the Medal of Honor, the first given to a woman and the only one awarded to a woman during the Civil War, was bestowed on Mary Walker by the U.S. Congress. Deciding in 1919 that too many Medals of Honor had been issued during the Civil War, Congress rescinded Walker's award. The spirited woman refused to surrender it, and in 1977 Congress reinstated the medal and authorized a commemorative stamp about Mary Walker. ■

Union stockades guarding railroad bridges along the Louisville & Nashville Railroad were of little protection against raids by Confederate cavalry. [HARPER'S WEEKLY]

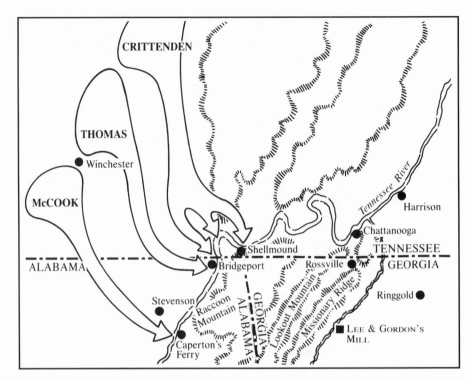

Map 9: The route Federal armies took in crossing the Tennessee River.

Because of illness and desertions, the Army of Tennessee counted only 30,000 men, but Bragg was promised more from Mississippi and Alabama. Polk held Chattanooga, watching Walden's Ridge to the north, with Hardee placed to the northeast to guard the approaches from Knoxville, recently occupied by the Federals. When Hardee was reassigned to Mississippi, President Davis promoted General Daniel Harvey Hill to assume his command.

Bragg had again been completely duped by Rosecrans. It was September 7 before he became aware that the Federals were in his rear. Bragg then evacuated Chattanooga, retreating into northwest Georgia to protect his railroad supply line and the industrial center of Atlanta. Crittenden quickly occupied Chattanooga and continued south. As their sweeping marches continued, Union armies under Crittenden, Thomas, and McCook became dangerously separated as they slowly traversed the steep, narrow, and rough mountain roads.

When Bragg learned the location of the three Federal corps, he finally managed to turn the tables on Rosecrans. The Confederates were not fleeing for safety, as the Federal general was led to believe by reports from "deserters." They were about to turn and loose a savage counterstroke against the Army of the Cumberland.

Rosecrans, convinced that the Army of Tennessee was in full retreat, continued his rapid pursuit through the mountains. Thomas advised Rose-

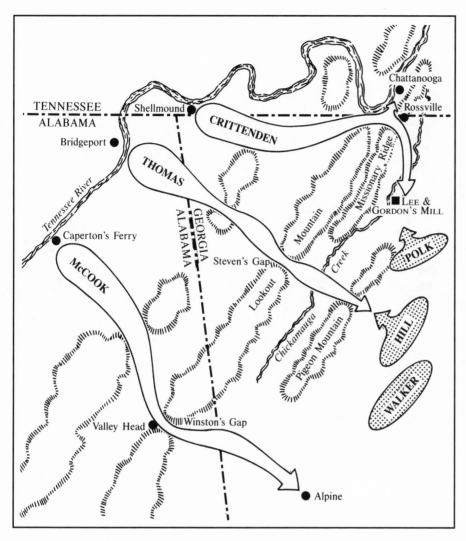

Map 10: The Federal approach to Chickamauga.

The Murder of Earl Van Dorn

There was no doubt that Confederate general Van Dorn was a fighting man. He was wounded five times in Mexico and captured three Union ships at Galveston, Texas, but began an unfortunate losing streak when his forces lost the battles of Pea Ridge, Arkansas, and Corinth, Mississippi. Besides his reputation as a soldier, there were many tales concerning Van Dorn's notorious womanizing.

During the spring of 1863, Van Dorn brought his cavalry to Middle Tennessee to assist Braxton Bragg. At Spring Hill he reportedly had an affair with Jessie Helen McKissack Peters, who was described as "incredibly beautiful," and a "beguiling temptress." Jessie was the young cousin and third wife of Dr. George B. Peters, who had grown wealthy through real estate holdings in Tennessee and Arkansas.

When Dr. Peters returned from a business trip on April 12, he heard that Van Dorn had visited his wife every night. On May 7 a jealous Dr. Peters entered Van Dorn's headquarters and shot him once in the head. Peters was never tried for the general's murder.

In 1866 Dr. Peters filed for divorce from Jessie, claiming she had abandoned him on the day he killed Van Dorn. Curiously enough, they later remarried and she bore him three children. Explaining why she wore black to Peters's funeral in 1899, Jessie reportedly said, "I never cared for George, but I guess I owe him this much." ∎

crans to gather his troops at Chattanooga and consolidate his gains, but Rosecrans refused. Believing Bragg was in full flight, he decided to pursue and defeat him.

Far from fleeing, on September 9 Bragg had his entire army concentrated at La Fayette, just south of Pigeon Mountain. Bragg had Rosecrans's columns under constant surveillance and knew that Thomas's isolated 20,000-man corps would descend Lookout Mountain via Steven's Gap, which leads into a wide, fertile valley called McLemore's Cove. Narrow Dug Gap on Pigeon Mountain, held by Bragg, would prevent Thomas from marching east, and to the south Pigeon Mountain and Missionary Ridge merge to form a natural barrier. When Thomas entered the cove, Bragg planned to strike him from the north, where the valley broadens and leads to Lee and

Chattanooga as seen from the north bank of the Tennessee River; Lookout Mountain is to the right. [HARPER'S WEEKLY]

Gordon's Mill along Chickamauga Creek, and from the east via Dug Gap. The Federal corps would be trapped in the cove.

Bragg had taken time to reorganize the Army of Tennessee. He divided his forces into four corps of two divisions each, led by Polk, Hill, Simon B. Buckner, recently arrived from Knoxville, and General William H. T. Walker, who had brought reinforcements from Mississippi.

Late on the evening of September 9, as Thomas's lead division ventured into the valley, Bragg massed 23,000 men and considerable artillery north of McLemore's Cove. He ordered one of Polk's divisions to attack Thomas from the north in the morning, as one of Hill's divisions struck the Federals from Dug Gap. Bragg impatiently awaited the sounds of combat on the following day, but Polk's division tarried to make sure the second division was in position. Meanwhile, Hill's divisional commander made a long list of reasons, several of them patently false, why he could not attack. Late in the day Bragg tried again. Sending Hill's other division to join Polk's original division, Bragg ordered an assault. It also failed to materialize, leaving Bragg livid by this casual disregard of his orders. While the Confederates were wasting opportunities to attack, the commander of Thomas's lead division recognized his danger and escaped out of harm's way up Steven's Gap.

After occupying Chattanooga, on September 12, Crittenden had advanced south toward La Fayette, Georgia. Two of his divisions were at Ringgold, while the other was dangerously isolated at Lee and Gordon's Mill, at the head of McLemore's Cove. Bragg ordered Polk, who now had four divisions under his command, to gobble up the exposed Federal division, then turn and destroy the other two. Polk initially followed incorrect directions, and by the time he arrived at the mill Crittenden's command was united. Once again, Polk took it upon himself not to attack.

Despite these close calls, Rosecrans was slow to believe that Bragg was making a stand. He dismissed the alarming reports of Thomas and Crittenden until September 13. Finally recognizing the truth, he ordered Thomas and McCook to close up with Crittenden at Lee and Gordon's Mill. McCook, thirty miles to the south, required four exhausting days to retrace his route, wrestling cannon and wagons over the ridges of Alabama and Georgia. He descended Lookout Mountain at Steven's Gap and followed Thomas down the valley to the mill. After his initial aggressiveness, Bragg returned to his cautious form and did not molest Rosecrans while the Union army was concentrating.

Rosecrans received further bad news while he waited anxiously for McCook to arrive. Rumor had Bragg being reinforced from Mississippi and Virginia, and the stories were true. General James Longstreet was bringing his 12,000-man corps by train from Robert E. Lee's army in Virginia. On the incredible 900-mile journey through the Carolinas, the troops changed trains sixteen times. Coincidentally, all the mistakes and delays allowed just enough time for the full strength of each army to arrive on the battlefield.

On September 18 Bragg ordered an attack against the Union left, held by

The Strange Case of Clement C. Vallandigham

Clement C. Vallandigham had been a leading Democratic congressman from Ohio until 1860. He viciously criticized Lincoln and the war, stating that he preferred a "Union of free will, not of arms." Vallandigham opposed using force to hold states in the Union and claimed that Lincoln was a man of "wicked and desperate cunning" who initiated the war and violated the Constitution to perpetuate it.

Vallandigham continued his attacks after being defeated for reelection. For expressing these beliefs, he was branded a Copperhead, a Northerner who supported the Confederacy.

Vallandigham was arrested in Ohio and transported to Cincinnati where a military court found him guilty of "sympathies for those in arms against the Government of the United States." He was ordered imprisoned for the duration of the war, but Abraham Lincoln changed the sentence to expulsion.

Vallandigham was sent by rail to Murfreesboro, where he entered the camp of William Rosecrans on May 24, 1863. He was immediately taken to Confederate lines under a flag of truce. Braxton Bragg accepted Vallandigham as a "distressed wayfarer." This

"man without a country" was not a Confederate sympathizer, as he bluntly informed Bragg: "I am a citizen of Ohio and the United States, still claiming and owing allegiance to both. I am within your lines against my will and by military compulsion, and therefore surrender myself as a prisoner of war."

Despite the last claim, Vallandigham was free to travel where he wished in the Confederacy. He made his way to Wilmington, North Carolina, and escaped the Confederacy on a blockade runner, then took passage to Canada, where he spent the remainder of the war. ∎

Lee and Gordon's Mill on Chickamauga Creek made meal for Civil War armies.

The Confederate Reinforcement at Chickamauga

In the spring of 1863, Confederate general James Longstreet advised Robert E. Lee to reinforce Braxton Bragg with his corps and the troops of Joseph Johnston in Mississippi. This concentration would destroy William Rosecrans, drive the Federals back to the Ohio River, and force Grant to abandon Mississippi, Longstreet predicted. Never willing to part with any troops, Lee countered that plan with his campaign to invade the North, which ended in disaster at Gettysburg.

On August 15 Longstreet wrote the Confederate secretary of war, James A. Seddon, stating that Georgia was the heart of the Confederacy and the nation would die if Rosecrans conquered the state. He wanted Lee to go on the defensive against George Meade, while he reinforced Bragg and crushed Rosecrans before

Union reinforcements could be rushed from Virginia and Mississippi.

Longstreet also took the issue to Lee. When "Marse Robert" conferred with Jefferson Davis in Richmond, they decided that Longstreet would go to Georgia with the divisions of John B. Hood and Lafayette McLaws, a total of nine infantry brigades and six artillery batteries.

Arrival of the reinforcements was delayed when Ambrose Burnside cut the Virginia & Tennessee Railroad, which connected Chattanooga with Bristol via Knoxville. Starting on September 9, 12,000 men were routed instead through Richmond, Petersburg, Wilmington, Augusta, Atlanta, and then north to the battlefield. This was the largest force ever moved such a distance—925 miles—yet it was accom-

plished in eight days.

General A. R. Lawton, quartermaster general of the Confederate army, assembled every functioning rail car he could locate—passenger, box, baggage, platform, coal, and mail. As many men rode atop the cars as within them. These miles of cars wobbling along the poor Southern railroads must have been a colorful sight. The men often had to march from one side of town to the other because the rails did not extend through a number of communities; and since Southern states had different rail gauges, the men had to detrain, then board another train at state lines. Cheering crowds, bearing food, drink, and clothing for the ragged warriors, met the trains at every stop.

"Now, General," Lee had said in a fatherly manner to

Longstreet, "you must beat those people in the West."

"If I live," Longstreet replied, "but I would not give a single man of my command for a fruitless victory." Those words seem to have been a premonition of the outcome at Chickamauga.

Longstreet's men were delayed a day in Atlanta as Johnston's Mississippi troops, the divisions of Bushrod Johnson and John C. Breckinridge, and two divisions of William H. T. Walker's Reserve Corps, arrived from the west and traveled north first. Simon B. Buckner's corps from Knoxville soon joined Bragg.

Rosecrans was slow to realize that he was outnumbered by this logistical feat. When battle was joined, the disparity in numbers was decisive. ∎

Crittenden at Lee and Gordon's Mill. Bragg hoped to turn the Federal left flank and drive Rosecrans's entire army into McLemore's Cove for easy destruction. Three Confederate divisions marched, countermarched, and crowded together on the same roads while their commanders suffered from lack of communication and coordination. To reach Crittenden, the Confederates had to cross Chickamauga Creek, but they were delayed by Union cavalry. By day's end, one division had partially crossed the creek, a second found its bridge destroyed and had to ford the stream at a different location, and only the third, the first division of Longstreet's to arrive—Texans led by General John B. Hood—was where Bragg wanted it. No attack developed, but by morning three-fourths of the Army of Tennessee was in position.

On September 17 Crittenden had extended his left flank to keep Bragg from turning it. After watching the dust of marching Confederate columns all day on September 18, Rosecrans ordered Thomas to pass behind Crittenden and extend the vulnerable left. By the morning of September 19, the Union line stretched for three and one-half miles to the north of Lee and Gordon's Mill.

The action at Chickamauga started early on September 19. Believing a Confederate brigade had crossed the creek, Thomas sent a brigade to drive it back. The Federals were repulsed by hordes of Rebels, and Thomas committed a division, which steadied his line. Bragg responded with a Confederate division that drove the Federals and captured five cannon. Thomas quickly realized he was facing the bulk of the Confederate army and requested additional troops from Rosecrans, who dispatched one of McCook's

American Vice President and Confederate General ■ John C. Breckinridge

Breckinridge, born near Lexington, Kentucky, in 1821, graduated from Centre College in 1839 and studied law at Transylvania University. After establishing a law practice in 1845, he entered politics.

Breckinridge spent two years in the Kentucky legislature, then four years in the U.S. House of Representatives before becoming James Buchanan's vice president at the age of thirty-five. He resigned that office in 1859 to enter the Senate, and in 1860 was the presidential candidate for the Southern Democrats. Although he opposed the war, Breckinridge resigned from the Senate and offered his services to the Confederacy, rising to the rank of major general. His parting statement to fellow

Kentuckians was, "To defend your birthright and mine, I exchange with proud satisfaction a term of six years in the Senate of the United States for the musket of a soldier."

The former vice president commanded a reserve corps at Shiloh. Dispatched to Louisiana during the summer of 1862, he was repulsed in an effort to recapture Baton Rouge. This action prevented his participation in the Perryville campaign, which was unfortunate for the Confederacy because he may have been the only person who could have persuaded any number of Kentuckians to join the cause. Breckinridge performed well at Stone's River, leading his beloved Orphan Brigade, then traveled to Mis-

sissippi with Joseph Johnston in an attempt to relieve the siege of Vicksburg in the summer of 1864. He returned to the Army of Tennessee in time to participate in the bloody battle of Chickamauga, where the Orphans distinguished themselves on the morning of September 20. Breckinridge went on to command the Department of Southwest Virginia, accompanying Jubal Early on his Washington, D.C., raid in the summer of 1864.

Jefferson Davis appointed Breckinridge to be his secretary of war in February 1865, and the two fled Richmond together at the end of the war. Breckinridge escaped to England, where he lived for a time. Finding himself destitute when he returned home to Kentucky

in 1869, eight years after his departure, Breckinridge renewed his law practice and died in Lexington in 1875. ■

[DICTIONARY OF AMERICAN PORTRAITS]

The Gordon-Lee House at Chickamauga, Rosecrans's pre-battle headquarters and Union hospital. [BATTLES AND LEADERS]

The Origin of Pup Tents

Brigadier General Samuel Beatty's brigade, which fought at Chickamauga, made an important contribution to America's military terminology. When issued tents so small that they could not stand inside, the soldiers called them "dog tents" or "pup tents." Signs reading "Sons of Bitches Within" or "Pups for Sale" were hung on the tents. When William Rosecrans inspected these troops, they fell upon their hands and knees and barked at their commander, who promised to find them more suitable shelter. ■

divisions, which stopped the Confederates. Bragg flung another division forward to blunt the Federal drive. When a fresh Union division threatened the integrity of the Confederate battle line, yet another Southern division entered the fray and forced the Federals to retreat again, although one-third of its men became casualties within minutes. This Confederate effort broke the Union line and captured the La Fayette Road, temporarily isolating Thomas from Crittenden. With the Rebels threatening to capture the Chattanooga Road, which was Rosecrans's line of retreat, Thomas committed another division, which stemmed the Confederate advance.

The impetuous Hood had waited throughout the day for permission to attack. Frustrated, at 4:00 P.M. he sent in two divisions without orders. The Texans fell upon a single Federal division and drove it until one of the last two Union divisions remaining uncommitted counterattacked and endangered Hood's flank. At twilight a Confederate division arriving from the mill hit Thomas, capturing three guns and advancing a mile until stopped by darkness.

By committing his units to battle piecemeal throughout the day, Bragg had squandered a perfect opportunity to achieve a decisive victory. One full assault would have ruptured Thomas's line, turned the Union left flank, and trapped the Union army in McLemore's Cove.

About midday, Rosecrans had moved his headquarters from the mill to the front, but he and a visitor, Assistant Secretary of War Charles A. Dana, could see little of the wilderness battlefield. Like all participants at Chickamauga, they followed the action by the sounds of battle. Both sides had suffered staggering casualties, but as darkness fell the Confederate and Union lines had stabilized.

The autumn night in the north Georgia mountains turned cold, and few

CONFEDERATE LINE OF BATTLE IN THE
CHICKAMAUGA WOODS.

Confederates advance to the attack through the wilderness of Chickamauga. [BATTLES AND LEADERS]

soldiers had blankets. Confederates shivered in clothes wet from fording Chickamauga Creek; but they held the water, leaving Union soldiers thirsty. No fires could be built, and jittery pickets fired continually, with occasional discharges of artillery also disturbing the night. Soldiers lay amidst the dead and dying, and the wounded stranded between the lines cried and groaned in agony. The rumbling of ambulances and artillery being repositioned and the sounds of marching men were heard as plans for renewing the battle were made. Few slept during this night as men in blue and gray erected crude log breastworks on the thickly forested battlefield.

Bragg met with Polk and reorganized his army into two wings for an assault at daybreak. The right wing, led by Polk, consisted of the divisions of Polk, Hill, and Walker. The left wing included the troops of Hood, Buckner, and Longstreet. They would be led by Longstreet, if he appeared in

Foremost of the "Fighting McCooks" ■ Alexander McDowell McCook

McCook held the highest rank of the fourteen brothers and cousins from the McCook clan who fought in the Civil War. Born in Ohio in 1831, he required an extra year to graduate from West Point. McCook served on the frontier, taught infantry tactics at West Point, and saw his first Civil War action at Manassas. He led a brigade under Don Carlos Buell at Shiloh and Corinth, and was promoted to major general in 1862. His corps fought hard at Perryville and Stone's River, but at Chickamauga the troops were routed. Rosecrans placed part of the blame for the defeat on McCook, who requested a court of inquiry which cleared him. Despite official exoneration, McCook waited a year for orders which never came.

McCook received unusual treatment from the army. Although he was brevetted brigadier and major general in the regular army at the end of the war, in 1866 he reverted to his prewar rank of captain. McCook was promoted to lieutenant colonel in 1867, but became a major general again by the time he retired in 1895. His postwar years saw service on the frontier and as William Sherman's aide. McCook died in 1903 and is buried in Cincinnati. ■

49

Longstreet Almost Gets Captured at Chickamauga

When the train bearing James Longstreet arrived at Catoosa Station at 2:00 P.M. on September 19, the general was upset that no one was present to greet or guide him. He and his chief of staff, Colonel G. Moxley Sorrel, and chief of ordnance, Lieutenant Colonel P. I. Manning, waited impatiently for two hours while listening to the distant sounds of a heavy battle. When a train with their mounts arrived, the three jumped their horses from a boxcar and followed the debris of war—ambulances, stragglers, and supply wagons—toward the fighting.

As the autumn darkness enveloped the woods, the party strayed from the main road. At length a challenge rang out from a sentry. "Who goes there?"

"Friends," Longstreet responded, noting the picket seemed to have a northern accent.

The sentry, equally suspicious, asked for further identification. When Longstreet asked what unit the guard was with, the response was in numerals. This was bad news, for Confederate units were usually named after their commanders, while Federal outfits were identified by numbers.

Noticing that the road ahead was barricaded, Longstreet announced loudly to his companions, "Let us ride down a little and find a better crossing."

The picket fired but missed as the Confederates rode into the woods. They galloped to the main road and finally located Bragg, asleep in an ambulance. After an hour's conference to plan the next day's battle, Longstreet and his aides went to sleep beneath a tree. ∎

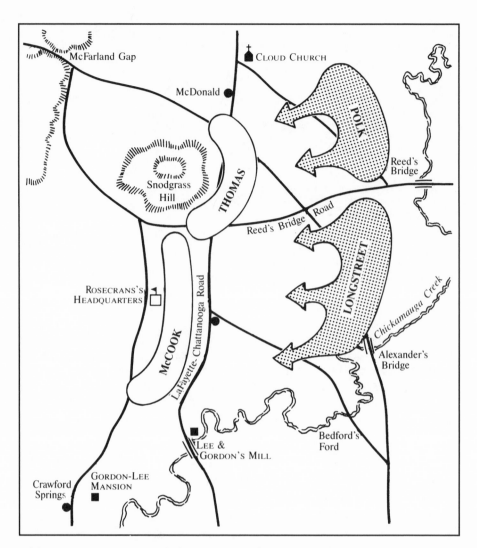

Map 11: Morning action at Chickamauga, September 20.

time. At that moment Longstreet was very angry. He had arrived at Ringgold in the afternoon, but no one had met him. Longstreet had wandered for hours through the Georgia woods, following the sounds of battle; at one point, he almost blundered into Union lines. When Longstreet eventually located Bragg at 11:00 P.M., the two decided to continue the strategy of the first day. In echelon, the divisions of Polk's wing would strike Thomas in succession, followed by Longstreet. Once again they would attempt to shatter the Federal left wing and drive Rosecrans into McLemore's Cove.

The atmosphere in the Union camp was grim. Rosecrans's line had nearly broken several times during the day, and there was evidence that Longstreet was on the field. Sheridan noted that "much depression prevailed" at

Confederate forces splashed across Chickamauga Creek to attack the Federals in September 1863.

A Tale of Chickamauga

Confederate general William B. Bates relentlessly drove his brigade forward against fierce Union resistance at Chickamauga, capturing twelve enemy cannon along the way. A story is told that when Jefferson Davis inspected the battlefield a month later, he noticed a dead horse that had obviously belonged to an officer and inquired to whom it had belonged. "General Bates," he was told. A bit further on Davis came upon a second horse. "General Bates," his escort said. Astride the Union log breastworks Davis saw a third horse. "General Bates," was again the answer. Impressed, Davis promoted Bates, who was a very junior brigadier, to the rank of major general. ■

headquarters. He considered their situation to be "a bad strait unquestionably." Rosecrans decided to remain on the defensive. Thomas would hold the left and McCook the right, with Crittenden held in reserve.

During the night, Hill's two divisions were ordered to march from the extreme left of the Confederate line to the extreme right to open the attack at dawn. Hill, who did not receive the order until daylight, allowed his men to eat breakfast before they moved. Furious, as the hours passed with no attack, Bragg sent an officer to locate Polk, who was found reading a newspaper and waiting for his breakfast. At 9:45 A.M. the assault finally stepped off.

Breckinridge's division hit Thomas first, his men overlapping the Union left flank. Confederate Kentuckians fought Federal Kentuckians at a distance of thirty yards. The Rebels briefly seized the road to Chattanooga but were unable to hold it. The next Southern division met a withering fire from Union soldiers crouched behind log breastworks. Finding shelter behind trees, the Confederates returned fire as best they could. Polk's two divisions were next in line, but they reeled from the volleys of musket and cannon fire that spewed from the works.

The Union line remained intact, but Thomas was being sorely pressed. He begged Rosecrans for reinforcements, which arrived regularly. At 10:30 A.M., one of Thomas's officers reported a gap in the center of the Union

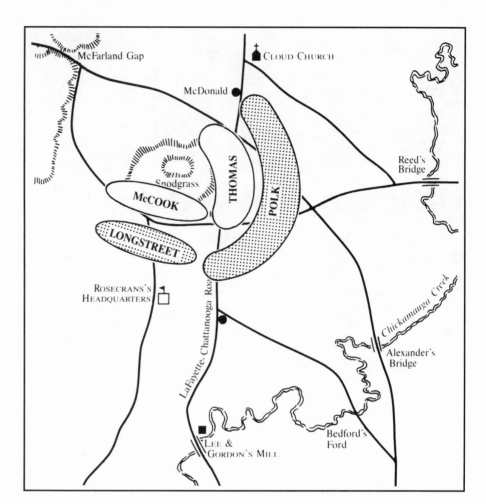

Map 12: Afternoon action at Chickamauga, September 20.

Chickamauga Wood

The battle of Chickamauga was so fierce that trees in the forests were riddled with bullets, grape shot, and shrapnel. Until 1900, local sawmills refused to accept timber from the battlefield because the metal ruined their blades. ■

line. Believing it had been left by a unit sent to reinforce him, Thomas reported the dangerous hole to Rosecrans. Rosecrans ordered General Thomas J. Wood to shift his division to cover the gap. Wood knew there was no gap at that position, that the division covering it was merely concealed in the thick forest. Unfortunately, earlier that morning Wood had received a severe public tongue-lashing from Rosecrans and did not care to question his commander's judgment. At 11:30 Wood moved his division. Rosecrans called in reserve troops to fill the gap left by Wood, and he also sent most of the division beside Wood to reinforce Thomas. Three Union divisions were now on the march behind Union lines, and a quarter-mile-long hole was left in Rosecrans's position.

At that exact moment of peril, Longstreet's three divisions charged past the Brotherton farm and poured through the opening in the Union lines. Over 23,000 Confederate soldiers rampaged in Rosecrans's rear. Union soldiers panicked as Longstreet captured two Federal batteries, shattered the

At Snodgrass Hill Thomas repulses numerous Confederate attacks at Chickamauga. [HARPER'S WEEKLY]

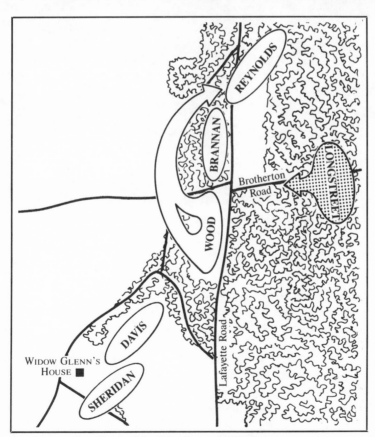

Map 13: The collapse of the Federal army at Chickamauga.

Union general George Thomas's stand at Snodgrass Hill saved the Union army at Chickamauga. [HARPER'S WEEKLY]

division belonging to General Jefferson C. Davis, then scattered Sheridan's division. Most of McCook's corps—five divisions—fled for Chattanooga.

Assistant Secretary of War Dana had been taking a nap when he was awakened "by the most infernal noise I ever heard." His first sight was of Rosecrans, a devout Catholic, crossing himself. *"Hello!"* Dana thought, *"we are in a desperate situation,"* a position Rosecrans reinforced by announcing, "If you care to live any longer, get away from here." Dana watched the Union line "melt away like leaves before the wind."

On the Confederate side, Longstreet was heard shouting, "They have fought their last man, and *he* is running." Bragg had hoped to crack the

Union soldiers fight behind improvised log barricades at Chickamauga. [LESLIE'S ILLUSTRATED]

Colonel Wilder and the Lightning Brigade

John T. Wilder was a successful businessman who owned an iron foundry in Indiana that employed 200 people. When the Civil War erupted, Wilder raised an artillery company, then rose to be colonel of the Seventeenth Indiana Infantry. It became known as the Lightning Brigade because of the innovative tactics and weapons the unit employed. The soldiers were mounted for swift travel but fought on foot, like the cavalry of Nathan Bedford Forrest. In May 1863 the brigade received seven-shot Spencer repeating rifles, which gave them the firepower of three brigades. Wilder took out a personal loan for the valuable weapons, and his men agreed to reimburse him through payroll deductions. When the war department learned of Wilder's exploits, it paid for the rifles. Ironically, Abraham Lincoln had wanted to distribute Spencers to all Union troops, but Secretary of War Edwin Stanton ignored his advice and relied almost exclusively on old-fashioned muzzle loaders.

At Hoovers's Gap in 1862, Wilder's brigade held off a force five times its number until reinforcements arrived. During the engagement at Alexander's Bridge, just before the battle of Chickamauga was joined, Wilder's men with four cannon held off a Confederate corps and its artillery for several hours. Confederate losses were considerable, which Confederate general John R. Liddell attributed to the "efficiency of the new weapons."

Two days later, when half the Union army collapsed, Wilder checked the Confederate advance and even drove a Confederate brigade back one mile, buying time for Thomas to establish a position on Snodgrass Hill and for many wounded at hospitals in Crawfish Springs to escape to Chattanooga. ∎

Federal left, but the right had been dissolved more completely than any other action in the war.

The Federals, their backs against Missionary Ridge, could only escape to Chattanooga through McFarlan Gap. "Men, animals, vehicles, became a mass of struggling, cursing, shouting, frightened life," a participant observed. The surging mass caught Rosecrans, who had his headquarters behind McCook, in its tide and swept him through the gap. He and his chief of staff, General James A. Garfield, the future president, rode five miles to Rossville, where a road led back to Chickamauga. Rosecrans intended to return to battle. He started to recite a list of orders to Garfield that would prepare Chattanooga for attack, but Garfield convinced Rosecrans that he had more authority to defend the city. Rosecrans agreed, and Garfield rode to Thomas. In Chattanooga Dana wired Washington, "Chickamauga is as fatal a day in our history as Bull Run."

Because of reinforcements received during the morning, Thomas commanded half the Army of the Cumberland: six divisions. His line was anchored on Snodgrass Hill, but the prominence would soon become famous as Horseshoe Ridge. This position, which protected the road to Chattanooga, must be held.

Colonel John T. Wilder's "Lightning Brigade," mounted infantry equipped with Spencer repeating rifles, bought some time for Thomas by staggering the advancing Confederates with their firepower at the Widow Glenn's house, site of Rosecrans's headquarters the previous day. While Longstreet paused to organize his winded men after the breakthrough, many Union stragglers joined Thomas and threw up low log breastworks.

Around 2:00 P.M., Longstreet resumed the offensive. His first attack ebbed just forty feet from the Union line. Two Rebel divisions arrived and captured the crest of Snodgrass Hill, but they were thrown back by a determined counterattack. Thomas was in a desperate situation. His men were running out of ammunition. If this position was lost, his troops would be cut off from Chattanooga. During the day Thomas had commanded 25,000 men, but now only a quarter of them remained in action.

Back in Rossville, Federal general Gordon Granger had waited with a division of inexperienced reserves since the previous day. Knowing Thomas was in trouble, he tired of waiting on orders. At length he cursed and announced, "I am going to Thomas, orders or no orders," and led his men into battle.

Thomas despaired of holding the hill when he spotted Granger in the distance. At first he feared they were another swarm of Rebels, but Granger's arrival stabilized the line, bolstered the spirits of the besieged Federals, and provided them with badly needed ammunition.

In the early evening Longstreet sent his last fresh division into battle. The Confederates fearlessly leaped over windrows of dead and dying comrades, but after hand-to-hand fighting at the Union line, the Rebels were thrown back. Garfield arrived with the first word Thomas had received of the disaster. Garfield ordered a retreat, but Thomas replied that a withdrawal would destroy his command. He would hold until dark, then slip away. Garfield sent word to Rosecrans that Thomas was "standing like a rock."

At dark Thomas started removing divisions from the battle line and sending them toward McFarlan Gap. The Federals threw back a Confederate

The Late Afternoon Ride of James Garfield

When James Longstreet split William Rosecrans's army, the right half took hasty flight toward Chattanooga, bearing with it Rosecrans and his chief of staff, Colonel James A. Garfield, the future president. The left half made a stand at Snodgrass Hill with George Thomas. At an intersection where a road led back toward Thomas, Rosecrans directed Garfield to continue into Chattanooga and ready it for defense while he returned to the battlefield. Garfield protested, stating, "I can go to General Thomas and report the situation to him much better than I can give those orders."

Convinced, Rosecrans said,

"Very well, I will go to Chattanooga myself. You go to Thomas."

Rosecrans then rode to Chattanooga. Later he was charged with abandoning his command by, of all people, Garfield.

Garfield's return to the battlefield was full of martial adventures, although they were probably exaggerated by his postwar biographers. He rode quickly through rugged forests, briars, marshes, and fields while under fire. Garfield later said that the most dangerous situation he encountered required him to leap a rail fence at a gallop and zigzag across an exposed cotton field. "Now is

your time," he remembered telling himself. "Be a man, Jim Garfield." Two orderlies accompanying him were shot dead from the saddle, and a third suffered a broken leg when his horse was killed and fell on him. Wounded twice, Garfield's own horse fell dead moments after he reached Thomas.

Garfield gave Thomas his orders from Rosecrans, which were to retreat immediately. "It will ruin the army to withdraw it now," Thomas replied calmly. "This position must be held until night."

"Thomas standing like a rock," Garfield informed Rosecrans, creating a legend both for Thomas and for himself. ∎

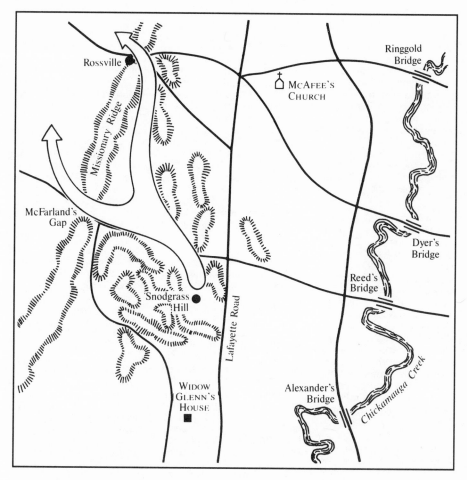

Map 14: Defense of McFarland's Gap at Horseshoe Ridge.

A Scapegoat for Chickamauga ■ Thomas Leonidas Crittenden

Crittenden, son of U.S. senator John J. Crittenden and younger brother of Confederate general George B. Crittenden, was a cousin of Union general George Thomas. Born in Kentucky in 1819, he became a lawyer and served in the Mexican War with John C. Breckinridge. After Simon B. Buckner joined Confederate service, Crittenden was appointed commander of the Unionist militia troops in Kentucky. He joined the Federal army, made brigadier general in September 1861, and commanded a division when Buell's Army of the Ohio reinforced U. S. Grant at Shiloh. Allowing his corps to be immobilized by Confederate cavalry at Perryville, Crittenden took no part in that action. He was a major general at Stone's River and led a corps which was swept from the field at Chickamauga. Although Rosecrans blamed the disaster on Crittenden and others, a court of inquiry found him blameless.

Crittenden was transferred to the East with Grant in the spring of 1864. He fought in the Army of the Potomac at Spotsylvania and Cold Harbor, then resigned from service in December 1864. President Andrew Johnson gave Crittenden a commission in the regular army in 1866, and he remained in the service until 1881. He died in 1893 in New York. ■

charge at 5:30 P.M., and only three regiments were left as Longstreet pressed another attack, the last of twenty-five assaults launched against Thomas. Out of ammunition, the remaining Federals fixed bayonets and counterattacked. Almost all of the heroic men were killed, wounded, or captured.

The Confederates suddenly found themselves shooting at each other as they closed in on the horseshoe-shaped position. Thomas had gone—"like magic"—wrote a respectful Longstreet.

The bloody battlefield was wholly in Confederate possession. Spontaneously, the entire Rebel army loosed the loudest Rebel yell that was heard on any field. The triumphant noise, which resounded across the Georgia mountains, was "the ugliest sound that any mortal ever heard," wrote Ambrose Bierce, a Union lieutenant and later a noted author.

(Continued on page 61)

Chickamauga Stories

As Confederate general A. P. Stewart's division approached Chickamauga, it came upon the home of Mrs. Debbie Thedford, who had several sons in the unit. When the soldiers, her sons included, fell upon Mrs. Thedford's potato crop, an officer attempted to chase them away. "Hold on, Mr. Officer," Mrs. Thedford shouted, "they are my potatoes, and my boys. Let 'em take 'em."

Mrs. Thedford had two other sons in James Longstreet's corps. Both were wounded and carried to her home for care.

* * * * *

On the first day of battle, Rosecrans attempted to pry information from a Captain Rice of Texas. The captain refused to respond to some questions and gave misleading answers to others. Frustrated, Rosecrans admonished the man, "Captain, you don't seem to know much for a man whose appearance seems to indicate so much intelligence."

"Well, General," the Texan drawled, "if you are not satisfied with my information, I will volunteer some. We are going to whip you most tremendously in this fight."

* * * * *

During the slaughter at Viniard's Field on September 19, an owl and several crows were seen engaging in aerial combat. "Moses, what a country," proclaimed a Confederate Irishman. "The very birds are fighting."

* * * * *

Another Southern Irishman was firing as quickly as he could reload when the regimental colors fell to the ground and Colonel William Grace ordered him to pick up the flag. Knowing the enemy concentrated their fire at color bearers, the Irishman replied, "By the holy Saint Patrick, Colonel, there's so much good shooting here I haven't a minute's time to waste fooling with that thing."

* * * * *

Late in the evening of September 19, John Hood led his division into the contest, the first Confederate troops from the East to fight in the West. Passing through Tennessee troops, they shouted, "Rise up, Tennesseans, and see the Virginians go in!" After Hood's men were forced to retreat, a Western soldier cried, "Rise up, Tennesseans, and see the Virginians come out!"

* * * * *

At Viniard's Field, Edmund Brewer Tate, one of eight brothers from Elberton, Georgia, who served in the Confederate military, was hit in the left side of his chest by a bullet that exited near his spine and made sixteen holes in his rolled blanket. Doctors, amazed that he was still alive, found his heart beating on the right side. Although it is known today that some people are born with their heart on the right side of the chest, at this time it was believed the force of the bullet had knocked the heart to the wrong side.

* * * * *

On the morning of September 20, General Leonidas Polk ordered B. F. Cheatham's division to advance. "Forward, boys, and give them hell!" the profane, hard drinking Cheatham cried. Polk, the dignified bishop-general, was caught up in the moment but hesitated to curse, so he shouted, "Give 'em what General Cheatham said, boys," or words to that effect. Actually, this story is told about every battle in which Polk and Cheatham participated. It may have occurred at Perryville or Stone's River, but it is too prevalent a story to be completely a myth.

* * * * *

Captain Sanford C. Kellogg, a courier who was carrying requests for reinforcements from George Thomas to Rosecrans, recognized Joseph J. Reynold's division but failed to see John Brannon's division in the dense trees and undergrowth. Thinking that Reynold's flank was "up in the air," or unsupported, he told Rosecrans that "Brannon was out of line and Reynold's flank exposed." As a result, Rosecrans shifted Thomas J. Wood's division and left a gap in the line that led to the terrible defeat.

Long after the Civil War, Captain Kellogg became intimate with the terrain of Chickamauga when he became the official mapmaker of the newly created Chickamauga National Military Park.

* * * * *

Hood's favorite horse, a roan named Jeff Davis, had been wounded in the leg early in the decisive battle at Gettysburg. The general was riding a different mount when he was wounded, which cost him the use of an arm. On the first day at Chickamauga, Jeff Davis was again wounded, and Hood borrowed another horse for the following day's battle. Riding into the fierce fight, he was wounded in the right leg, which had to be amputated. Hood's troops became convinced that he was only safe when riding his own horse. The amputation was performed by Dr. T. G. Richardson, later president of the American Medical Association.

* * * * *

As Confederates swarmed past the Widow Glenn's house and routed the divisions of Jefferson C. Davis and Philip H. Sheridan, William H. Lytle decided an audacious attack by his brigade might slow the Confederates and give Rosecrans time to establish a second line. "All right, men," he shouted, "we can die but once. This is the time and the place. Let us charge." Pausing for a moment, he added, "Boys, if we whip them today, we will eat our Christmas dinner at home." The brave charge was quickly overwhelmed, and Lytle died from four bullet wounds.

* * * * *

After dark on September 19, an eighteen-year-old boy clad in homespun found Captain H. W. Henry of Company I, Twenty-second Alabama, and asked to enlist. Certainly, Henry answered, but there will be a great battle tomorrow. The young man replied that was of no concern. On the following day, the company was lying low under a terrible Union fire, but the young volunteer was seen fully erect, loading, taking deliberate aim, and firing, over and over again.

"Lie down, you fool!" Henry shouted. "You will be riddled with bullets. Get behind a rock or a tree and shoot."

"I was just as safe as you was behind a tree," the boy later explained to the captain, "for a man don't get killed until his time comes nohow."

* * * * *

A Confederate private named Challon, a kindly man nearly sixty years old, was loved for the stories he spun around the campfire. At Chickamauga a bullet broke his thigh bone, then raging fires almost consumed him. After being rescued by his comrades, Challon said, "No matter if the old man dies; we whipped the rascals."

* * * * *

As a Union officer tried to rally the troops streaming for Chattanooga, he heard one soldier call, "We'll talk to you, my son, when we get to the Ohio River."

* * * * *

The Snodgrass Hill position was first occupied by Colonel Morton C. Hunter of Indiana. Although his regiment fought well, it was forced to retreat; but he ordered it to pause every fifty yards for a half-mile to fire on the victorious Confederates. When Hunter reached the hill, he muttered, "I will not retreat another inch."

* * * * *

Colonel William C. Oates of the Fifteenth Alabama came upon fifteen-year-old Bryant Skipper trailing his company by a considerable distance with tears streaming down his cheeks. Seeking tc console the boy, Oates observed that he was not wounded and would probably survive the battle, so he should not be scared. "Afraid, hell!" the boy retorted. "That ain't it. I am so damned tired I can't keep up with my company." The boy survived to sire ten children and serve as a sheriff in Alabama.

■　■　■　■　■

Thomas struggled magnificently to hold his perilous position on Snodgrass Hill. Riding up to General Charles Harker, he announced, "This hill must be held, and I trust you to do it." Harker replied that his brigade would "hold it or die here." Riding up to Colonel Emerson Opdycke, Thomas demanded, "This point must be held." Opdycke responded, "We will hold this ground, or go to heaven from it." For its resolute stand, Opdycke's 125th Ohio became known as the "Tiger Regiment."

■　■　■　■　■

Union general James B. Steedman reached Snodgrass Hill at a critical moment, leading 7,500 Union reinforcements who carried 95,000 rounds of ammunition. As one of his green regiments began to break under the furious Confederate attacks, Steedman grabbed its banner and roared, "Go back, boys, go back; but the flag can't go with you." The soldiers rallied and recharged into the battle. When words failed to sway another group of men, Steedman hurled rocks at the soldiers until they reentered the fray.

■　■　■　■　■

Colonel Edward A. King had commanded the Sixty-eighth Indiana when the Union garrison at Munfordville, Kentucky, was surrendered in 1862. At that time he had wrapped the regimental flag around his body to keep it from falling into Rebel hands. Confederate general Simon B. Buckner, who had seen King in Indiana several

months earlier while he was a Union prisoner following the Confederate capitulation of Fort Donelson, commented that the Federal officer had gained weight.

When King was killed at Chickamauga, his soldiers placed the body on a caisson as they retreated. "He saved our flag at Munfordville," one of his men later stated, "and we saved his body at Chickamauga, the only one brought off that bloody field." King's remains were eventually buried in Dayton, Ohio, following the largest funeral in that city's history.

■　■　■　■　■

During the Federal retreat from Snodgrass Hill, General John B. Turchin, a Russian fighting for the North, successfully led his brigade to clear some Confederates out of a woods. Later, when asked if he had considered surrendering during that terrible day, Turchin replied,

"What, surrender! No sir, never. I shoost my prigade, and cuts my way right out. When I tells my men to sharge, de sharges, right through. I tells, sir, we never surrender."

■　■　■　■　■

As a Union regiment was withdrawing, a Captain Rodarmel suddenly screamed and tore through the underbrush. "Oh, my God, only think of it," he wailed. "I am shot in the hind end."

■　■　■　■　■

When Jefferson Davis addressed the Confederate troops around Chattanooga, he tipped his hat and said, "Man never spoke as you did on the field of Chickamauga, and in your presence I dare not speak. Yours is the voice that will win the independence of your country and strike terror to the heart of a ruthless foe." ■

Union general George Thomas stood like a rock here at the re-created Snodgrass cabin.

The Southern Illustrated News *ridiculed Rosecrans's retreat from Chickamauga: "We have fought the Battle of Chickamauga to gain our position at Chattanooga, and here we are!"*

The Rock of Chickamauga, The Sledge of Nashville ▪ George H. Thomas

During the Civil War, a number of notably incompetent generals rose to command Union armies, but one of their greatest leaders has long remained unheralded. Thomas, born in Virginia in 1816, was part of the West Point class of 1840 which included William T. Sherman. He served as an officer of artillery, taught at West Point, was twice brevetted in Mexico, and fought the Indians, where he was wounded by an arrow in the face. He lost his family in 1861 when he chose to fight for the North. His sisters turned his picture to the wall and never spoke his name again. When visitors inquired about George, they replied, "We have no brother."

Thomas assumed an early role in the Army of the Ohio, and later the Army of the Cumberland. He decisively defeated the Confederates at Logan's Crossroads in January 1862, fought under Buell at Shiloh, advanced to Corinth with Halleck, served well at Perryville and Stone's River, and very probably saved the Union at Chickamauga. When the Federal army was put to flight, Thomas and his men established a precarious hilltop position and repulsed furious Confederate attacks until nightfall, preventing the Rebels from completely detroying William Rosecrans's force. For this heroic action Thomas was nicknamed the "Rock of Chickamauga." The siege of Chattanooga was raised by a memorable charge of his troops up Missionary Ridge.

After Thomas' steady service in the Atlanta campaign, where he commanded half the massive Union army, Sherman dispatched him to contain Hood in Tennessee. Hood laid a pathetic siege to Nashville while Grant harried Thomas to attack. When "Old Slow Trot" was ready, and Grant was boarding a train to relieve him, Thomas launched a shattering assault which inflicted the worst defeat suffered by a Confederate army in the entire war. This gained Thomas yet another nickname, the "Sledge of Nashville."

Thomas was one of the Union's best tacticians, but when many of his plans were successfully implemented, more colorful generals reaped the rewards. Thomas refused to seek the presidency in 1868 and died two years later, at his post as commander of the Department of the Pacific in San Francisco.

As a public demonstration of Thomas' contributions to the outcome of the Civil War and of the regard in which he was held, over 10,000 people attended his funeral in New York. ▪

[LIBRARY OF CONGRESS]

The road to Chattanooga was littered with bodies of Federal soldiers who had dragged themselves off the battlefield. While Rosecrans prepared Chattanooga for an attack by the victorious Confederates, Thomas formed his exhausted men for a rearguard action in Rossville. On the field Longstreet replenished his ammunition and awaited orders to continue the attack. The orders, and the attack, never came.

Appalled by his losses, Bragg could not be convinced that this battle had been a victory. After Thomas left the field, Polk roused Bragg from sleep and informed him of the Union army's rout. Forrest and other officers urged Bragg to pursue Rosecrans. The Federal army could be destroyed, they argued, and Chattanooga recaptured. The generals presented a Confederate soldier who had been captured, saw the Union rout, and then escaped; but Bragg would not believe him. "Do you know what a retreat looks like?" he asked. "I ought to, General," the soldier retorted. "I've been with you during your whole campaign." Bragg could only think of his staggering casualties. Immediate pursuit was out of the question. A frustrated Forrest asked angrily, "What does he fight battles for?"

The Confederates had won a great victory. Fortunately for the Union cause, they had suffered such terrible losses and were so spent by the bloody battle that Bragg chose not to follow up this singular opportunity to destroy Rosecrans. Later he explained that his men were exhausted, one-third of his artillery horses and other draft animals were dead, and the army was short of supplies.

Chickamauga Telegrams

Upon reaching Chattanooga after the rout at Chickamauga, Assistant Secretary of War Charles A. Dana wired news of the disaster to Washington, D.C. "My report today is of deplorable importance," it read. "Chickamauga is as fatal a name in our history as Bull Run."

Two days later, after a tardy investment of Chattanooga, Braxton Bragg informed Richmond: "It has pleased Almighty God to reward the valor and endurance of our troops by giving our arms a complete victory over the enemy's superior numbers. Thanks are due and rendered unto Him who giveth not the battle to the strong." ■

Rosecrans Rebukes Wood

As the sun rose on the morning of September 20, William Rosecrans expected Braxton Bragg to resume battering his left flank. In preparation for the assault, the Union commander continued to shift divisions to reinforce George Thomas. Rosecrans had a great deal of trouble getting James S. Negley's division in motion. After giving Negley a direct order to march, he rode off to direct Alexander McCook and Thomas Crittenden to close up on the position Negley would vacate. Upon inspecting Thomas's position on the left, Rosecrans found that Negley had not moved an inch and McCook had not taken any action. Growing more anxious as the hours passed, Rosecrans gave up hopes of shifting McCook and instructed Crittenden to move Thomas J. Wood's division into Negley's former position. The general then rode away to confer with McCook. Upon his return, Rosecrans found neither Negley nor Wood in position. Negley blamed Wood for the delay, then marched in a direction that took him away from the battlefield until an officer corrected him.

Rosecrans located Wood and apparently vented all the frustration that had accumulated during the morning on the unsuspecting officer. "What is the meaning of this, sir?" he shouted angrily at Wood in the presence of his subordinate's entire staff. "You have disobeyed my specific order. By your damnable negligence, you are endangering the safety of the entire army, and, by God, I will not tolerate it. Move your division at once, as I have instructed, or the consequences will not be pleasant to yourself."

Without responding to Rosecrans's tirade, Wood saluted and started his three brigades in motion. Rosecrans was known for being quick to anger and for having a sharp tongue, but this incident cost him his command, his place in history, and nearly his army. Hours later, when Rosecrans ordered Wood to fill a gap that Wood knew did not exist, he obeyed without question, leaving a real opening that the Confederates exploited to spectacular advantage. ■

The staggering toll of casualties—34,000 in two days of hard fighting—made Chickamauga the second bloodiest battle of the Civil War. Bragg lost 18,454 men, Rosecrans, 16,179. The Union had suffered a demoralizing defeat, and Chattanooga was now under siege. News of the battle at Chickamauga was met with wild celebration across the South, but the Confederacy could not afford such costly successes. ■

A DRIVING TOUR
■ The Chickamauga Campaign ■

From the entrance to the Visitors Center at Stone's River National Battlefield Park, turn right onto the Old Nashville Pike. After .4 turn left for .3 to cross the railroad tracks, then right to drive south on U.S. 41.

In southern Rutherford County, just before I–24 crosses the route, you will pass through Hoover's Gap, a natural passage through a rugged ridge called the Highland Rim. This ridge is an oval belt of low hills that encircle Middle Tennessee. Hoover's Gap is a narrow, four-mile-long gap that allowed only two wagons to pass in 1864, with 1,100-foot-high ridges towering on each side.

As Rosecrans started south from Murfreesboro in the early summer of 1863, the Confederates occupied a line through Shelbyville, Bell Buckle, and Wartrace. Thomas used Hoover's Gap to outflank Bragg and force the Confederate evacuation of the Duck River line. On June 24 the Federal XIV Corps struck two Confederate brigades here and drove them back to Fairfield, five miles to the southwest of Hoover's Gap. Maneuvering around the ridge toward Bradyville and McMinnville, southeast of Murfreesboro, Crittenden followed Thomas through Hoover's Gap. McCook, stopped by Hardee at Liberty Gap, sidestepped to Hoover's. Granger, moving to the southwest on the route of U.S. 231 through Guy's Gap, occupied Shelbyville when Polk evacuated the town on June 27. When the Federals united at Manchester on June 30, they were in the Confederate rear. Thus they forced Bragg to retreat closer to Chattanooga through Tullahoma.

Liberty Gap, where Hardee stopped McCook, is two miles to the west, on Short Creek Road, and Bell Buckle Gap, defended by Polk with the bulk of Bragg's army, is another two miles west of Liberty Gap, on Bell Buckle Road. The railroad still runs through Bell Buckle Gap. Bell Buckle Gap and Liberty Gap are both on the line between Rutherford and Shelby counties.

At the intersection of U.S. 41 with TN 64 is Beech Grove, where a cemetery contains the graves of un-identified Confederate soldiers who fell in battle here and at Hoover's Gap June 24–26, 1863. The cemetery, established after the war, has a memorial that honors the Confederates who died in the area. Nearby was the boyhood home of Henry Watterson, a Confederate soldier and founder of the Louisville *Courier–Journal.*

Bell Buckle got its name from a bell and a buckle that were carved on a large beech tree by Indians or a long hunter. It is known today as the "Quilters Capital." Of historic interest is the Webb School, established in 1870 by W. R. Webb, the "father of

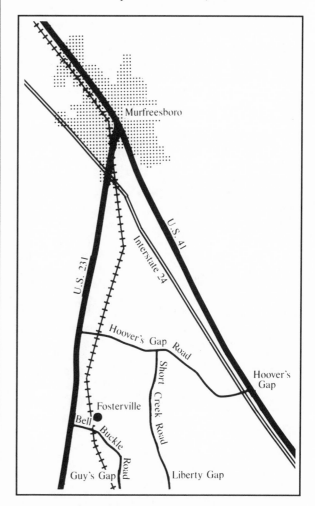

Map 15: From Stone's River National Battlefield to the gaps through the Highland Rim.

preparatory school education in the South." This small school has produced ten Rhodes scholars and governors of five states. On display is the Junior School, a one-room, wood-shingled, clapboard-covered structure that was warmed by a pot-bellied stove.

From January until June 1863, Hardee camped at Wartrace, between Beech Grove and Shelbyville in Bedford County. He covered the Confederate right with a defensive line that stretched along the ridge between Wartrace and Fairfield. He and Polk were protected by strong breastworks, with 600 yards of entangling abatis in front, along Duck River. Rosecrans avoided the Southern fortifications and surprised Bragg by crashing through Hardee's flank at Hoover's Gap, which Bragg thought was not suitable for large armies, thus gaining the Confederate rear.

Wartrace was established along the Nashville & Chattanooga Railroad in 1851. Its claim to fame is the Walking Horse, a unique breed developed by local planters. The Walking Horse Hotel, a three-story brick building with wide verandas, was opened for railroad passengers in 1917. It is still in service. The hotel displays a large collection of material dealing with Walking Horses. Strolling Jim, the first World's Champion Tennessee Walking Horse in 1939, is buried out back. Across the street is the old well house, a public gathering place. Main Street looks much as it did one hundred years ago.

To the east, in Cannon County, is Woodbury, one of the places threatened by Rosecrans's feints in June 1863. On July 12, 1862, Forrest rested his 1,400 cavalrymen here before the raid on Murfreesboro. On the day after the raid, Forrest camped at Readyville, just west of Woodbury on U.S. 70 South, and continued through McMinnville the next day. One-half mile west of Woodbury is a boulder and plaque erected to the memory of Lieutenant Colonel John B. Hutchenson of Morgan's command who was killed in January 1863 in one of numerous skirmishes that occurred in this vicinity.

To the west is Shelbyville, Polk's headquarters. His position at Guy's Gap, north of town, was attacked by Granger's reserve corps and Federal cavalry on June 27, 1863, as a feint while Rosecrans used Thomas to flank Bragg to the east.

In Confederate Square of Shelbyville's Willow Mount Cemetery is a monument, dedicated October 17, 1899, that honors Southern veterans. A marker indicates the grave of Sumner A. Cunningham, founder and publisher of *The Confederate Veteran* magazine. The Church of the Redeemer (1817) has been

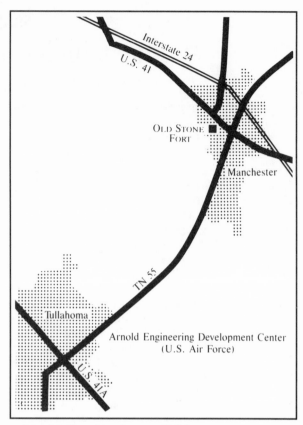

Map 16: From Manchester to Tullahoma.

used by several denominations. Shelbyville was the birthplace of Henry Davidson, West Point class of 1853, who was a Confederate colonel when he was captured at Island No. 10. After being exchanged, Davidson was promoted to general and commanded a brigade of Wheeler's cavalry. He surrendered with Johnston at Greensboro, North Carolina, in April 1865. Andrews' Raiders, the Union soldiers who stole the engine General in Georgia and attempted to disrupt the railroad north to Chattanooga, met just east of Shelbyville before the plan was set in motion. Both armies established signal stations atop nearby Horse Mountain.

A Confederate cemetery is on TN 64 to the west of Shelbyville, at Farmington School in Marshall County. It contains the remains of the men who died at Liberty and Guy's gaps and later during a raid by Forrest.

After 33.3 turn right into the Old Stone Fort State Park. The Museum–Visitors Center is .7 down the road.

This park preserves an ancient mile-long circular wall made of stone and earth. Twenty feet thick and five feet high, the wall encloses fifty acres of a peninsula formed by the Duck River bluffs. For years debate raged over who had created the enclosure and for what purpose. The builders were variously identified as Hernando de Soto, thirteenth-century Vikings, migrant Hebrews around A.D. 100, and Phoenicians in 1,000 B.C. The wall was thought to be a fort, built for protection against hostile Indians, but archaeology has proved that the Old Stone Fort was built by the Woodland Indians about 2,000 years ago. Because very few artifacts have been found inside the enclosure, its purpose is thought to have been religious or ceremonial. Dozens of such structures have been found from Georgia to Ohio. The park museum explains the different theories concerning the origins of the fort. Exhibits and an audio-visual presentation illustrate the archaeology of the area. The park has camping and picnicking facilities; trails lead through the fort and beside the river. Falls here powered paper, rope, and gunpowder mills during the Civil War.

Return to U.S. 41 and turn right. The Coffee County Courthouse is to the left after .1.1.

The Coffee County–Manchester Museum is a block northeast of the courthouse. In Manchester Rosecrans concentrated his army before moving against Bragg, who had withdrawn to Tullahoma, to the west.

Continue south on U.S. 41. After .7 turn right onto TN 55. After 11.3 turn left onto U.S. 41A in Tullahoma.

From this intersection, three blocks to the southwest, on Maplewood, is a Confederate plot in the city cemetery, where are buried 407 soldiers who died in hospitals between January and June 1863, when Bragg had his headquarters here. The plot, surrounded by a large chain and entered through a metal arch, has a monument in the center. At one time individual headstones had been erected, but they are now laid flat on the ground and are nearly obscured by the grass. This may make for easier mowing, but the act seems disrespectful to the soldiers who rest here. The Confederate cemetery is now a large, flat, grassy plot of land.

Just north of Tullahoma, at scenic Shippman's Creek, is the Ledford Mill and Museum, listed on the National Register of Historic Places. Built in 1880 by Stanford Ledford and operated by the family until

A marker honors more than four hundred Confederates who died while Braxton Bragg established his headquarters in Tullahoma during winter and spring 1863.

1942, the mill has a turbine powered by water carried through an iron pipe flume. The turbine generates thirty-five horsepower to turn the forty-two-inch stones in the mill. Meal, flour, and crafts are offered for sale. In the museum is an outstanding collection of tools from the eighteenth and nineteenth centuries. Slide shows illustrate coopering, or barrel making, and basket weaving.

From the intersection in Tullahoma follow U.S. 41A south.

The railroad along which Bragg retreated is on the left, and the Elk River is crossed on this route. Union cavalry tried to wreck the heavily defended railroad bridges over the river to the east, but they were foiled by a trained mobile force of Confederate infantry. Our route also passes through tiny Estill Springs, where Camp Harris was established to train Confederate soldiers. Bragg made temporary camp here in June 1863, as he retreated toward Chattanooga.

After 12.4 you may turn left on TN 50 for .9 to Decherd, on the Nashville & Louisville Railroad.

The railroad, which has paralleled U.S. 41A, now veers east to pass through Cowan. Bragg formed a

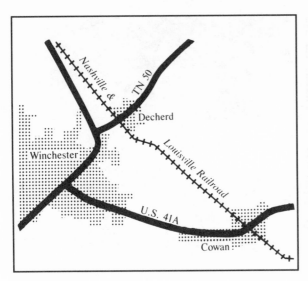

Map 17: Decherd, Winchester, and Cowan areas.

battle line along the Elk River near Decherd and Winchester, but he decided against giving battle and resumed his retreat. Thomas and McCook followed Bragg through these communities, while Crittenden marched to McMinnville, crossed the Cumberland Mountains into the Sequatchie Valley at Pikeville, and moved to Jasper near the Alabama line.

Continue on U.S. 41A for 1.6.

The Old Jail Museum in Winchester is on the left. Built in 1897 beside the Boiling Fork Creek, it functioned as the county jail for seventy-five years. In 1972 it became a museum operated by the Franklin County Historical Society. There are rooms devoted to the Civil War, both world wars, Indians, and pioneers. The security cell block looks as it did when the jail was in operation.

Also in Winchester was Hundred Oaks, one of the original American castles. It was built in 1890 by Arthur H. Marks, who admired the castles he had seen in England and Scotland while working in the consular service. After marrying a Scottish girl, Marks returned home to build a castle on his property, which was shaded by towering oaks. The enormous brick structure had a crenelated four-story tower. The study, a duplicate of the one in Sir Walter Scott's Scottish home, was two stories high. Tragically, soon after the castle was completed, Marks died of typhoid fever at age twenty-eight. The building has served as a restaurant, and its towers and cloisters were being re-

stored to their 1890 splendor when the building was destroyed by fire.

Mary Sharp College, a women's school established in 1851, closed for the duration of the Civil War. The buildings were used as a Federal hospital, but it reopened following the war and operated until 1896.

The people of this county were so eager to join the Confederacy that in a mass meeting on February 24, 1861, they voted to secede from Tennessee and petitioned Alabama for annexation. Things quieted down when Tennessee seceded on June 2. Winchester County organized 1,200 men for the First Tennessee Regiment, the original complement of soldiers which the state sent to serve the Confederacy.

On U.S. 64 to the south, near Belvidere, is the site of Davy Crockett's farm. His first wife, Polly, is buried there. Twelve miles west of Winchester is Falls Mill and Country Store. The mill was built in 1873 as a cotton and woolen factory, and in the early 1900s it was converted to a cotton gin. After another life as a woodworking shop, the mill was restored in 1969 and opened as a flour and grist mill. Visitors can watch the century-old thirty-two-foot overshot waterwheel—thought to be the largest used regularly in the country—turn the original mill stones as they grind corn into yellow and white meal and grits and whole wheat, rye, and buckwheat flours. Milled products and crafts are for sale. Visitors may tour the mill, picnic beside the old mill stream, and hike to the dam and falls on Factory Creek. The Museum of Power and Industry houses interesting exhibits.

A little further to the west is the Tims Ford Dam, which inundated 10,700 acres of land, creating 250 miles of shoreline. There are a marina, cabins, and camping.

From the jail return to U.S. 41A and turn left. After .2 at the courthouse follow the signs for U.S. 41A around the square. After 6.1 the Cowan Railroad Museum is on the right.

The railroad, a strategic asset during the Civil War, continues south here, skirting the rugged Cumberland Mountains on its roundabout route through northern Alabama to Chattanooga. The museum, housed in a 1904 depot, displays railroad watches, caps, lanterns, and a fifty-inch-long wooden engine model crafted in 1910. Beside the depot is a 1920 Porter steam locomotive, a flatcar, and a caboose.

The depot and nearby Cumberland Mountain Tunnel are both listed on the National Register of Historic Places. The 2,228-foot-long tunnel was bored through

A plaque in Cowan commemorates the completion of the Cumberland Mountain Tunnel, an engineering feat and strategic objective during the Civil War.

limestone between 1845 and 1847 by 400 slaves owned by the Nashville & Chattanooga Railroad. Their tools were picks, shovels, hand drills, and sledge hammers. The tunnel was not the only engineering feat performed here. From Cowan, a spur line was built to Sewanee up the steepest incline ever attempted at that time. Pusher engines from the rail yard here helped trains up the grade to the Cumberland Plateau.

In the railroad park is Franklin County's first courthouse, a simple one-story log building used between 1807 and 1814.

Bragg deployed the Army of Tennessee here at the foot of the Cumberlands. He again decided against fighting and retreated over the mountains into Alabama. Cowan was the site of Peter Turney's house, burned in 1863 because of his secessionist activities. He commanded the First Tennessee Infantry and later became governor and a justice of the state supreme court.

The intersection of U.S. 41A–64 and TN 56, east of Cowan, was the scene of the last fighting in Tennessee during Rosecrans's campaign against Bragg in the summer of 1863. Protecting Bragg's withdrawal to Chattanooga, Wheeler repulsed an attack by Union cavalry under Colonel Lewis Watkins.

Continue east toward Sewanee on U.S. 41A, up the steep, scenic Cumberland Mountains. Near the top note the pullover to the left at Lone Rock, a large stone formation that offers a fantastic view of the valley 1,000 feet below.

After 6.5 turn left into the picturesque 10,000-acre campus of the University of the South, generally called Sewanee. After .7 the Shapard Tower, housing the fifty-six-bell Polk Memorial Carillon, which offers concerts on Sundays, is among the striking buildings to the right. After .3 the Kirby Smith Monument is on the left. The stone memorial, dedicated May 5, 1939, bears a metal likeness of the controversial general who initiated Bragg's Kentucky invasion.

This beautiful mountaintop college was established July 4, 1857, by the Episcopal Church. Bishop Leonidas Polk, who was soon to be a Confederate general, laid the cornerstone of University Hall in 1860. After the Federals occupied Sewanee during the summer of 1863, they burned the building and broke up the cornerstone for souvenirs. One eighteen-inch-square block of the cornerstone is embedded in the wall of All Saints Chapel (1907). Inside the chapel are historic paintings, flags, memorials, English stained glass, and a massive pipe organ. In the DuPont Li-

Following the Civil War, Confederate general Edmund Kirby Smith taught at the University of the South at Sewanee, atop the Cumberland Plateau.

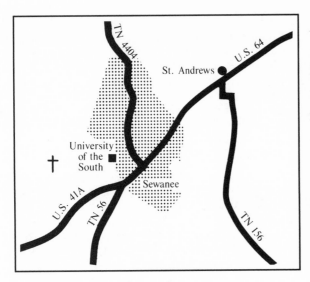

Map 18: Sewanee and St. Andrews areas.

brary are collections of rare books, literary manuscripts, and artifacts concerning the confederacy and the Episcopal Church. In the Breslin Tower of Convocation Hall are the Douglas Chimes and a Seth Thomas clock. These Victorian Gothic buildings, constructed with lovely pink sandstone from local quarries, were patterned after those of England's Oxford University.

Following the Civil War, Confederate veterans were often employed at southern schools. Kirby Smith, naval captain Jack Eggleston, and General Josiah Gorgas all taught at Sewanee. Gorgas, the Confederate official responsible for manufacturing war materiel or importing it through the Union blockade, was vice chancellor from 1872 until 1878. Smith and Eggleston are buried here.

Samuel Tracy, founder of the Sewanee Mining Company, donated 5,000 acres of land, one million board feet of lumber, 20,000 tons of free transportation, and 2,000 tons of coal to help establish the University of the South.

Sewanee was the site of Rebel's Rest, a pre-Civil War home of Leonidas Polk.

At the Sewanee Memorial Cross, a fifty-five-foot-high monument dedicated to Franklin County men who served in World War I, is a beautiful view of the valley.

Return to U.S. 41A and turn left for two miles into Saint Andrews. Turn right onto TN 156–Midway Road, turn left after .3, and another right at .1 to remain on TN 156. *Most of this route is through a peaceful national forest, and near the end it descends the mountain in steep curves. After 24 miles, in South Pittsburg, turn right onto U.S. 72 West.* (Tom Mix was night watchman at a cement factory here for several years before he became a famed actor in western movies.) *The shortest route to Chattanooga is to follow U.S. 72 east along the Tennessee River to Interstate 24; but we signed on for the longer, and considerably more scenic, historical route. Rosecrans led Bragg to believe he would cross the Tennessee River to the east near Chattanooga, but instead crossed far to the west. Enter Alabama, and Bridgeport is reached after 5.5. Tour information for Bridgeport may be found in the "Perryville A Tour" in* Piercing the Heartland.

Turn left onto County Road 91 and follow the signs for 91 to the river, turning right at .3, left at .1, right at .1, left at .5, and right at .2 to reach the ferry.

The ferry, which operates from 6:00 A.M. to 4:30 P.M., Central Standard Time, does not run on Sundays, and its staff breaks for lunch from 11:00 until 11:30 A.M. If this poses a problem, simply remain on U.S. 72 until Stevenson and turn right to cross the Tennessee River on AL 71, a route that is much quicker. However, the Confederate army, and later part of Rosecrans's army, Thomas's corps, crossed the river on ferry boats and pontoon bridges, so going that way provides a greater feeling for the history of the campaign. The original railroad bridge, at the site of the current one to the left, was very important during the struggle for Tennessee and Georgia. McCook marched down the Tennessee River to cross at Caperton's Ferry near Stevenson, while Crittenden moved from Jasper to cross the river at Shellmound, closer to Chattanooga.

Once across, turn right to parallel the river on AL 91. Enjoy the meadows and mountain scenery to the left. After 9.3 turn left (the Tennessee River bridge to Stevenson is to the right) to climb up steep Sand Mountain on North AL 117. This long, broad mountain is a productive agricultural area. At a four-way stop after 8.7, turn left onto AL 71, and right to stay on AL 71 after 8.7. The route crosses into Georgia and Al 71 becomes GA 136. There are wonderful views at Magby Gap on the descent to Trenton. Pass under Interstate 59, which connects Chattanooga with Birmingham, and after 7.4 stop at the intersection with U.S. 11–GA 58 in Trenton.

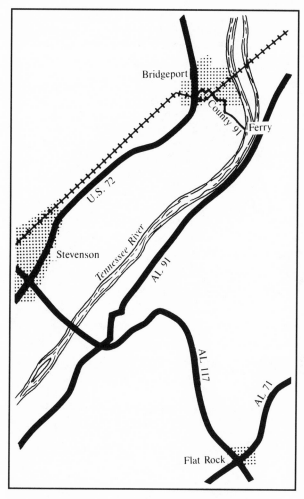

Map 19: *Bridgeport, Stevenson, and Flat Rock areas.*

Turn right for .1, then left to follow GA 136, which zigzags up Lookout Mountain. The broad plateau atop Lookout Mountain, which ranges in height from 1,750 feet to 2,392 feet, has sheer limestone cliffs near the summit. After six miles the entrance to Cloudland Canyon State Park is on the left. The canyons are 1.5 down the park road.

Cloudland Canyon, developed in 1938, consists of 1,917 acres of mountain plateau and deep canyons. The canyons form an inverted *Y* as Bear Creek and Daniel Creek form the two forks, then combine into Sitton Gulch Creek, which has carved the huge central canyon. This dramatic geological feature has been forming for 250 million years.

Several trails lead along the branch canyons to a point where the canyons intersect. From this point, with the canyons branching to each side, visitors can peer into the depths of the central chasm. The height here is 1,800 feet; the canyon floor is 800 feet below. This is one of the most beautiful and inspiring views in the entire Southeast.

A rather strenuous trail, containing 400 stairs, leads down the canyon wall to a sixty-foot waterfall on Daniel Creek, which also has a ninety-five-foot waterfall. A wonderfully shaded glade is surrounded by enormous boulders that have fallen from the cliffs.

Five miles of trails lead through oak forests where forty-two different types of trees and shrubs may be seen. The park, which is situated near attractions in three states, including Chickamauga, Chattanooga, and Russell Cave, has cabins and a campground.

Return to the park entrance and turn left to follow GA 136. Just after the intersection with GA 157 this highway enters Stevens Gap to descend Lookout Mountain. George Thomas's 20,000-man corps emerged from this gap. After 7.9 we are in the center of McLemore's Cove.

To the right the valley is blocked by a ridge, and to the left was the direction from which Bragg's forces were supposed to march and destroy Thomas, but did not.

Turn right onto GA 193 and follow that highway as it turns sharply east.

Dug Gap, on Pigeon Mountain, is just south of the intersection with GA 341. A Confederate division was ordered to march through it to attack Thomas but failed to do so, claiming the gap had been obstructed with felled timber by the Southern rearguard retiring before Thomas.

Trenton, originally named Salem, became the seat of Dade County in 1840. From 1860 until 1908 coal was mined in this area, and iron ore smelting operations began in 1874. During that period the state leased prisoners to work in the mines, often under the worst imaginable conditions. A narrow limestone valley is sandwiched between Sand Mountain and Lookout Mountain, near the end of the vast Appalachian Range. Until 1937, when GA 2 was built over Lookout to connect Trenton with La Fayette, Dade County was isolated from Georgia and could only be reached from Alabama or Tennessee. The county occasionally threatened to secede when its concerns were ignored by Georgia.

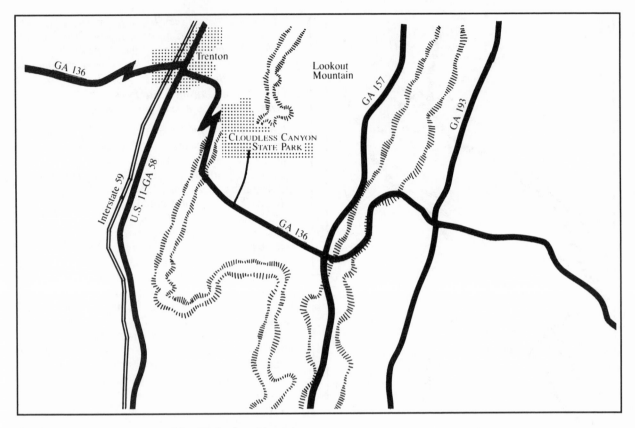

Map 20: Lookout Mountain area.

After 13.3, turn left onto U.S. Business 27 in La Fayette, and at .5 Gordon Hall is to the right.

Erected in 1836, this two-story, red-brick Georgian structure served as a school until 1920. It has recently been restored by the La Fayette Area Chamber of Commerce. Gordon Hall, named for John B. Gordon, an outstanding Confederate general and state politician who lived nearby and attended the school as a child, is on the National Register of Historic Places. Used as Union headquarters in 1864, the building was in the line of fire during the battle of La Fayette. It had been Bragg's headquarters in September 1863. According to tradition, Bragg planned the battle of Chickamauga under an oak tree in the front yard. The famed Bragg Oak was destroyed by lightning in 1920. A Confederate monument, dedicated April 27, 1909, and a stack of cannonballs mark the site of Bragg's headquarters.

The La Fayette Presbyterian Church, built of brick

in 1848, was used as a field hospital by both armies during the Civil War. Planks laid across pews formed crude operating tables.

In June 1864, while Sherman operated against Atlanta, 450 Union soldiers were quartered in the Walker County Courthouse in La Fayette when 1,000 Confederate cavalry launched a surprise attack at 3:00 A.M. The outnumbered Federals fought desperately and managed to hold off the Confederates until reinforcements arrived to drive off the attackers.

While attempting to draw Sherman away from Atlanta in October 1864, Confederate general John B. Hood established a defensive arc around La Fayette. The Union army deployed opposite Hood, but the Confederate leader withdrew into Alabama without giving battle.

South of here in Chattooga County are two places important to the Chickamauga campaign. Between Pigeon Mountain and Taylor Ridge is Alpine, two miles south of Menlo. Union general Daniel McCook's corps

Braxton Bragg planned the Battle of Chickamauga at Gordon Hall in Lafayette, Georgia.

reached Alpine on September 11, 1863. After almost being isolated from the rest of the Union army, McCook was forced to withdraw and follow Thomas's route to Chickamauga. A skirmish was fought at Summerville during the maneuvers preceding Chickamauga.

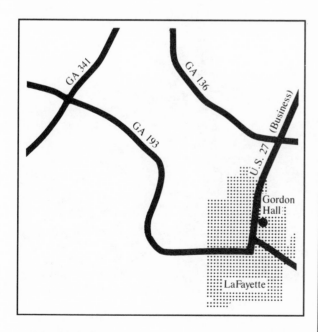

Map 21: Lafayette area.

Turn right onto U.S. 27 for 2.4, then turn left onto GA 136 West. After 5.6 turn right onto GA 341 to follow the route of Thomas and McCook from Steven's Gap through McLemore's Cove to Chickamauga. At 6.4 pull into the parking area on the right. The Gordon–Lee House is on the left, Crawfish Springs to the right.

This is the village of Chickamauga, which is a corruption of the Cherokee word *Tsikamagi*. The spring in the ravine below was named for Chief Crawfish, an Indian leader. When the Cherokee Nation was organized, the land was divided into districts—like counties—and a council house was built to provide local government. One such house, a log structure, was built in 1820 on the bluff here. When Walker County was established in 1833, the council house was used

The Gorden-Lee House in Chickamauga was headquarters of William Rosecrans and the site of seven Union divisional hospitals during the battle.

as the courthouse until a larger structure could be built. On this land Fort Cumming, a stockaded blockhouse, was built by the U.S. government in 1836 to facilitate the removal of the Cherokees to Oklahoma. Union troops marching to battle stopped to fill their canteens at Crawfish Springs.

After James Gordon acquired 2,500 acres here, he built a mill, sawmill, store, and this twelve-room, redbrick Greek Revival home in the 1850s. Made on the property by slaves, the bricks form eighteen-inch-thick walls. The famous Gordon–Lee House, used as

Rosecrans' headquarters before the battle, was a Federal hospital during the fighting. When Confederate troops took possession of the field, thirty Union doctors remained behind to care for their wounded. Seven divisional hospitals, one in the house and six more on the grounds, had been established here. Restored in 1974, the house is now a bed and breakfast inn.

A house that stands nearby on the edge of the battlefield was occupied during the war by Mrs. Clarissa Hunt, a widow. A Federal battery posted on a hill near the house fired one misdirected cannonball, which sailed through her back door, punched holes in two interior doors and a piece of furniture, then plowed through the front door. No one was hurt.

Continue .1 to the center of town and turn right onto Gordon Street, following it carefully around a curve. After 1.3 turn right, then left onto U.S. 25 after .7 and drive through the Chickamauga battlefield.

U.S. 25 is the old La Fayette Road, and the contending armies fought furiously for its possession. On a small road off to the right is the Gordon–Lee Mill. The first mill established on this site was built by James Gordon in 1836. His son-in-law, James Morgan Lee, was operating it when Polk established his headquarters in the mill. Polk had been sent by Bragg to destroy Federal general Thomas Crittenden's isolated corps before the great battle occurred. When Polk dallied, the opportunity was lost. Crittenden used the mill for his headquarters for several days, requiring Lee to grind corn for his troops. The mill was between the lines during the battle, and constant skirmishing occurred around it. The mill burned in 1867 but was soon rebuilt. It has not been used for many years and is not open to visitors.

After 4.1 turn left into the parking area beside the new Visitors Center at the Chickamauga and Chattanooga National Military Park.

America's largest and most frequently visited battlefield, the park consists of 8,000 acres of woodland, meadows, and mountains in Georgia and Tennessee. It was established by Congress in 1895 at the request of Union and Confederate veterans.

The twenty-nine states that provided soldiers who fought here (four states had men fighting for both sides) have since erected over 600 monuments. Visitors are guided by 700 cast iron plaques (blue signifies Union actions; red, Confederate) which describe troop movements; and 250 artillery pieces scattered across the 5,000-acre park indicate significant sites in the battle. Large triangular mounds of cannonballs mark the places where eight brigade commanders died, including Benjamin H. Helm, Lincoln's brother-in-law; smaller mounds designate the location of army and corps headquarters. Acorn-topped monuments represent the Fourteenth Corps, which stood solid as an oak tree with Thomas at Snodgrass Hill. Because the South could ill afford monuments following the Civil War, most of the memorials were erected by Northern states. For example, Alabama has one monument here, while Illinois has 143. Over an area of 1,600 square miles in Georgia and Tennessee, there are 1,400 historical markers describing the battles of Chickamauga and those for Chattanooga. The scripts were written and placed by men who actually fought on these fields.

In 1881 the Society of the Army of the Cumberland held its annual meeting in Chattanooga. When their members visited the battlefield of Chickamauga, they

The Georgia monument at Chickamauga honors the three branches of service during the Civil War: infantry, artillery, and cavalry.

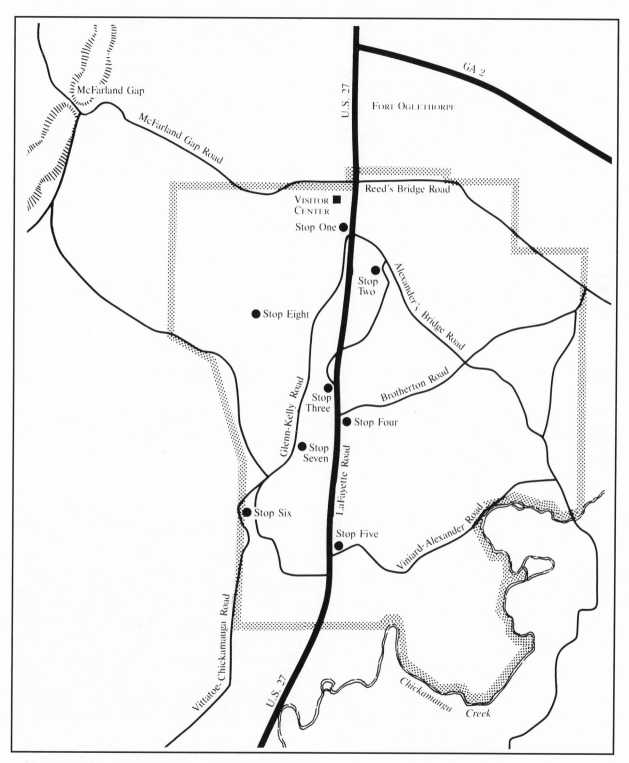

Map 22: Chickamauga and Chattanooga National Military Park.

were upset to discover that landmarks had vanished and the terrain was altered. In 1888 two former Union officers toured the grounds and produced a series of newspaper articles about the importance of preserving the battlefield. They thought that a memorial park jointly planned by veterans who had fought for the North and the South would help heal the wounds of war. The project started at Crawfish Springs on September 20, 1889, with the largest barbecue ever held in the South. Fifteen thousand pounds of meat—hogs, sheep, goats, and cattle—and 12,000 loaves of bread were consumed. Over 14,000 people attended, and many made a five-dollar donation to the Chickamauga Memorial Association.

Ohio congressman Charles H. Grosvenor, who was a colonel at Chickamauga, introduced a bill in the House of Representatives that would preserve not only the field of Chickamauga but also important battle sites in Chattanooga. The proposal, which met with no opposition in Congress, was signed into law by President Benjamin Harrison, who had fought in Georgia with Sherman. After property costing $400,000 was obtained, veterans visited the battlefields to help mark important places. Ohio, which had the most Union men fighting in the battle, spent $90,000 to erect monuments in the park, and other Northern states quickly followed suit.

Ceremonies to dedicate the park began on September 18, 1899, with 10,000 veterans of the Army of the Cumberland attending. Seventy special trains brought visitors into Chattanooga, where people were housed in tent cities erected around the city. On the following day forty-four cannon fired a salute at Snodgrass Hill. After Vice President Adlai Stevenson's opening remarks, former Union and Confederate officers spoke. Observances continued on September 20 with a parade and dedication services held at Lookout Mountain, Missionary Ridge, and Orchard Knob.

Chickamauga has recently celebrated its 100th anniversary in grand style. Friends of the Park planned the commemoration, which kicked off in September 1989 with a Blue and Gray Barbecue at the Gordon–Lee House. The organization raised three million dollars for construction of an extensive addition to the Visitors Center, which opened on August 19, 1990.

The original Visitors Center, built in 1935 on the site of Fort Oglethorpe's golf course, was occupied by the McDonald family's log cabin during the Civil War. The striking addition was designed by MetaForm, which organized the exhibits at the Statue of Liberty and Ellis Island. The seventy-foot-long screen in the theater is thirteen feet high and encloses the audience

180 degrees. The result is a feeling that visitors are on the battlefield. A new state-of-the-art, twenty-four-minute multimedia presentation concerning the battles of Chickamauga and Chattanooga is unique, innovative, and dramatic. It utilizes forty-three slide projectors which flash 1,300 slides, five video players, and seven stereo speakers to enhance an understanding of the battle here and subsequent actions around Chattanooga. Ten miles of cable tie the display together. The park already attracts 900,000 people a year, and this addition is expected to increase that number.

A special feature in the museum is the Claude E. and Zenada O. Fuller Collection of American Military Shoulder Arms, 355 impressively displayed infantry weapons. It is one of the most complete collections in the world and includes weapons from colonial times until World War I, with an emphasis on Civil War rifles. Many of them are one of a kind, and their condition ranges from good to excellent. A unique specimen is a Sharps 1863 carbine with a coffee mill built into the stock. The idea was that one of these rifles would be distributed to each company so the men could have freshly ground coffee.

In 1935 the Fullers retired and moved to Chattanooga. Mr. Fuller wrote five books about the history of American firearms and built several structures to house his collection. In 1954 he donated the weapons to Chickamauga, which constructed a special wing for

The Wilder Tower honors the men of Col. John Wilder's Brigade, which slowed the Confederate onslaught at this spot.

their exhibition. A restored battery wagon and traveling forge are also displayed with the weapons.

An outdoor artillery park displays different types of guns used during the Civil War. Volunteer reenactors regularly demonstrate cannon and rifle firing. New interpretive signs are also being erected around the park. These fiberglass panels use historic drawings, maps, and other artwork to explain what occurred at different locations on the battlefield. Thirty are being erected at Chickamauga and ten on Missionary Ridge and Lookout Mountain.

Miles of roads and footpaths crisscross the large battlefield. A brochure available in the Visitors Center outlines an easily followed seven-mile auto tour route with eight major sites identified. Monuments, markers, and cannon are liberally distributed along the tour route.

The battle of Chickamauga is described at *Stop One.* Skirmishing developed late in the evening of September 18 as Forrest's troopers captured Reed's Bridge, which spans Chickamauga Creek, from Union colonel Robert H. G. Minty's cavalry. The way was cleared for Confederate infantry to cross the creek and engage Rosecrans's forces. The site of the bridge is outside park grounds to the east. Combat erupted early on the following morning and rapidly moved south for three miles along the route of the La Fayette Road (U.S. 27) as Bragg attempted to crack the left flank of the Union line and isolate Rosecrans from Chattanooga. Savage fighting occurred in the dense woods and tangled undergrowth as additional divisions were thrown into the fighting throughout the day. Although the integrity of the Federal line was threatened several times, it never broke.

Stop Two is situated halfway down Battleline Road on part of the Kelly farm, which was the site of renewed fighting on September 20, a Sunday morning. During the night Federal troops, expecting Bragg to continue hammering their left, built substantial log breastworks as Rosecrans dispatched heavy reinforcements to Thomas. Polk attacked late, as usual, at 10:00 A.M. His troops were slaughtered by a fierce fire that came from behind those works. By noon, Polk's attack had lost its momentum, and Longstreet assumed the offensive on the Confederate left. This road follows the Union line where fierce fighting raged; the Confederate line was 75 to 250 yards east of the road. Note the number and variety of monuments along the route, most of them erected by Northern states.

The fatal confusion in the Union command is described at *Stop Three.* A courier riding nearby on the

Gen. James Longstreet sent three Confederate divisions past the Brotherton cabin to achieve the greatest southern victory in the Civil War.

Glenn–Kelly Road was unable to see a Federal division concealed in the thick woods. After he reported a gap in the line, Rosecrans ordered another division to that position, leaving a real opening in his line. More monuments, markers, and cannon indicate where the unseen division was lurking.

The grandest action of the Confederacy during the Civil War occurred at *Stop Four.* Rosecrans had removed a division near the Brotherton Cabin to plug the nonexistent gap. Two other divisions which had been ordered to extend their line into this area had not yet arrived when Longstreet sent a column of three divisions streaming into the unsuspected hole at 11:00 P.M. Of all the charges meant to pierce a line of battle—Pickett at Gettysburg, Hood at Franklin, Grant at Spotsylvania, and dozens of others—this was the only one that achieved a breakthrough, and it occurred only by accident. When Longstreet routed two Union divisions and shattered two more, Rosecrans's right was destroyed. The Confederates then turned to attack Thomas on the left. The Brotherton Cabin here is the original structure. Across the highway is the imposing Georgia Monument, with figures representing the three arms of military service: infantry, artillery, and cavalry. A flag bearer stands atop the seventy-one-foot column.

Stop Five describes the cost of the battle of Chickamauga. Of 66,000 Confederate troops, 2,300 were killed, 14,500 wounded, and nearly 1,500 missing. Rosecrans's 58,000 men suffered 1,600 killed, 10,000 wounded, and 5,000 missing. These casualties, which

Monuments with an acorn indicate actions of George Thomas's corps, which stood solid as an oak tree at Chickamauga.

total almost one-third of all the men involved, made Chickamauga the second bloodiest battle of the Civil War, ranking only behind Gettysburg.

This site, Viniard Field, was one of the bloodiest in the battle. On September 19 Hood's division, the vanguard of Longstreet, attacked the Union right at 3:30 P.M. On the wilderness battlefield the combat degenerated into charge and countercharge, a stand-up combat with little cover for the combatants. Hood almost severed Rosecrans's route of retreat to Chattanooga, but Union reinforcements drove the Confederates back to their starting point. A forest of monuments, historical markers, and artillery pieces interprets the battle. The Viniard House, which stood here, was frequently mentioned in accounts of the battle.

The most impressive monument on the battlefield is found at *Stop Six*, Wilder Tower, an eighty-five-foot-high structure constructed of Chickamauga limestone. A spiral staircase inside leads to an observation deck on top, which offers a grand view of the area. The tower commemorates the heroic stand made by Colonel John Wilder's mounted infantry brigade, who delayed Longstreet with their seven-shot repeating rifles and gave Thomas time to organize a position at Snodgrass Hill. The survivors of Wilder's Brigade raised $9,714.27 for the monument, which was dedicated in September 1899. A unique monument here, honoring the First Wisconsin Cavalry, is a riderless

horse. Ironically enough, Wilder returned to Tennessee following the war and became mayor of Chattanooga. This is now the site of popular concerts on July 4.

This was the site of the Widow Glenn's home, used as Rosecrans's headquarters the day before the breakthrough. It was burned to the ground by an exploding shell. Mrs. Eliza Camp Glenn, widowed when her husband, John, was killed in battle after enlisting in the Confederate army, was left alone to raise a two-year-old son and a daughter who was born after her father's death.

The collapse of Rosecrans's right is told at *Stop Seven*. After Longstreet's breakthrough, two Federal divisions ran headlong for McFarlan Gap, which led to Chattanooga. Infantrymen abandoned their rifles, and artillerymen jumped on their horses and left their cannon in the disorganized retreat that passed through these fields. Rosecrans, whose headquarters were in

One of seven hundred monuments erected to honor soldiers who fought for the North and South at Chickamauga.

this area, and two of his corps commanders were caught in the rout. Of the two other divisions that were scattered by Longstreet, some of the men fought at Snodgrass Hill while others ran for safety.

Stop Eight, Snodgrass Hill, is another of those magic places in Civil War history. After the Union right was destroyed, Longstreet turned on the left, commanded by Thomas, who had the only Federal fighting unit remaining on the field. If Thomas could be overrun, the Union Army of the Cumberland would be destroyed. Thomas had one full division and parts of three others when Longstreet approached. The Federals hurriedly built crude breastworks of logs, fence rails, and rocks. When Longstreet attacked the Union left at 1:00 P.M., he was repulsed. A determined attempt against the right was close to success when Granger arrived with reinforcements and ammunition. Assaults continued until dark, when Thomas successfully extricated his command. He will forever be remembered as the Rock of Chickamauga, upon whom waves of Southern attackers were dashed. George Thomas, arguably the third most accomplished general in the Union army, has never received the recognition he deserves.

After the fighting at Chickamauga ended, thousands of dead from both armies were buried on the grounds. Later, the Federal dead were reinterred in Chattanooga, the Confederate dead, in Marietta, Georgia. Despite stories that the battlefield is still a vast graveyard, officials believe only one man remains buried in the field. John Ingraham, a Confederate soldier from the area, was found on the field by his family and by his fiancee, Abigail Reed, who buried him where he lay, near Reed's Bridge.

There are several sites just north of Chickamauga National Military Park that were important to the battle fought here. Off U.S. 27 on McFarlan Gap Road is McFarlan Gap, through which the Army of the Cumberland fled to Chattanooga. Just off U.S. 27 on East Lake Drive in Rossville is the two-story log John Ross House, built by an important Cherokee chief. It was the headquarters of Rosecrans's reserves, led by General Gordon Granger, who rushed to bolster the magnificent defense of Thomas. It is open to the public. Along U.S. 27 in downtown Rossville is a monument honoring the Tennessee cavalry. ■

The Siege of Chattanooga

By September 22, 1863, Rosecrans, who was surprised but pleased by Bragg's failure to follow up his smashing victory at Chickamauga, had strongly fortified Chattanooga. Two large artillery positions, Fort Negley and Fort Grose, had been built in the valley south of town.

When Bragg finally advanced, he placed his troops in a six-mile semicircular line that started on Missionary Ridge to the east, ran down to the Chattanooga Creek Valley, and up to Lookout Mountain on the west, overlooking the Tennessee River. Hardee held the right on Missionary, and Longstreet the left on Lookout. Bragg's strategy was simple. He expected to starve Rosecrans into surrender. The Southern position was formidable, but incomplete. Perhaps because the Rebel generals spent much of their time fighting with Bragg, no one had bothered to seize the ground west of Lookout Mountain, the valley of Lookout Creek and Raccoon Mountain, which would have truly isolated the city.

The Union army was in desperate shape. Supplies were transported by rail from Nashville south to Stevenson, Alabama, then east to Bridgeport, twenty-seven miles west of Chattanooga. Because portions of the rail line running east to Chattanooga lay in Confederate territory, supplies were loaded on wagons and transported via a poor road northeast up the Sequatchie Valley to Anderson's Crossroads, then southeast on a steep, twisting path over rugged Walden's Ridge to cross the Tennessee River on a pontoon bridge at Chattanooga. The distance was sixty miles, and the journey took eight to twenty days, depending on the weather. Heavy rains often created mud that reached the bellies of mules. Wagons frequently required sixteen mules to complete the journey, with one whip-equipped soldier to encourage each mule and other men to help push. The route was soon lined with the carcasses of 10,000 animals, dead of exhaustion or hunger. The road was so jammed that empty wagons could not return for additional loads.

The 35,000 Union soldiers packed into Chattanooga were hungry, but the remaining civilians were starving. After their houses were commandeered or dismantled for fuel, women and children made cold, hungry journeys over the mountains to seek refuge.

The Execution of Sam Davis

The trial and execution of Sam Davis, the "Boy Hero of the Confederacy," resulted from U. S. Grant's relief of Chattanooga. Scouts in southern Tennessee and northern Mississippi and Alabama were tracking the movements of William Sherman's troops from Vicksburg and Memphis along the railroad from Corinth to Chattanooga. Discovering a corps led by Union general G. M. Dodge in the vicinity of Pulaski, Tennessee, a number of couriers attempted to enter Confederate lines at Decatur, Alabama, and deliver the vital intelligence to Bragg.

Sam Davis was captured with this information, a detailed map of Union fortifications at Nashville, and three toothbrushes and three bars of soap, credible evidence of a visit to Nashville, on his person. After the execution, General Dodge remarked sadly, "He was too brave to die." ■

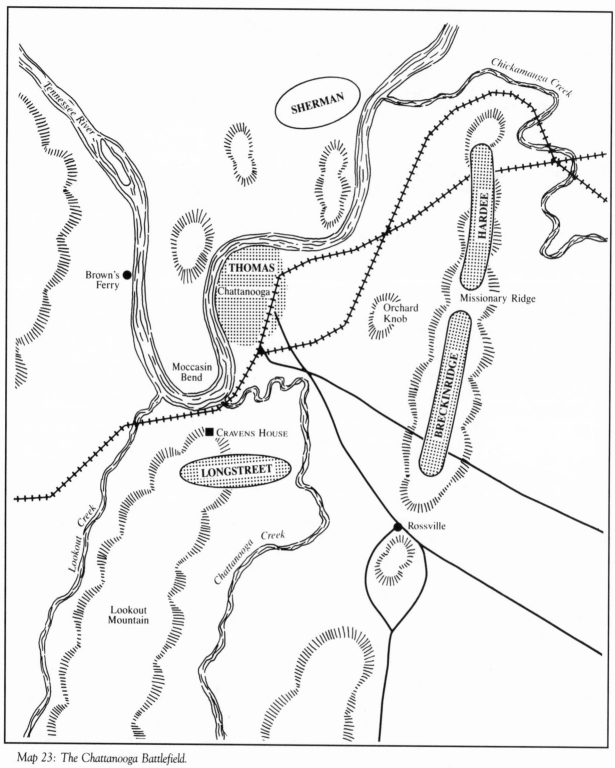

Map 23: The Chattanooga Battlefield.

Batteries of Confederate artillery dominated Union-held Chattanooga during fall 1863. This cannon is on Missionary Ridge.

Grant Takes Charge

Following the battle of Chickamauga, Secretary of War Edwin Stanton ordered U. S. Grant to Cairo, Illinois, as soon as possible. At Cairo he received further instructions to meet with war department officials at the Galt Hotel in Louisville. As Grant was about to depart by train, a messenger ran up and announced that Stanton's train was approaching. While the two rode to Louisville, Stanton gave Grant a choice of two orders. Both appointed him commander of the Military Division of the Mississippi, which amounted to most of the territory west of the Alleghenies, but one order retained William Rosecrans in besieged Chattanooga, while the second would replace him with George Thomas. Grant chose the second and was soon in personal command in Chattanooga, where his decisive leadership raised the Confederate siege.

Early in 1864 Congress revived the grade of lieutenant general, a position previously held only by George Washington. On March 9 Abraham Lincoln bestowed the rank upon Grant, for the "nation's appreciation." After inspecting the Army of the Potomac, Grant decided it was plain that here was the "point for the commander to be." When he took charge in Virginia, Sherman was given Grant's former position and ordered to destroy the Army of Tennessee and capture Atlanta. Grant concentrated his attention on the Army of Northern Virginia. One year later, Grant and Sherman had brought the war to a successful conclusion. ■

The Union position worsened when Bragg sent Wheeler to raid the Union supply route. In early October, 5,000 gray cavalrymen destroyed 500 wagons, killed 1,000 mules, and destroyed several railroad bridges. Wheeler was finally driven off by the arrival of Union general Edward McCook's cavalry division, which inflicted 700 casualties on the raiding Rebels.

While Rosecrans did nothing to relieve his plight, he did grind axes. He fired McCook and Crittenden for their roles at Chickamauga and promoted Gordon Granger. Assistant Secretary of War Charles A. Dana wired Stanton that Rosecrans seemed stunned and incapacitated "to an astonishing degree."

Stanton responded to the crisis by rushing reinforcements to Chattanooga. Convinced that George Meade and his Army of the Potomac, inactive since Gettysburg in July, would take no action until the spring of 1864, Stanton ordered 20,000 men from two corps, led by General Joseph Hooker, west by train. The force, including ten artillery batteries and 3,000 horses and mules, traveled 1,150 miles but still managed to reach Bridgeport on September 25, only six days after they left Virginia. This feat surpassed Bragg's move from Corinth to Chattanooga a year and a half earlier, and Longstreet's recent transfer to Georgia. With no food available in

A union signal station at Chattanooga during the siege. [HARPER'S WEEKLY]

Chattanooga, Hooker remained on the Union supply line in northern Alabama.

On the Southern side, Bragg relieved Polk for failing to attack before Chickamauga. Bragg's four commanders—Polk, Hill, Longstreet, and Buckner—petitioned President Davis for Bragg's removal. They claimed the Army of Tennessee was effectively paralyzed because of lack of leadership. Davis traveled through the Carolinas to Atlanta and north to Confederate headquarters to resolve the situation. With Bragg present, the president asked the dissenters to express their opinions of the commanding general. Longstreet said Bragg would be of "greater service elsewhere," and the others concurred with this mild rebuke. Davis retained Bragg, who then reorganized the army. Polk was reassigned to Mississippi in exchange for Hardee. D. H. Hill went home, with Breckinridge taking his corps; and Longstreet was stripped of half his force.

In Vicksburg, U. S. Grant received a telegram from Henry Halleck, Lincoln's general-in-chief, ordering him to Cairo, Illinois. After arriving on October 16, Grant was directed to Louisville. There he met Stanton, who gave him command of the Military Division of the Mississippi. Grant chose to relieve Rosecrans, replacing him with Union general George H. Thomas as

Federal troops build a pontoon bridge as part of the "Cracker Line." [HARPER'S WEEKLY]

commander of the Army of the Cumberland. Grant passed Rosecrans at Stevenson as he began a journey over the mountains that brought him to Chattanooga on October 23.

On the following day Thomas started in motion a plan devised by his chief engineer, General William F. Smith. This plan took advantage of the peculiar geography of the region. Chattanooga lies on the southeastern bank of the Tennessee River. Just south of the city, the river turns sharply north to create a loop. By crossing the river at Chattanooga and traveling two and a half miles west across Moccasin Point, Brown's Ferry on the Tennessee River is reached. From this point the river continues northwest for five miles around Walden's Ridge, then turns southwest for seven miles, creating a peninsula. A road across this neck of land crossed Raccoon Mountain via Running Creek Gorge and connected Brown's Ferry with Kelly's Ferry, which could be reached by steamship from Bridgeport without being exposed to Confederate fire from Lookout Mountain. If Brown's Ferry and the road west were captured from the Confederates, supplies could be hauled eight miles from the river to Chattanooga. From that point to the city, the river was not only commanded by Rebel artillery, but a narrow, swift gorge known as "the Suck" made water transportation hazardous.

Rosecrans built this bridge over the Tennessee River at Chattanooga in October 1863. [BATTLES AND LEADERS]

Smith's plan called for a division to march across Moccasin Point and attack Brown's Ferry, while a second division floated down the river from Chattanooga on pontoon boats to surprise the Confederates protecting the landing. The pontoons would then be used to bridge the river. At the same time, Hooker would send three divisions across the Tennessee River at Bridgeport and march south of Raccoon Mountain to Wauhatchie, near Lookout Mountain, to support the assault.

At 3:00 A.M. on October 27, 3,500 men and three batteries advanced across Moccasin Point while 1,800 men drifted down the Tennessee on fifty

The Man Who Won the Civil War ■ Ulysses Simpson Grant

Grant, born in Ohio in April 1822, with the name Hiram Ulysses, later decided to keep Ulysses Simpson, which was the name his sponsor used when appointing him to West Point. He was a poor student, graduating twenty-first of thirty-nine in 1843, but was perhaps the best horseman in the country. As Grant's luck would have it, there were no cavalry slots available, and in the Mexican War he was a regimental quartermaster. Despite this rear echelon position, Grant managed to find the front often enough to be brevetted twice, usually where William J. Hardee, a close West Point friend (Grant's wife, Ellen, was Hardee's cousin), was fighting.

Grant could not seem to function in the peacetime army. Stationed in the Pacific Northwest in 1854, he left the army

when his commanding officer warned him about his excessive drinking. For the next six years Grant tried farming, selling real estate, and clerking. All these enterprises failed, and the beginning of the Civil War found him clerking at a store in Galena, Illinois, which was owned by his brothers.

In June 1861, Grant was appointed colonel of the Twenty-first Illinois, and made brigadier in August. After capturing Forts Henry and Donelson, he became a national hero known as U.S. ("Unconditional Surrender") Grant. Despite the enmity of Henry Halleck and being surprised at Shiloh, Grant's stature grew in the American military. He spent a year cracking Vicksburg, then relieved Chattanooga and routed Braxton Bragg at Missionary Ridge. Early in 1864 he

was made lieutenant general, a rank bestowed only upon George Washington until that time, and was put in charge of all military forces in the country. Grant rode with the Army of the Potomac in Virginia and whittled away the fabled Army of Northern Virginia at such bloodbaths as the Wilderness, Spotsylvania, Cold Harbor, and the nine-month siege at Petersburg, where he ultimately destroyed Robert E. Lee's force.

The Republican party ran Grant for the presidency in 1868. He spent two terms in the White House. His administration was renowned for its corruption. Grant was personally honest, but incredibly gullible, and his appointees took financial advantage of their positions. Afterward, he toured Europe for two years, then lost

his fortune in a business swindle. In an attempt to raise money for his family, Grant spent his final years writing his memoirs while dying from throat cancer. Grant died in July 1885 and is buried in New York City. ■

[LIBRARY OF CONGRESS]

Union soldiers landing at Brown's Ferry rout the surprised Confederate sentries. [HARPER'S WEEKLY]

pontoons and two flatboats. It took two hours to traverse seven miles of Confederate-held territory, but the force landed safely at daybreak and captured the landing. While securing the road to Kelly's Ferry, six Confederate companies mounted a brave, but unsuccessful, counterattack. The Southerners retreated to Lookout Mountain when Union reinforcements arrived. The Federals had suffered only 138 casualties.

On the night of October 28, Hooker was camped in the vicinity, with General John W. Geary's division at Wauhatchie, three miles south of Brown's Ferry. From the heights of Lookout Mountain that afternoon, Longstreet and Bragg had watched Geary march past. Recognizing the threat to his position, Bragg ordered an attack on Brown's Ferry with three divisions. For reasons which were never disclosed, Longstreet sent only one division to strike Geary at Wauhatchie.

At 2:30 A.M. Longstreet's men launched a savage night attack that severely pressed Geary. Reinforcements rushing from Brown's Ferry ran into

Troops of the Army of the Cumberland traveling on the Louisville & Nashville Railroad in 1863. [HARPER'S WEEKLY]

a Confederate ambush but managed to drive off the Rebels after fierce fighting. Just as Geary thought he would be overrun, the Confederates broke off the engagement and abandoned Lookout Valley. Grant dispatched additional troops to secure the route west of Chattanooga, and the supplies situation improved dramatically. The "Cracker Line," named for the hardtack that was a staple of the army, was open.

To reinforce Thomas and Hooker in Chattanooga, Grant ordered 20,000 men under General William T. Sherman to march from Memphis and Vicksburg. Their advance was slowed by the necessity of repairing the Central Alabama Railroad, which ran from Nashville southeast to Decatur, Alabama, where it joined the Memphis & Charleston line and continued east to Chattanooga. Regular visitations by Confederate raiders had resulted in 102 miles of ruined track and 182 burned bridges. Sherman's four divisions rebuilt the route with amazing energy, finishing the task in only forty days. Sherman's force reached Chattanooga on November 20.

While the Federals worked feverishly to save a desperate situation, the Confederate position deteriorated rapidly. Bragg's sick, hungry men lacked adequate ammunition and shelter. As Grant massed 60,000 soldiers in Chattanooga, Bragg's 50,000 men were reduced by 15,000 when Longstreet was sent to Knoxville for a campaign that had been suggested by President Davis. Longstreet urged Bragg to withdraw south to a better position in Georgia, but Bragg rejected the idea.

The War Child ■ Joseph Wheeler

Wheeler, born in Augusta, Georgia, in 1836, graduated from West Point in 1859 and resigned to join Confederate service just two years later. He led infantry into battle at Shiloh, but by July 1862, when he was twenty-six, Braxton Bragg had made him commander of all the cavalry of the Army of the Mississippi. Wheeler protected Bragg's flank on the invasion of Kentucky, then rode completely around William Rosecrans's army just before the battle of Stone's River and destroyed hundreds of supply wagons. During the siege of Chattanooga, Wheeler's forces contributed to the hunger in the Union camp by raiding supply lines and torching entire wagon trains.

Wheeler's reputation, fearsome during the Tennessee campaigns, began to tarnish in 1864. He adequately scouted Union maneuvers and screened Confederate movements during the Atlanta campaign, but, unlike Nathan Bedford Forrest's tireless raiders, Wheeler's men were unwilling to do the physical labor necessary to seriously impair Sherman's railroad supply line. At the close of the campaign, when his services were most needed, Wheeler had embarked on a fruitless expedition into Tennessee, leaving the Confederate army without its eyes and ears.

When John B. Hood marched to Nashville, Wheeler was left in Georgia to harass William Sherman's March to the Sea, which he accomplished with such vigor that Jefferson Davis praised him for constricting Sherman's area of destruction. In the final month he was subordinated to Wade Hampton because he was unable to prevent his troopers from murdering captured Union soldiers. At war's end Wheeler was arrested near Conyers and served a month in prison.

Wheeler, a self-professed "war child," fought in an incredible 127 battles and skirmishes, suffered three wounds, and lost sixteen horses in combat. The attrition rate among his staff officers was legendary; eight were killed and thirty-two wounded.

After the Civil War, Wheeler settled in Alabama and entered business. In 1868 he won the first of eight terms to the U.S. House of Representatives. When the Spanish–American War broke out, Wheeler joined the United States Army and led a division of cavalry against the Spanish in Cuba. His service became the symbol of a reunited nation and fulfilled Sherman's belief that if America fought a foreign nation, that "Joseph Wheeler is the man to command the cavalry of our army."

Wheeler retired as brigadier general in the U.S. Army. He died in Brooklyn in 1906 and was buried with full military honors in Arlington Cemetery. ■

[LIBRARY OF CONGRESS]

Grant and the Confederate Pickets

The day after his arrival in Chattanooga, U. S. Grant inspected the Union fortifications. Walking along the Tennessee River with his staff, he saw twenty Confederate pickets on the opposite bank, "within easy range," Grant later wrote. Although his party obviously consisted of officers, the Rebels made no reaction to their presence. Grant thought the Confederates "looked upon the garrison of Chattanooga as prisoners of war, feeding or starving themselves, and thought it would be inhuman to kill any of them except in self-defense."

Several days later Grant again rode to the front. Seeing him approach, a Union picket cried, "Turn out the guard for the commanding officer." Knowing the Confederates were nearby, Grant muttered, "Never mind the guard," and the men returned to their duties.

Moments later, Grant heard a Confederate across Chattanooga Creek shout, "Turn out the guard for the commanding general, General Grant." The Southerners formed a line facing north and saluted their adversary, who returned the honor.

On the creek was a fallen log where soldiers from both armies drew water. Spying a Confederate sitting on the log, Grant "rode up to him, commenced conversing with him, and asked whose corps he belonged to. He was very polite, . . touching his hat to me. . . . I asked him a few questions—but not with a view of gaining any particular information—all of which he answered, and I rode off."

These incidents reflect the typically friendly relations that existed between Union and Confederate soldiers when battle was not imminent. ■

Confederate batteries atop Lookout Mountain shell Union works on Chattanooga Creek in October 1863. [Harper's Weekly]

Grant was now prepared to take the offensive. He would threaten Bragg's supply line to the south and communications with Longstreet to the east. Grant had little faith in Thomas's men, who recently had been routed at Chickamauga, or Hooker's Easterners, similarly roughly handled by Lee at Chancellorsville. Grant contemptuously considered these men to be second-class troops. He intended to use Sherman's Army of the Tennessee, formerly his command, to relieve the siege. Marching from Bridgeport, Sherman would feint on the Confederate left around Lookout Mountain with one division, while the remainder disappeared into the wooded hills north of Chattanooga to feint on Knoxville. At night they would cross the Tennessee River and capture Missionary Ridge, cutting off the Confederate line of retreat through Chickamauga Station. Hooker would circle around Lookout Mountain and threaten the Rebel rear at Rossville Gap, while Thomas assaulted the Confederate center and supplied artillery support.

The attack was set for November 21, but Sherman's twenty-seven-mile march was delayed by mud and high water. As he crossed the river at Brown's Ferry and faded into the hills, other Union troops crossed the Tennessee River into Chattanooga. Bragg was puzzled. He did not know which troops were going where for what purposes. Deciding that the expedition to Knoxville was endangered, he sent a division to reinforce Longstreet; a second division waited for rail transportation east.

This Confederate activity led Grant to wonder if Bragg was retreating. To

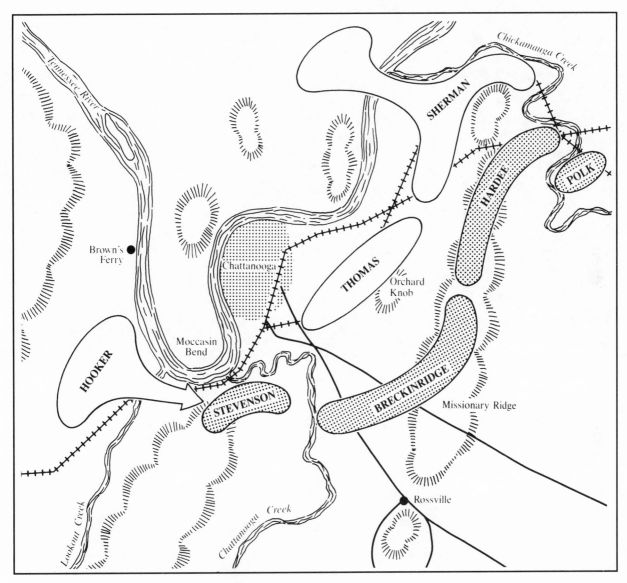

Map 24: The Battle of Chattanooga, November 24.

find out, on November 23 he ordered Thomas to capture Orchard Knob, a Confederate position on high ground in Chattanooga Valley between the city and Missionary Ridge. Thomas's men easily captured their objective. Bragg, alarmed by Grant's moves, ordered the division waiting to join Longstreet back to Missionary Ridge.

Sherman was hiding eight miles northeast of Chattanooga. Early on the morning of November 24, his men ferried across the Tennessee River on 116 pontoon boats and built a 1,350-foot-long bridge. At 1:00 P.M. Sherman attacked Missionary Ridge. After a difficult fight, he secured his goal but

Federal troops capture rifle pits in Lookout Valley in 1863. [HARPER'S WEEKLY]

was then shocked to learn that his maps were incorrect. He had captured an isolated hill. Missionary Ridge was actually across a small valley, and it would have to be assaulted at daybreak against a now-alerted enemy.

At dawn on the same day, Union general Joseph Hooker set out with 10,000 men to flank Lookout Mountain by occupying the valley between Lookout and Missionary Ridge and capturing Rossville Gap. His men splashed across Lookout Creek as Union artillery bombarded the heights.

Longstreet's departure had left the Confederate left virtually naked. Lookout Mountain and the valley between it and Missionary Ridge were held by 7,000 widely scattered Confederates commanded by a new officer who was unfamiliar with the terrain. Hooker's men crawled up the lower slopes of the mountain through a thick fog. At 10:00 A.M., 1,500 entrenched Rebels at Robert Cravens's farm, on a shoulder of the mountain about half-way to the summit, were attacked. Fierce fighting continued throughout the afternoon until dark. That night, which was graced by a full lunar eclipse, Bragg decided he could not hold Lookout Mountain and evacuated his troops to Missionary Ridge. Hooker had lost 500 men, the Confederates 1,250, many of them as prisoners.

When the sun rose on November 25, Union troops in the valley below cheered as they saw the Stars and Stripes flying from the forbidding mountaintop. Lookout Mountain had symbolized a besieged Chattanooga, and now it seemed to herald an imminent victory.

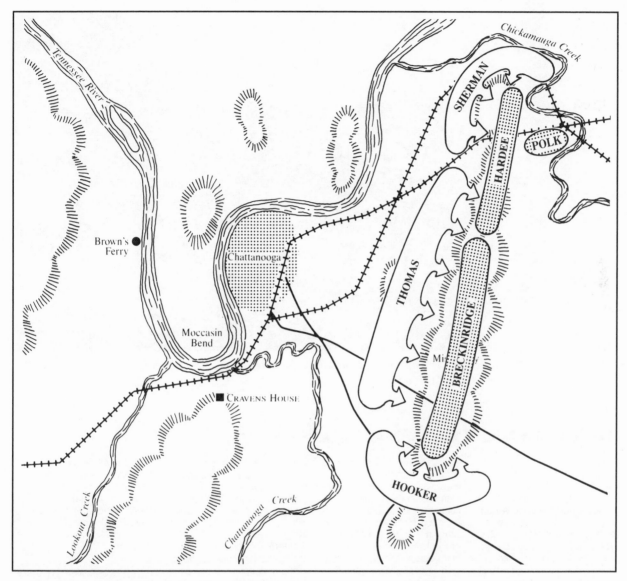

Map 25: The Battle of Chattanooga, November 25.

Hardee held the Confederate right on Missionary Ridge, with Breckinridge on his left. At dawn on November 25, Sherman's 26,000 men attacked Hardee's 10,000 soldiers at a point where a railroad tunnel pierced the mountain. The Federals charged across the valley and labored up the steep slope. The fighting was close and fierce until 3:00 P.M., when a Confederate counterattack drove Sherman from the ridge.

While Sherman assaulted from the east, Hooker continued around the Rebel left and captured Rossville Gap, which allowed his men to reach Missionary Ridge from the western end. Seeing Sherman's failure from his post

Fierce fighting rages around the Cravens House on Lookout Mountain. [HARPER'S WEEKLY]

The Man Who Defined War ■ William T. Sherman

Sherman, one of the greatest generals in American history, was born in Ohio in 1820. Initially named Tecumseh for the famous Indian warrior, William was added by his adoptive parents, U.S. Senator and Mrs. Thomas Ewing, whose daughter, Ellen, he later married.

Sherman graduated from West Point in 1840, sixth in his class, and served in California during the Mexican War. Weary of trying to earn a living in the military, Sherman entered civilian life in 1853 and worked in a California bank which failed. He was an unsuccessful lawyer in Kansas, but seemed to have found his niche in 1859 as commandant of a military school, which would become Louisiana State University. He resigned in January 1861 when required to accept military equipment seized from a U.S. arsenal,

then rejected a Confederate commission, one of the few offered a native Northerner. Sherman was managing a streetcar company in St. Louis when offered a commission in the U.S. Army in May. He led a brigade at First Manassas in August and became the North's seventh brigadier, eight ahead of U. S. Grant.

Sherman's volatile temper and absolute contempt for a free press embroiled him in conflicts which almost led to his dismissal. The general actually considered suicide when he had a nervous breakdown in Kentucky in September 1861 and was relieved of command. Sherman had returned to serve under U. S. Grant when the Confederates fell upon his division at Shiloh. Despite being surprised and mauled, Sherman fought well. His star began

to rise when he assisted Grant in the capture of Vicksburg, where he led a corps. After the pair relieved the Confederate siege of Chattanooga, Grant left his trusted friend in charge of the western armies.

Sherman's brilliant maneuvering won him Atlanta, and his virtually unopposed march to Savannah and through the Carolinas was a stroke of genius which pierced the hollow shell of an exhausted Confederacy. In appreciation, Congress made him a lieutenant general, the third since George Washington (Grant was the second). Paradoxically, when that devastating campaign was over, Sherman was harshly censured by Congress for granting generous terms of surrender to Joseph Johnston and the Army of Tennessee.

After the war, Sherman con-

tinued to serve the U.S. Army until his retirement in 1884. He rejected offers to run for the presidency that year and toured the country giving speeches. He died in New York City in 1891 and is buried in St. Louis. ■

[NATIONAL ARCHIVES]

Federal general Joseph Hooker's troops engage in fierce fighting "above the clouds" on Lookout Mountain, November 24, 1863. [HARPER'S WEEKLY]

Medals of Honor at Missionary Ridge

A small monument near the Bragg Reservation atop Missionary Ridge marks the spot where the Twenty-first Wisconsin reached the crest. The unit was staggered near the top by heavy enemy fire, and one regimental color bearer was shot, a second bayoneted, and a third decapitated by a cannonball. A young first lieutenant bravely seized the standard, shouted, "On, Wisconsin!" and planted the flag atop the Confederate works. Inspired, the men surged forward to drive back the defenders. For his decisive action, eighteen-year-old Arthur MacArthur, Jr., received the Congressional Medal of Honor, although it arrived twenty-seven years late due to bureaucratic nonsense. The regimental commander wrote that MacArthur was "most distinguished on a field where many of the regiment displayed conspicuous gallantry." According to one account, after the battle General Philip Sheridan hugged MacArthur and announced, "Take care of him. He has just won the Medal of Honor."

(Continued on page 94)

on Orchard Knob, Grant ordered Thomas to seize Confederate trenches at the foot of the ridge to relieve the pressure on Sherman.

There were only three Confederate divisions defending a four-mile line atop Missionary Ridge. Bragg had only 26,000 men available for duty that day, and he had unwisely placed a third of them on top of the ridge, a third halfway down the slope, and the remainder at the bottom. Soldiers stationed below the crest had orders to retreat up the mountain if attacked. This prevented their comrades from firing until they had reached the summit. To make the situation worse, the Rebel works had been poorly engineered. Instead of being located below the northern slope where the soldiers would have protection and clear fields of fire, a position known as the "military crest," the breastworks were situated on the actual crest. The Confederates would be unable to see an attacking force until the enemy was on top of them.

At 3:30 P.M. Thomas's Army of the Cumberland surged toward Missionary Ridge with flags flying and bands playing. Braving a devastating artillery fire, his 25,000 men quickly secured the bottom of the heights. As the Confederates scrambled up the slope, which clearly resembled a rout to the Federals, Thomas's men impulsively gave chase. Union soldiers clawed and scratched their way up the slope as Grant demanded to know who had given the order to assault the ridge. The Confederates held their fire until the men stationed below them reached the crest, then they tried to stop the Federals. They threw rocks at the Yankees, lit artillery shells and rolled them down the ridge, and shouted "Chickamauga" as if words might stop the mighty advance. Nothing could stem the Northern tide, and soon entire

(Continued from page 93)

MacArthur's son, General Douglas MacArthur, won the Medal of Honor seventy-nine years later for his service in World War II. They are the only father–son combination ever to win the distinguished award.

Because of disciplinary problems, Axel H. Reed of the Second Minnesota was placed under arrest just before the battle of Chickamauga and imprisoned in the rear. When the desperate battle erupted, Reed walked to the front, found a rifle, and fought so bravely that the charges against him were dropped. At Missionary Ridge his unit, Company K of the Second, led the Union charge and was one of several that claimed to have been the first to reach the summit. Reed was awarded the Medal of Honor for his service around Chattanooga. Despite losing an arm at Missionary Ridge, he remained in the army until the end of the war. ■

Union soldiers triumph atop Lookout Mountain. [HARPER'S WEEKLY]

Rebel brigades broke and fled. A Union soldier shouted, "Come and see them run!"

As Thomas pierced the Confederate center, Hooker advanced from the left. The Confederate line collapsed as sixty Union regiments reached the top of Missionary Ridge. Breckinridge's corps panicked. Bragg, whose headquarters were situated just behind the breakthrough, tried to rally the men, but they jeered their commander and kept running. Victorious Union soldiers wept, cheered, and danced in celebration.

Only Confederate general Patrick Cleburne's highly disciplined division, which had stopped Sherman, remained intact. His men guarded the Confederate rear as the Army of Tennessee trudged through Chickamauga Station toward Dalton, Georgia. Cleburne blunted Hooker's pursuit at Ringgold, Georgia, prompting Grant to call off the chase and send Sherman to relieve General Ambrose Burnside in Knoxville. After this disaster, Braxton Bragg finally tendered his resignation, which Davis accepted. The general left the army on December 3.

(Continued on page 98)

Stories From the Siege of Chattanooga

Believing that William Rosecrans would evacuate Chattanooga, U. S. Grant telegraphed General George Thomas, ordering him to hold the city "at all hazards." The Union government was much encouraged by Thomas' reply: "We will hold the town till we starve."

- - - - -

Commenting in his *Memoirs* on the decision by Jefferson Davis to weaken Bragg's forces by sending James Longstreet to besiege Knoxville, Grant noted that on several occasions the Confederate president "came to the relief of the Union by means of his *superior military genius*."

- - - - -

According to Grant, by the time cattle had been herded to Chattanooga from Nashville, and over the mountains during the autumn in a country scoured clean of forage, the soldiers said they received "beef dried on the hoof."

- - - - -

When ordered to attack Confederate rifle pits at the base of Missionary Ridge, General August Willich, a native of Germany, muttered, "Vell, I makes my vill."

- - - - -

Union general Joseph S. Fullerton wrote that when the soldiers continued up Missionary Ridge, Grant asked Thomas, "Who ordered those men up the ridge?"

"I don't know," Thomas answered. "I didn't."

Grant turned to Gordon Granger and inquired, "Did you order them up, Granger?"

"No," Granger responded, "they started up without orders. When those fellows get started, all hell can't stop them."

Grant, unable to find someone to take responsibility for this risky venture, muttered something like, "If this charge fails, somebody will suffer."

- - - - -

At the foot of the ridge, General Philip Sheridan borrowed a silver flask of whiskey from another officer, took a swig, shook the container at several Confederate officers who stood atop Missionary Ridge near Braxton Bragg's headquarters, and shouted, "Here's at you!"

Two Confederate cannon fired at that moment, the explosions from the shells showering Sheridan with dirt. "Oh," Sheridan said, "that was ungenerous. I shall take those guns for that."

Sheridan drew his sword and, waving it in one hand and his hat in the other, shouted, "Forward, boys, forward! Give 'em hell! We will carry the line!" When his horse was shot, Sheridan continued on foot with his men.

- - - - -

The flag of the Twenty-fifth Illinois reached the crest of Missionary Ridge in the hands of the seventh color bearer of the day. The banner had been pierced over thirty times.

- - - - -

When Colonel Henry J. Angelbeck of the Forty-first Ohio saw a blazing Confederate caisson, which was filled with ammunition, he cut loose the wounded team and pushed the vehicle down the east slope after the retreating Confederates, where it exploded.

- - - - -

Finding his army disintegrating around him, Bragg rode among his men in an effort to rally them, shouting, "Here is your commander!"

Many of the soldiers replied with a classic Civil War line, "Here's your mule!" (The expression was typically thrown at passing cavalrymen, whom the infantry hated.)

- - - - -

Confederate general Patrick Cleburne's younger brother, Christopher, a private, was one of many Rebels who threw stones at the Yankees climbing the ridge. When a captive Irishman spotted Chris, he shook his fist and shouted, "Ah, you are the little devil who hit me jaw with a rock!"

- - - - -

After the successful assault, Granger told his troops, "I am going to have you all court-martialed! You were ordered to take the works at the foot of the hill, and you have taken those on top! You have disobeyed orders, all of you, and you know that you ought to be court-martialed." ■

The Army of the Cumberland captures a Confederate battery as they overrun Missionary Ridge. [HARPER'S WEEKLY]

Charge of the Mule Brigade

The night battle of Wauhatchie was a fierce, swirling, confused affair that severely pressed the Federals. At the moment when it looked as if the North would be overwhelmed, the Confederates broke off the fight and withdrew back up Lookout Mountain.

This fortunate deliverance sparked one of the great myths of the war. Some Union sources, including Grant, who was not present, claim that Federal teamsters abandoned their mule teams in fear that they were about to be overrun. According to legend, the frightened mules stampeded toward the advancing Confederates, who thought they were being charged by cavalry and fled before the onrushing animals. Union soldiers on the field testified that their opponents skillfully withdrew from the field.

With this story in mind, an anonymous Union soldier sat down and wrote a parody of Alfred Lord Tennyson's classic poem "The Charge of the Light Brigade," an actual account of British military action during the Crimean War.

Half a mile, half a mile,
　Half a mile onward,
Right towards the Georgia
　troops,
　Broke the two hundred.
"Forward, the Mule Brigade!
　Charge for the Rebs!" they
　neighed:
Straight for the Georgia
　troops
　Broke the two hundred.

"Forward, the Mule Brigade!"
Was there a mule dismayed?
Not when the long ears felt
　All their ropes sundered.
Theirs not to make reply,

Theirs not to reason why,
Theirs but to make them fly:
Oh! to the Georgia troops
　Broke the two hundred.

When can their glory fade?
O the wild charge they made!
　All the world wondered.
Honor the charge they made!
Honor the Mule Brigade,
　Long-eared two hundred!

In a comment on the common practice of giving men "brevet" promotions for meritorious service in battle, Union general Horace Porter claimed that after Wauhatchie the officer in charge of the mules made the following recommendation: "I respectfully request that the mules, for the gallantry in this action, may have conferred upon them the brevet rank of horses." ■

Nathan Bedford Forrest Threatens Braxton Bragg

Bragg never had much use for Forrest, whom he considered to be unprofessional and uncooperative. After Chickamauga, the Confederate commander decided to reinforce Joseph Wheeler's cavalry by stripping Forrest of all his force except a single regiment and battery. What made this particularly difficult for Forrest to accept was that Bragg had done something similar during the Perryville campaign, giving Wheeler command of a unit that Forrest had raised. Because of a bungled joint operation over a year earlier, Forrest considered Wheeler an idiot and refused to work with him.

Forrest protested this new directive, and when Bragg brusquely repeated it, the rough cavalryman became incensed. Convinced that Bragg was carrying out a vendetta against him, Forrest stormed into Bragg's headquarters and ignored the hand that Bragg offered in greeting. According to Forrest's personal physician, Dr. J. B. Cowan, who was present, Forrest launched into a lengthy diatribe.

"I am not here to pass civilities or compliments with you," Forrest began. "You commenced your cowardly and contemptible persecution of me soon after the battle of Shiloh, and you have kept it up ever since. You did it because I reported to Richmond facts, while you reported damned lies." Forrest charged that Bragg "robbed me of my command in Kentucky . . . men whom I armed and equipped."

Now, he continued, Bragg had stolen his forces a second time. "I have taken your meanness as long as I intend to," he announced. "You have played the part of a damned scoundrel, and are a coward, and if you were any part of a man, I would slap your jaws. You may as well not issue me any orders, for I will not obey them," he warned. In conclusion, Forrest stated, "If you ever again try to interfere with me or cross my path it will be at the peril of your life."

Forrest resigned from the Confederate military, but Jefferson Davis recognized his ability even if Bragg did not. Interceding, he convinced Forrest to accept an independent command further west, where he bedeviled the Federals until war's end. ∎

Bragg Finally Bows Out—Without Grace

After establishing a position at Dalton, Georgia, on November 28, Bragg telegraphed Richmond, asking "relief from command and an investigation into the causes of defeat."

Two days later, he blamed the debacle of Missionary Ridge on his men, writing, "The shameful conduct of our troops on the line," allowed them to be overrun. Bragg stated that a position so strong should have been held by "a line of skirmishers." He accepted some blame for the rout, saying the Chattanooga campaign was "justly disparaging to me," but then he attacked his officers. "The warfare against me has been carried on successfully, and the fruits are bitter." Bragg believed John C. Breckinridge was drunk and "totally unfit for any duty," and Benjamin Cheatham "is equally dangerous."

"I feel we both erred in the conclusion for me to retain command here after the clamor raised against me," Bragg conceded to Jefferson Davis. "A panic which I had never before witnessed seemed to have seized upon officers and men, and each appeared to be struggling for his personal safety, regardless of his duty and character." ∎

These long lines of artillery were captured by Federal troops at Missionary Ridge. [HARPER'S WEEKLY]

Braxton Bragg's Third Crisis

This crisis was the worst. It began immediately after Bragg bungled the opportunity to destroy the Union army at Chickamauga. The morale of the army fell to unprecedented low levels, and Bragg's generals were almost mutinous.

On September 22, Bragg attacked Leonidas Polk and Thomas C. Hindman for their failure to attack at McLemore's Cove, and for Polk's tardy attack on the second day at Chickamauga. Bragg suspended the two, and when Jefferson Davis asked that Polk, an old friend, be reinstated, Bragg refused. Polk traveled to Atlanta, where he defended himself to hordes of visiting supporters and demanded a court of inquiry into the charges against him. An immensely popular figure, he gained considerable sympathy. The Confederacy was in an uproar.

Bragg's generals held a secret meeting at which they planned their commander's ouster. They drafted a petition, which was signed by twelve generals, and sent it to Jefferson Davis. The president reacted by sending an assistant to the Confederate camp. The aide reported such animosity against Bragg that Davis quickly traveled to Georgia for a conference. He met with Polk in Atlanta, then continued on to see Bragg, whom he had already decided to retain. When Davis met with Bragg and his corps commanders, most of the generals said Bragg should be removed.

Davis kept Bragg, who dropped charges against Polk who was then sent to command the Department of Alabama, Mississippi, and East Louisiana in exchange for Joseph Hardee. Feeling vindicated again, Bragg reorganized his army to punish his chief critics, Daniel H. Hill, Nathan Bedford Forrest, and James Longstreet, transferring some, taking troops away from others.

If the Confederate humiliation at Missionary Ridge seems surprising, this is the explanation: Bragg fought his own subordinates so hard that he had little time left for the enemy. ■

In the three days of battle, Bragg suffered 6,700 casualties, with an additional 4,000 men captured, along with forty cannon and countless rifles abandoned. Grant's losses were only 5,800. The danger to Chattanooga, and to Tennessee, had been eliminated. The road to Atlanta and an opportunity to split the Confederacy asunder were open. ■

A DRIVING TOUR
■ The Siege of Chattanooga ■

From the exit of the Chickamauga National Bat-
tlefield Park Visitors Center, turn left onto U.S. 27
for .1, then turn left onto McFarland Gap Road.

It passes through the community of Fort Oglethorpe,
which was once an 810-acre military reservation established in 1903 and named for James Oglethorpe,
the founder of Georgia. The fort was garrisoned by
the Sixth Cavalry and became a mobilization and training center during World War I. The community of Fort
Oglethorpe retains much of the camp's facilities, including barracks, officers' quarters, and parade
grounds.

This is McFarlan Gap, where Rosecrans's crushed
army fled the field at Chickamauga. Imagine the route
strewn with dead and dying soldiers and animals, discarded weapons, and wrecked wagons.

At the stop sign after 2.1 drive straight. At the first
red light turn right toward Rossville, then continue
straight at the second light to remain on McFarland
Avenue.

Rossville was named for John Ross, whose Indian
name was Kooweskoowe. Ross was the principal chief
of the Cherokee Nation for thirty-eight years, from
1828 until his death in 1866. In 1797 his Scottish
grandfather, John McDonald, built a simple, two-story
hewn-log house here beside a spring on an Indian trading path that led to Augusta. The logs were fastened
with wooden pegs, chinked with mud, and covered
with clapboard. Ross inherited the home and grew
prosperous with a ferry, a warehouse in Chattanooga,
and a large farm with slaves. In 1817 he became
postmaster of the area. The fact that Ross had fought
with General Andrew Jackson meant nothing when
President Jackson ordered the Cherokee Indians to
leave Georgia. Although Ross was only one-eighth
Cherokee, he accompanied the Indians on the Trail of
Tears to Oklahoma. His wife, who was half Cherokee,
was one of thousands who died on the tragic journey.
In the west Ross devoted his life to establishing
schools to educate and train his people.

The Ross House still stands in Rossville. In 1963 it
was moved several hundred feet to prevent its demoli-
tion when a new building was constructed. Ten logs

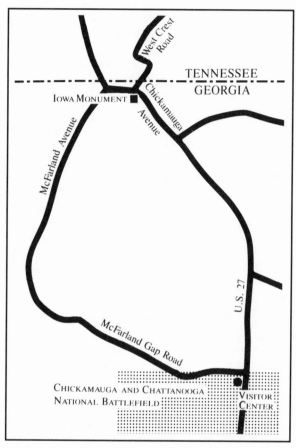

Map 26: *From the national battlefield to the Iowa Monu-*
ment.

and some of the floor planking were replaced, and new
shingles were added. According to legend, at its original location a hidden tunnel led from the house to a
cave where secret Cherokee council meetings were
held. The house is open to visitors. On display are
belongings of Ross donated by descendants in
Oklahoma, and a secret room, which was discovered
when the house was moved, can be examined. A door
has been cut into the chamber, but it remains a mys-
tery how the room was originally entered. A stone
monument honoring Ross is on the grounds.

The house was headquarters for the Union reserve troops under General Gordon Granger during the battle of Chickamauga. Knowing that the army was in trouble, Granger marched to the battlefield without orders and saved Thomas. When the Federals withdrew from Chickamauga in the early evening, they formed a rear guard here in Rossville; but the expected Confederate pursuit never materialized. On the following day, Thomas entered Chattanooga.

After 2.9 turn right onto Chickamauga Avenue. At .4, beside the towering Iowa Monument, turn left onto West Crest Road.

The marble shaft of this monument rises fifty feet into the air. Four soldier figures guard the base, and a fifth stands atop the column. On November 24 Hooker's men advanced from the west to threaten the Confederate left on Missionary Ridge.

After .5 go straight at the stop sign and immediately bear left. This is Missionary Ridge, named for the Brainerd Christian Mission, which was established nearby to convert the local Indians. After 2.9 turn right and immediately left to circle through the Bragg Reservation, which is dominated by the imposing Illinois Monument.

When the Chickamauga–Chattanooga park was established, the U.S. Congress had many veterans who had served in both armies during the Civil War. They recognized a unique opportunity to preserve the battlefields in honor of the soldiers who had fought here and to educate future generations of military leaders. The mountains, forests, fields, and streams represented every type of terrain and obstacle American soldiers might encounter. This 150-mile battlefront afforded the chance to study strategy and maneuver and to apply those lessons in light of the actual decisions made by commanders on these fields. In 1896 Congress declared Chickamauga–Chattanooga a field "for military maneuver" by the army and national guards. Historians and professional soldiers traveled from around the world to walk these grounds.

Lookout towers were erected around the area, including one here at the Bragg Reservation, where students undoubtedly learned not to imitate the strategy of Bragg and Jefferson Davis here and at Snodgrass Hill at Chickamauga.

In 1898 a sprawling tent city of 45,000 men was erected on the Chickamauga battlefield, designated Camp Thomas, where men were trained to fight in the Spanish–American War. Military uses of the Chickamauga–Chattanooga park passed to Fort Oglethorpe in 1902, until the program was canceled in 1940.

The Chattanooga part of the national park consists of detached "reservations" here on Missionary Ridge, in the valley below at Orchard Knob, atop Lookout Mountain, and at Signal Mountain.

This reservation marks the site of Bragg's headquarters when Thomas's troops shattered his line. From this spot Bragg could clearly observe developments in Chattanooga and on Lookout Mountain to the left. The tall Illinois Monument here is a marble column topped by a figure called Victory. Statues of four soldiers ring the base.

This elevation was not the impregnable position it has been made out to be. The ridge is actually several low hills separated by ravines, and it was difficult for artillery to fire on attackers. During the siege of Chattanooga, much of the timber was cut to improve visibility and fields of fire, and for use in defensive works. The Confederate line was very thin when Thomas attacked the center, with only two divisions manning the entire front. Hooker was driving down the ridge from the west, and Sherman had hammered the eastern flank all day. Union soldiers reached the crest at a dozen different locations, spreading panic among the defenders. Thousands of Confederates threw down their rifles and dozens of artillery pieces were abandoned as soldiers fled. Triumphant Federals screamed in victory as the Southerners ran down the southern slope to safety.

Missionary Ridge is 400 feet high and seven miles in length. By the time the park was established, the ridge was a prime residential area, and few parcels of land were available for purchase. The government managed to secure five reservations, ranging in size from less than one-half acre to fifty acres. On many lawns are monuments, historical markers, and cannon that point out the location of troop positions and batteries. The road is twisting and very narrow, and the reservations have limited parking. Stop only in designated areas.

Return to West Crest Road and turn right. After .2 turn left to cross the interstate on a bridge. To the left at .6 is the Ohio Reservation.

The Ohio Monument here was dedicated on September 18, 1895, by William McKinley, then governor of that state, to commemorate the participation of Ohio soldiers in the battle for Missionary Ridge.

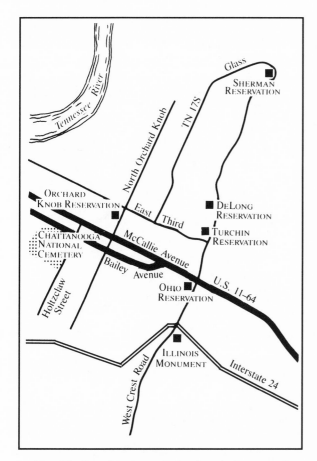

Map 27: From Missionary Ridge through the national cemetery.

Resume the tour and drive carefully straight ahead after the stop sign, as visibility is extremely limited. At .8 the Turchin Reservation is on the left. The De-Long Reservation is on the left after .3.

This was the center of the long Confederate line on Missionary Ridge. The Minnesota Monument honors soldiers who had fought hard at Chickamauga and were among the first Federals to crack this mountaintop position. Many different units claimed to have been the first to reach the summit.

Continue east. After two miles turn right and immediately left to the Sherman Reservation at .3.

Here on the eastern end of the ridge is the largest of the five reservations. On November 25 Sherman had occupied a neighboring hill, thinking it was the extreme right flank of Bragg's line. His maps were in error. When he advanced against Missionary Ridge on the following morning, the Confederates, who belonged to Patrick Cleburne's division, one of the finest in the South, were alerted. The Southerners had been waiting for train transportation to Knoxville at Chickamauga Station and had arrived just hours before Sherman attacked. Repeated assaults were beaten off, and at a critical moment Cleburne ordered a counterattack which cleared the slope. When the Confederate line on Missionary Ridge was shattered, Cleburne's tough division, whose resistance had prompted Grant to order Thomas to attack, remained the only intact Confederate unit on the field. It fell back to protect Bragg's retreat through Chickamauga Station, and on the following day it blunted an attack by Hooker at Ringgold, Georgia, which allowed the Army of Tennessee to escape to Dalton.

The Chattanooga campaign ended on this ridge in the late evening darkness of November 25, 1863. It brought to an end nearly two years of bloody fighting for the city. The struggle resulted in 753 Federals killed, 4,722 wounded, and 349 missing from Grant's strength of 56,000. Of the 46,000 men Bragg started the siege with, 361 were killed, 2,160 wounded, and an incredible 4,146 missing, most of them captured after the disaster at Missionary Ridge.

The Confederacy had lost complete control of Tennessee and its most important railroad center. The corridor to Atlanta, which had been one of Lincoln's primary goals, was at last open.

As a result of this dismal campaign, Bragg finally resigned his commission; but Jefferson Davis called the disgraced Confederate general to Richmond to serve as his military adviser. For Grant, the only consistently successful Union general, the relief of Chattanooga meant command of all Federal armies. His coordinated offensive in the spring of 1864 sent Sherman to capture Atlanta and march through the empty shell that the Confederacy had become. Grant proceeded to Virginia, got his teeth in Lee, and did not let go until the Army of Northern Virginia disintegrated on the road from Petersburg to Appomattox.

Return to the road you have been following, which has become Campbell, and turn right. After .2 turn left onto Glass for .7, then left on TN 17 South for 1.9, and turn right onto East Third. At .3 turn left onto North Orchard Knob. The entrance to the Orchard Knob Reservation is on the right after .2.

This prominent hill was a forward Confederate position between Missionary Ridge and Chattanooga. To

101

discover if the Confederates were lifting their siege, a question raised when Bragg dispatched reinforcements to Longstreet at Knoxville, Grant ordered Thomas to occupy the knob. His troops started forward at 1:30 P.M. on November 23, and after a short, sharp fight which lasted half an hour, the hill was secured. An alarmed Bragg recalled Cleburne's division, which was waiting for train transport to Knoxville, to its original position on Missionary Ridge. Grant and Thomas made their headquarters here when Sherman attacked Missionary Ridge on November 25. When the assault was stopped cold, Grant instructed Thomas to capture Confederate rifle pits at the base of the ridge to relieve the pressure on Sherman.

Because the troops of the Army of the Cumberland had been treated with contempt by Grant's Army of the Tennessee for being routed at Chickamauga, they had something to prove. After the Federals easily took the rifle pits and upon seeing the Confederates retreating up the slope, they impulsively gave chase, screaming "Remember Chickamauga!" Watching the action through his field glasses, Grant murmured, "Someone will pay if the charge fails." The charge was one of the handsomest in the war; it completely shattered the siege of Chattanooga and the Army of Tennessee.

On the hill are monuments, cannon marking the position of supporting artillery batteries, and tablets that describe the events which occurred here.

Continue down Orchard Knob for .2, turn right onto McCallie for .5, then left onto Holtzclaw. After .4 turn right into the entrance to the Chattanooga National Cemetery. Almost directly ahead is the General Monument and the graves of Andrews' Raiders.

This cemetery was established in 1865 by General George Thomas for the burial of Union dead from Chickamauga, Wauhatchie, Orchard Knob, Lookout Mountain, Missionary Ridge, and other actions in the area. Of 12,956 Civil War dead, 5,000—over one-third—are unknown. Since the war, many veterans from America's conflicts have also been buried here.

A wonderful story concerns Thomas and this cemetery. When a chaplain who was helping to lay out the grounds asked if the soldiers should be buried according to the state they were from, which was the custom, Thomas said wearily, "No, no, mix 'em up, mix 'em up. I'm tired of states' rights."

Confederate dead from Chickamauga were moved to Marietta, Georgia. Southern casualties from the battles for Chattanooga are buried in the Chattanooga Confederate Cemetery, between Lansing and Pal-

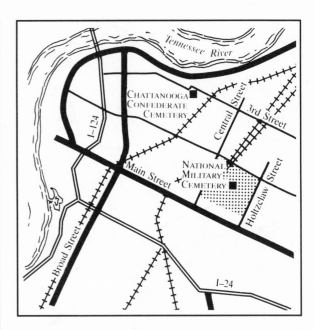

Map 28: Downtown Chattanooga.

metto streets, from East Third Street to East Fifth Street. Established in 1865, it has markers identifying the units of those buried, with only veterans buried following the war having individual markers. If the cemetery is closed, call the Chattanooga Parks Department (615-757-5054) for admission.

This monument in the Chattanooga National Cemetery honors Andrews' Raiders, who stole the General in an attempt to burn railroad bridges in northern Georgia.

After their capture nearby, Andrews' Raiders were held in Swimm's Jail, a private establishment. It was a two-story building, thirteen feet by twenty-six feet. The chained and handcuffed Raiders were held there for three weeks. Andrews managed to escape and made his way to Williams Island in the Tennessee River, several miles downstream from the city along the route of TN 27. He was recaptured a week later and hanged the following week. Eight Raiders, including Andrews, were tried in Knoxville, then transported to Atlanta for execution. The rest escaped from jail in Atlanta. Several reached Union territory, and the remainder were exchanged.

The executed Raiders were buried originally in Atlanta's Oakland Cemetery but were reinterred here. The granite stone monument in the center of the eight graves, topped by a bronze model of the General, was dedicated May 30, 1891, Memorial Day. The names of twenty-two Raiders (two were omitted) are engraved on the side of the monument. The gravestones indicate that the men were awarded the Congressional Medal of Honor for their bold mission and sacrifice. Andrews, a civilian, was not eligible for the medal.

The General, the locomotive they stole near Marietta, Georgia, and drove north toward Chattanooga, hoping to burn a number of railroad bridges, was badly damaged when Hood blew up his munitions trains at Atlanta in September 1864. Captured by the Federals,

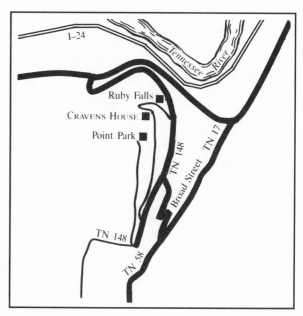

Map 29: The Lookout Mountain area.

it saw service following the war but was soon forgotten. Found in poor condition on a siding near Atlanta, the General was restored, and from 1901 until 1961 it was displayed at Chattanooga's Union Station between trips to historical celebrations. In 1961 it was taken to Louisville and prepared for a centennial run the following year along the original route of the "Great Locomotive Chase." When the Georgia legislature asked for permanent ownership of the General in 1967, the mayor of Chattanooga obtained a court order to keep it in his city. In 1970 the U.S. Supreme Court refused to hear the case, which meant the railroad company owned the General and could dispose of the engine in whatever manner it chose. In 1970 the locomotive was permanently enshrined in a museum at the place where it was stolen, in Kennesaw, near Marietta (see *Fields of Glory*).

Return to Holtzclaw and turn right for .3, then right on Main Street. After 1.5 turn left on Broad Street. After 1.8 turn left to follow TN 17.

Lookout Mountain rises abruptly to tower 1,400 feet above the Tennessee River Valley. The Confederama is on the left, and just down the road the Lookout Mountain Incline Railway is on the right.

The terrain surrounding Chattanooga and the military actions which occurred around the city are diffi-

Southern dead from battles around the city are buried in the Chattanooga Confederate Cemetery.

cult to describe, much less understand, without an intimate knowledge of local geography. That knowledge can be obtained at the Confederama. Chattanooga's unique position has been dramatically recreated on a table 480 feet square. The city, railroads, river, mountains, and ferry points are depicted in a clear manner; and a taped narration, accompanied by rousing martial music ("Dixie" and the "Battle Hymn of the Republic"), and battle sounds explain each action in the campaign for Chattanooga. Over 5,000 specially crafted toy soldiers illustrate the battles, and 650 flashing lights signify combat as real smoke rises from the battlefields. The scene starts with Chickamauga and proceeds step by step through the Confederate siege, Grant's arrival, the opening of the Cracker Line, the battle of Wauhatchie, Sherman's army hiding in the hills, and the battles of Orchard Knob, Lookout Mountain, and the final attack against Missionary Ridge when the Confederate line collapsed. Three miles of electric wiring hold this three-dimensional display together.

Another diorama depicts what Chattanooga bills as the "Last Battle of the Revolution." John McDonald, a Scottish trader who was adopted by the Cherokee Indians, was a British agent during the Revolution. He accumulated a large stock of supplies which were to be used by Indians to start a revolt on the frontier. In reaction to increased Indian activity, a force of militia from Virginia and North Carolina marched here and destroyed the stores. When a second cache was suspected, the Americans returned and burned it in 1780. In 1782, a year after fighting in the Revolution ended, the frontiersmen, commanded by John Sevier, Tennessee's first governor, launched a third expedition that destroyed the supplies and Tuskagee, a town of the Chickamauga Cherokees that was located on Moccasin Bend.

On this trip Indians taunted the Americans from the opposite bank of the Tennessee River. Thereupon the militia crossed the river and fought the Cherokees, led by Chief Dragging Canoe, in the thickly wooded lower slopes of Lookout Mountain.

The Incline, established in 1897, is billed as "America's Most Amazing Mile." With a slope of 72.7 percent near the top, it has one of the steepest grades in the world. Two electric trolley cars take visitors to and from the summit of Lookout Mountain at the breathtaking speed of eight miles an hour. Colorful St. Elmo Station, sometimes literally in the clouds on top of the mountain, has an observation deck with unspoiled views of the scene below. Visitors can observe the operation of the giant gears in the machine room.

Continue on TN 17. After .4 turn right onto TN 58, then bear right after 1.3, following signs for the Cravens' House. At the stop sign after .8 follow North TN 148 to the right. Turn left after .2 at the signs for the Cravens' House, and turn left after .5 to the parking area at the house. If you miss a turn just follow the directional signs.

This house, built by Robert Cravens, was the only permanent home on Lookout Mountain before the Civil War. Cravens moved his ironworks to Chattanooga in 1850 because the network of railroads that converged here provided easy access to markets. At his complex, which included a blast furnace, foundry, and machine shop, Cravens manufactured railroad engines and freight cars. He built a one-story, six-room house in 1856 on this shoulder of the mountain, about halfway to the top. Cravens named it "Alta Vista." The altitude afforded good views, cool breezes, and good water.

One account claims that during the siege, the Cravens family shared the house with Confederate officers, while enlisted men camped in the yard. During the fighting, they huddled in the stone dairy beneath the detached kitchen as shells fell around the house. Another story says the Cravens relocated to Ringgold, Georgia, before the battle.

The house was Confederate general E. C. Walthall's headquarters during the siege. At dawn on November 23, three divisions of Hooker's corps, 10,000 men, formed a line three deep, waded across Lookout Creek at the foot of the mountain, and started climbing up the west face through a thick fog, carefully picking paths through fields of slashed timber and deep ravines. Artillery from Moccasin Bend supported the attack, although the gunners below could see only snatches of fighting through the drifting fog. The Federals encountered a brigade of Confederates on the mountain terrace at the Cravens' House, and heavy combat erupted. At noon two additional Southern brigades arrived and fought from behind defensive works near the house. Confederate cannon at the top of the mountain fired on the Federals when they could see targets. After several hours of fierce fighting, the battle waned around 2:00 P.M. because the fog had become too thick to distinguish between friend and foe. When Bragg decided the mountain could not be held, the Confederate troops were withdrawn during the night.

The house became a nationally recognized landmark after the Federals captured Lookout Mountain. While camped here, northern newspaper correspondents

Near the rebuilt Cravens House is a monument that honors Union soldiers who captured Lookout Mountain.

The entrance gate to this eighteen-acre reservation was built in 1905 by the U.S. Corps of Engineers. It bears a replica of their seal.

This was the extreme left of Bragg's line at Chattanooga, held by Longstreet until he was dispatched to Knoxville. The siege might have accomplished its goal if the line had extended to the northwest and had occupied the valley of Lookout Creek and Raccoon Mountain, which would have commanded Moccasin Bend and a longer stretch of the Tennessee River. Confederates of General Carter L. Stevenson's division held the summit.

The first of three sets of cannon in the park, which represent the extensive batteries the Confederates hauled up the mountain to threaten Chattanooga, are two Parrott Rifles. Named for the inventor, Robert Parrott of New York, these 1,750-pound pieces had rifled barrels. Grooves inside the barrel gave projectiles a spin that resulted in greater accuracy and range, up to two miles. These rifles prevented Union shipping from passing on the river below.

It is easy to imagine how occupation of this mountain could dominate Chattanooga, the river, and the railroads. Below is the sprawl of Chattanooga. To the right is Missionary Ridge, which blocks access to Chattanooga from the south. Hooker captured Rossville Gap between Lookout Mountain and Missionary Ridge to cut off one Confederate retreat route. Directly in front is the seven-mile peninsula called Moccasin Bend, created by a huge loop in the Tennessee River. A village site for prehistoric and historic Indians, it has yielded hundreds of skeletons excavated from burial grounds, and innumerable artifacts have been found there. In the distance are Raccoon and Signal mountains, and Walden Ridge, which prevents easy access to the city from the north and west.

Two smooth-bore cannon indicate where Garrity's Battery was positioned. These twelve-pound Napoleons, so named because they were developed in France for Napoleon's campaigns, could fire a twelve-pound shot 1,700 yards. The most common cannon used during the Civil War, these guns were murderously effective at close range. During the fighting at the Cravens House below, however, they were useless; to attack Federal positions, the muzzles would have had to be depressed, causing the shot to roll out before they could be fired.

The last set of cannon marks Corput's Battery, near the western overlook. Nearby is Sunset Rock, where Bragg and Longstreet watched Hooker's reinforcements arrive on October 28, 1863. Bragg ordered a night attack with three divisions, but Longstreet sent

sketched and photographed the house and wrote accounts of the battle that raged around it. The house had been battered by fire from Confederate and Union cannon, and bullets had rattled against its walls throughout the battle. Union troops dismantled the house for firewood and to floor their tents, and remaining timbers were taken as souvenirs.

After the war, Cravens rebuilt the house and lived here until his death in 1886. The house was restored during the 1950s by the Chattanooga Chapter of the Association for Preservation of Tennessee Antiquities and was acquired by the National Park Service. Tour the house and examine the cannon and monuments on the grounds.

Return to the stop sign below the Cravens' House and turn right. After .5 turn right, and bear right after 1.1 onto East Brow Road at the signs to Point Park and the Incline. Point Park is reached after 1.2.

The arch at Point Park atop Lookout Mountain leads to stunning views of Chattanooga and the Tennessee River Valley.

only one, Hood's former command. Longstreet observed the midnight attack at Wauhatchie from this observation post. The battle resulted in fierce fighting that inflicted heavy casualties on both sides before the outnumbered Confederates were repulsed.

The Tennessee River may have been commanded by Confederate batteries, but the Cracker Line, across the northern neck of Moccasin Bend, was out of range. The Confederates could only watch helplessly as reinforcements and wagons loaded with supplies flowed into Chattanooga. This development ended the siege.

On November 24 the Confederates could not fire until the Federals reached the Cravens House below because fog obscured their vision. The cannon that were capable were used against the attackers, but fog again rolled in during the early afternoon, forcing the Confederates to cease fire. No combat occurred here. During the night the cannon were taken down the mountain and used to reinforce Southern positions on Missionary Ridge. Finding the summit evacuated, Union soldiers from Kentucky climbed on ladders to a rock ledge near here early on November 25 and planted the American flag. That sight was mightily cheered by the Federals in the city below. They had known hunger, cold, and despair because of those threatening guns atop Lookout.

In the center of the park is the New York Peace Monument, designed by R. Hinton Perry and dedicated in 1907. It is ninety-five feet high and fifty feet in diameter at the base. On top are the figures of a Union and a Confederate soldier shaking hands beneath a single flag, which represents unity and peace. This imposing monument is made of Tennessee marble and pink Massachusetts granite.

Several sets of stairs lead to the Ochs Museum and Overlook, 500 feet below the bluff. It offers a stunning view of the Tennessee River and the surrounding terrain. Dedicated on November 12, 1940, the Ochs Museum has a series of exhibits and photographs that describe the battles for Chattanooga and their significance. On a ledge nearby is the Umbrella Rock, where many Union luminaries, including U. S. Grant, posed for photographs. Twelve feet high, it consists of several stones with a large flat rock on top. It is unsafe to climb today.

The Bluff Trail, the primary hiking path on the mountain, leads downhill from here to rifle pits and the Cravens House. Along the trail is the spot where soldiers raised the U.S. flag on November 25.

The Visitors Center at Point Park has a slide show, a panoramic painting of the battles for Chattanooga, and one of the finest Civil War bookstores in the South.

In a gift shop next door to the Visitors Center is the Lookout Mountain Museum. It has life-sized dioramas that depict historical events in the area, in addition to Civil War weapons, swords, and equipment, and Indian artifacts.

Lookout Mountain, which is crowded with residences today, has long been a tourist attraction. The first settlement, called Summertown, consisted of the Lookout Mountain Hotel and a number of cottages. Trains and steamboats were met in Chattanooga by carriages, which transported visitors up the mountain via a toll road. Confederate and Federal troops occupied the structures, and Jefferson Davis rested here while traveling to his home in Mississippi after being released from prison in May 1867.

Lookout Mountain is occupied by two of the South's leading tourist attractions, Ruby Falls and Rock City. The name does not reveal that Ruby Falls is deep inside a cave. Actually, there are two distinct caves at Ruby Falls. The Historic Cave, situated 420 feet below the spot where the entrance is today, had a natural opening on the banks of the Tennessee River. There is evidence that Indians inhabited it, and during the Civil War soldiers found shelter in its huge chambers and intricate passages. On a wall of the cave is scribbled, "Andrew Jackson 1833." That entrance was sealed at the turn of the century when a railroad tunnel was built through the mountain.

In 1923 businessmen had the idea of drilling an elevator shaft through solid limestone from a shoulder of the mountain to the cave and opening it for commercial exploitation. The drillers were excited when they found a second cave 260 feet below the surface. They were further delighted when exploration revealed beautiful cave formations and a natural waterfall that plunges 145 feet into a large chamber.

Today elevators whisk visitors to the second cave. An hour-long, eight-tenths of a mile tour culminates at the illuminated waterfall, which is truly a wonder. The entrance to the cave, called the Cavern Castle, has been added to the National Register of Historic Places. Several observation decks at the castle offer wonderful views of Chattanooga, the Tennessee River, and surrounding mountains.

Rock City Gardens is a fifty-year-old delicious example of southern entrepreneurship. These ten acres of unique rock formations and lush gardens were once promoted on hundreds of barn roofs and thousands of bird houses erected at motor lodges across the eastern United States. "See Rock City" is an American advertising institution ranking right up there with Burma Shave signs. The Smithsonian Institution possesses one of the bird houses, and replicas are on sale at Rock City.

So what is Rock City? The Fairyland Trail is a flagstone path, winding through the gardens, where hundreds of native plants add color to any season. It passes towering stones with such names as the Squeeze, Needle's Eye, Mushroom Rock, and Goblin's Underpass, and goes over suspension bridges to Fairyland Caverns and Mother Goose Village. Lover's Leap commands a stunning view of seven states. Miniature golf was invented nearby, when the Tom Thumb course was established.

On the slopes of Lookout Mountain is Reflection Riding, which offers a three-mile drive and nature hiking trails through 350 acres of arboretum. There are 1,000 varieties of trees, shrubs, and wildflowers in this English-style garden. In the Chattanooga area are 300 kinds of trees and 900 varieties of wildflowers, 500 on Lookout Mountain alone. This region is believed to have more diversity than any other place on earth except China. The Chattanooga Nature Center is adjacent to this property. Historically, this was the starting point for Hooker's men as they assaulted Lookout Mountain.

The final part of the Chickamauga–Chattanooga park is the Signal Point Reservation, which overlooks the impressive Grand Canyon of the Tennessee River from the north bank, opposite Raccoon Mountain. Signal Mountain received its name because on its summit

Lookout Mountain was often shrouded in mist as Confederate gunners fired on the besieged city.

the Cherokee Indians lit signal fires, which were visible for twenty miles. The mountain towers 1,400 feet above the river and is the southernmost extension of Walden's Ridge. This was one in a series of signal stations established for communication with Bridgeport, Alabama, after Rosecrans was trapped in Chattanooga. The letters of coded messages were formed by swinging a pole holding a red and white flag by day or a torch by night, in combinations of left, right, and center. During good weather the station was constantly in use. The signals could be seen eight to fifteen miles with normal vision and up to twenty-five miles with field glasses. Displays at the reservation tell the little-known story of the Signal Corps. The beautiful views of surrounding mountains and the gorge are worth the effort to drive up Signal Mountain.

Below this spot, where Suck Creek enters the Tennessee River, is the Suck, a serious navigational hazard on the Tennessee River. Before the dams were built, boats passing this dangerous spot were kept close to the opposite shore by a system of cables. Indians attacked settlers as they moved slowly through the treacherous water. The pioneer expedition to Nashville that floated down the Tennessee on flatboats was almost destroyed here.

Stringer's Ridge north of Chattanooga, named for an early settler, Captain William Stringer, was the site where Federal general James S. Negley shelled Chattanooga for two days in early June 1863. As Rosecrans passed far to the southeast before Chickamauga,

Captain Eli Liley's Eighteenth Indiana Battery, part of Wilder's mounted infantry brigade, shelled the city on August 21, 1863. Other Union troops demonstrated loudly upstream to convince Bragg that Rosecrans would cross the Tennessee River there.

Red Bank, now a community along U.S. 27 north of the river, was the wooded ridge that hid Sherman's force. Completely fooled by his disappearance, Bragg decided that Sherman was reinforcing Burnside in Knoxville, so he weakened his army by sending a division to Longstreet. On the morning of November 24, Sherman bridged the river and began his move against Missionary Ridge.

Chickamauga Dam, which forms Chickamauga Lake in eastern Chattanooga, is 60 feet high and 5,685 feet long. The project cost thirty-one million dollars and employed 2,000 men. The TVA wanted to call it Sherman Dam, because the Army of the Tennessee crossed the river on a pontoon bridge near this location, but the United Daughters of the Confederacy and other southern groups protested vigorously.

Near the dam stood the Frankstone Inn (1840). According to legend, James A. Garfield, Rosecrans's chief of staff, was quartered there. He gave Mrs. Lewis Sheppard, wife of the owner, a letter of introduction to President Lincoln so she could plead for her son's release from a prisoner of war camp. The boy, Lewis Sheppard, Jr., had joined the Confederate army at age fifteen. He returned home safely, studied law, and became a respected citizen.

In the Wauhatchie Valley, along the route of U.S. 11–64–U.S. 41–72 which hugs the base of Lookout Mountain beside the Tennessee River, are several sites related to the opening of the Cracker Line. Near Tiftonia was fought the battle of Wauhatchie, October 28, 1863, which occurred at night between three brigades of Hood's division, led by Confederate general Micah Jenkins, and Union general John Geary's division. The Confederates were repulsed. Early on the morning of November 24, Hooker's men forded Lookout Creek here to scale the slopes of Lookout Mountain. The railroad, which connected Chattanooga with the West, crossed the Tennessee River at Bridgeport, then passed through Shellmound and Wauhatchie at this point below Lookout, as it still does.

Several small bits of land in this area are owned by the National Park Service, but they are undeveloped and unmarked.

The site of Brown's Ferry is several miles north of Tiftonia. It was established in 1800 on the Great War and Trading Path by John Brown. Legend says that some drovers, who camped here while taking herds of cattle to market, were robbed and killed. In October 1863 Hazen's brigade drifted downstream on pontoons and barges to seize the landing from the Confederates as Union reinforcements marched from Chattanooga across Moccasin Bend. Moccasin Bend Road, which runs the length of that important Civil War site, can be reached from U.S. 27 and TN 27 north of Chattanooga and the river, on the route to Signal Mountain and Red Bank.

North of Chattanooga and northwest of Walden's Ridge on TN 27 is the Anderson Highway, which was the only road connecting Chattanooga with the Union supply base in Bridgeport, Alabama, twenty-seven miles to the west. As wagon trains labored over these steep mountains to Anderson's Crossroads, they were constantly endangered by Wheeler's cavalry. When rain fell, as it did frequently during the fall of 1863, mud slowed the sixty-mile journey and thousands of mules died of exhaustion along this route. After his removal from command, Rosecrans passed this way, as did many Chattanooga citizens who had been starved out of their homes. Grant suffered a fall on the treacherous road as he traveled to take command in the besieged city.

U.S. 27 crosses Walden's Ridge north of Chattanooga and enters the Sequatchie Valley. This long ridge was both a blessing and a burden to Confederate defenders of the city before Chickamauga. It offered protection, but also shielded attackers. Bragg crossed the ridge to begin his invasion of Kentucky via this beautiful valley.

The Chattanooga area was attractive to prehistoric and historic Indians, who found plenty of game on the ridges, fish in the streams, and nuts and berries in the forests. Many Indian artifacts have been found here, and Civil War era photographs show a large Indian mound that has since been destroyed. The first European explorer in this region was Hernando de Soto, who may have visited a village beside the mound in 1540. Historians also believe that he might have rested at the palisaded settlement of Chiaha, on Burn's Island in the Tennessee River in June 1540, while his scouts looked for gold in surrounding areas. When the Spanish departed, they took with them 500 Indians to serve as carriers.

In 1815 Cherokee chief John Ross established a ferry and warehouse on the Tennessee River. The community that grew up around it was known as Ross's Landing until 1838, when the inhabitants decided they needed a fancier name. They chose Chattanooga, which is thought to be a Cherokee word for "rock coming to a point," describing Lookout Mountain. Others suggest that it means "hawk's nest," or that it came from *Tsatanuge,* an ancient village situated at the foot of the mountain. Chattanooga was incorporated in 1839.

When the Cherokees were removed to the West, some Indians were transported by steamboat from Ross's Landing. John Ross, who had established Chattanooga and served as chief of the Cherokees for nearly forty years, and his wife were among those expelled.

Chattanooga's geological position is unique among American cities. It is opposite a large loop (Moccasin Bend) in the Tennessee River. To the north is Signal Mountain, 2,080 feet high, and rugged Walden's Ridge; to the west is Lookout Mountain, 2,391 feet high, and Raccoon Mountain, 1,160 feet high; to the south is long Missionary Ridge.

Chattanooga's first railroad, the Western & Atlantic, which connected the city with Atlanta and the Atlantic coast, arrived in 1849. Two years later 45,000 bales of cotton were shipped from Alabama to Charleston and Savannah. The Nashville & Chattanooga was completed in 1854, and the rails were extended to Knoxville the following year. In 1857 the Memphis & Charleston opened Chattanooga to the Mississippi River. When the line to Knoxville was continued to Virginia, Chattanooga became the primary railroad hub in the South and one of the most important in the nation.

The railroad connections to the north, south, east, and west made Chattanooga a great prize in the Civil War. At the beginning of the war, President Lincoln said if the North could capture East Tennessee and Chattanooga, "the rebellion must dwindle and die." The Great Locomotive Chase was intended to isolate the city so it could be occupied by Union troops. Bragg's invasion of Kentucky was meant to relieve the pressure on Chattanooga, and Stone's River and the Chickamauga campaign were fought for possession of the city. The Confederates attempted to regain Chattanooga with the siege, which was broken by the battles engineered by Grant.

Chattanooga's prewar population of 5,000 people tripled during the Civil War, bloating the city with refugees, criminals, and fugitives. From November 1863 until the end of the war the city was an important Union supply depot, particularly during Sherman's campaign against Atlanta in 1864. It was protected by Union Forts Milhalotzy, Phelps, Wood, and Sheridan. Today a pyramid of cannonballs marks the site of Fort Sheridan.

The *Daily Rebel,* a newspaper published for Confed-

erate soldiers, was established in Chattanooga by Franc M. Paul on August 2, 1863. As the war turned against the South, the *Daily Rebel* fled with the Confederate army. It was printed in five towns in three states and from boxcars accompanying the troops. The last edition was issued April 11, 1865, in Selma, Alabama. Other editors besides Paul were Henry Watterson and Albert Powers. This paper was often the only source of news available to Confederate soldiers fighting in the West.

On the Hamilton County Courthouse lawn is a statue of Confederate general Alexander P. Stewart. It was dedicated April 22, 1919.

Chattanooga was the logical site for the Congressional Medal of Honor Museum because the first Americans to receive this award, which is presented for heroism in combat, are buried in the National Cemetery there. Veterans who received the medal in every conflict since the Civil War have special tombstones that commemorate their proud and distinguished honor. The museum is situated in temporary offices while a permanent building is being constructed. Displayed are uniforms, portraits, and photographs of men who have won the Medal of Honor.

Chattanooga has a number of other interesting museums. The Hunter Museum of Art is housed in a Classical Revival mansion (1904) and in a modernistic addition perched on a bluff over the Tennessee River. It has a permanent collection of American art, from pre-Revolutionary War to Andy Warhol, and changing exhibits. Across the street is the Houston Museum, which houses a collection of 15,000 glass pitchers, antiques, music boxes, and whale oil lamps. The Museum of Religious and Ceremonial Art displays artifacts related to religions of the world. The Jeffery L. Brown Institute of Archaeology, on the campus of the University of Tennessee, Chattanooga, preserves artifacts from ancient civilizations. The Chattanooga Museum of Regional History has exhibits that illustrate local history—prehistoric and historic Indians, early pioneers, the Civil War, and geology. The display, Colossal Fossils: The Living Dinosaurs, features nine life-size, robotic dinosaurs which will entertain the entire family. There are hands-on exhibits and a gift shop. Chattanooga even has a Knife Museum, which displays 5,000 blades, many of them unique.

Chattanooga has been the center of TVA activity for fifty years. The TVA Energy Center teaches visitors how energy is created by hydroelectric facilities, how coal is fired, and how nuclear steam is produced. There are many computer games, exhibits, and hands-on models and demonstrations in the 5,000-square-foot museum.

An interesting TVA enterprise is found atop Raccoon Mountain, where a 520-acre lake has been created. Water is pumped to the mountaintop reservoir, then released to turn turbines and create electricity. There are breathtaking views from three scenic overlooks, and visitors may descend 1,100 feet to view the workings of the turbine room. The Tennessee River Gorge, also known as the Grand Canyon of the Tennessee River, is visible from the mountain. On the Tennessee River here is the TVA's largest rock-filled dam, 8,500 feet in length. On the west side of Raccoon Mountain was Kelly's Ferry crossing the Tennessee River. A road connecting it with Brown's Ferry to the east passed through a gap in the mountain.

The high ground which the Confederates should have occupied to isolate Chattanooga—Raccoon Mountain on the south bank of the Tennessee River—has a variety of entertainment facilities, including Raccoon Mountain Caverns, which offers a forty-five-minute, half-mile stroll through beautiful cave formations, as well as a four-hour wild cave tour.

The first passenger rail connection between Cincinnati and Chattanooga was opened with great fanfare on March 5, 1880. A reporter at the festivities dubbed the train the "Chattanooga Choo Choo," a name that became world famous during the 1940s when the Glenn Miller Orchestra popularized a song by that name.

The Chattanooga Choo Choo is now a thirty-acre hotel/entertainment complex centered around the Terminal Station in downtown Chattanooga, the hub of activity in Chattanooga during the early 1900s. In the enclosed 34,000 square feet are restaurants, shops, rides on an antique trolley, swimming pools, tennis courts, and a model railroad museum. The complex offers 315 renovated guest rooms, and for those who have always imagined the romance of sleeping on a train, 45 sleeping parlors in authentic railcars are available. An important attraction is the Chattanooga Choo Choo, a woodburning locomotive identical to the one which made the original run from Cincinnati.

The Choo Choo is not the only railroading attraction in Chattanooga. The Tennessee Valley Railroad Museum occupies two sites, the East Chattanooga Depot and Grand Junction Depot, separated by Missionary Ridge. Organized in 1961 by railroad enthusiasts, this center has become the second largest railroad museum in America, featuring material from the "Golden Age of Steam Railroading."

The museum preserves six locomotives, including Engine No. 4501, the first of its type, bought by the Southern Railroad in 1916. A 1930 steam engine pulls a train along six miles of track (the route dates to 1852), which crosses four bridges, one over Chickamauga Creek near the site of a railroad station that was important during the siege of Chattanooga, and through Missionary Ridge via a 986-foot horseshoe-shaped tunnel built before the Civil War. Cleburne's division stopped Sherman's attack at Missionary Ridge above the tunnel. Day-long leaf-watching excursions through the mountains are scheduled each fall. At the East Station is an eighty-foot turntable to redirect the locomotive for its return trip, a repair shop, and equipment displays that are open for inspection by visitors.

The depots are reproductions of stations in the early 1900s. One was constructed with material from a railroad station that stood at Athens, Tennessee. Preserved at the museum are four former Air Force diesel engines, a 1925 Pullman car, a dining car, a 1929 caboose, and two coaches with first and second class compartments. There are exhibits of railroading artifacts, including telegraph keys and sounders, and time tables. A dining room and gift shop are open.

At the spot where Chattanooga originated, Ross's Landing, the Chattanooga Riverboat Company operates the 500-passenger *Southern Belle.* Cruises on the Tennessee River, complete with historic narration, offer views of the city, Lookout Mountain, and the other geological features that made Chattanooga a difficult military problem for defenders and attackers alike. ∎

The Knoxville Campaign

P resident Abraham Lincoln had long taken a personal interest in the welfare of East Tennessee's people. Largely small farmers who opposed slavery, they were Unionist in sentiment, and Lincoln felt they had been persecuted by Confederate authorities for their beliefs. Indeed, many had been imprisoned and stripped of property, while others were tortured and murdered.

Union general Ambrose Burnside had taken command of the 24,000 men in the Army of the Ohio in March 1863. While Rosecrans bedeviled Bragg, Burnside left Cincinnati for Knoxville in August with three divisions. Knoxville was defended by Confederate general Simon B. Buckner, who had only 2,500 soldiers. Before Burnside arrived, Buckner was recalled to help defend Chattanooga.

A direct route to Knoxville would have led Burnside through Cumberland Gap, which was defended by Confederate general John W. Frazer, who commanded 2,300 men and fourteen cannon. Rather than confront the Rebel fortifications, Burnside sent a division to demonstrate from the north, while his cavalry crossed the Cumberland Mountains through Winter's Gap and Big Creek Gap. The rest of the infantry swung forty miles to the south through Kingston and entered Knoxville to a warm welcome on September 3. When Frazer refused to surrender, Burnside led two brigades to block the rear of the gap, forcing a Confederate surrender on September 7. Cumberland Gap had changed hands for the fourth and final time in the war.

Burnside, who intended to drive east into Virginia to destroy valuable salt works, ignored over a dozen requests to march 100 miles southwest to help Rosecrans, first before the calamity of Chickamauga, and afterwards when Chattanooga was besieged. When Lincoln believed Knoxville was threatened in late October, he ordered Burnside to remain in the city.

On November 5 Longstreet left Chattanooga to attack Knoxville with 10,000 infantry and Wheeler's 5,000 cavalry. Jefferson Davis hoped the Federals would weaken their forces in Chattanooga to reinforce Burnside, which would help relieve Bragg's precarious situation. The move had little strategic purpose and left Bragg hopelessly outnumbered.

Longstreet's troops rode aboard troop trains so dilapidated that the soldiers had to disembark at every hill and walk. Eight days were required to

Union general Ambrose Burnside's artillery being drawn through the mountains of East Tennessee in fall 1863. [HARPER'S WEEKLY]

The Bearded General ■ Ambrose Everett Burnside

Burnside, although born in Indiana in 1824, was the son of a South Carolina slave owner. He was briefly a tailor's apprentice before attending West Point, from which he graduated in 1847. Burnside saw garrison duty during the Mexican War, but left the military for a business career in 1853. After developing an early breechloading rifle, he started a company in Rhode Island to manufacture them, but the enterprise failed.

Burnside reentered the army when war threatened. He led a brigade at First Manassas and served well during an amphibious operation on the North Carolina coast which gave the Union a strategic base of operations in the South. Burnside, a friend of Abraham Lincoln, was appointed major general and offered command of the Army of the Potomac in July 1862,

which he declined. He led two corps at Antietam, and although he captured an important bridge which bears his name, three hours were required to capture it from a mere 500 Confederates. His delay probably saved Robert E. Lee's army.

When Lincoln relieved George McClellan in November, he again called upon Burnside to lead the foremost Union army. Burnside did not believe he was capable of commanding such a large force and immediately set about proving this conclusion. His move against Richmond almost succeeded. The Federals stole a march on Robert E. Lee and reached the Rappahannock River opposite Fredericksburg unopposed, but the required pontoon bridges were delayed. When Burnside finally crossed

the river, Lee was strongly entrenched on a ridge commanding the town. In a senseless attack, the Federals lost 13,000 men. Burnside made another attempt to reach Richmond, the infamous "Mud March," before his relief.

Burnside, who received command of the Department of Ohio in March 1863, captured Knoxville and held it against a siege by James Longstreet. He left the service in April 1865.

Burnside embarked on a number of peacetime business endeavors. He was elected governor of Rhode Island three times and served in the U.S. Senate before his death in 1881. Burnside is best remembered for the luxurious muttonchop facial hair he wore during the Civil War, which have ever since been called "sideburns." ■

Confederate general James Longstreet assaults Fort Sanders at Knoxville in November 1863.
[HARPER'S WEEKLY]

cover the sixty miles to Sweetwater, where promised and desperately needed supplies and warm clothing failed to arrive. Longstreet sent Wheeler ahead to capture strategic high ground that overlooked Knoxville, but the position was found to be strongly fortified.

As Longstreet approached, Burnside decided to leave the city with 5,000 men and delay him. The Confederate general was pleasantly surprised on November 15 to meet Federal resistance when he crossed the Tennessee River thirty miles from Knoxville. If Longstreet could get around Burnside and cut him off from Knoxville, the Federals would be trapped.

Burnside recognized his danger and barely won a race to Lenoir's Station on November 16. Longstreet then found a shortcut to Campbell's Station, only fifteen miles southwest of Knoxville. Again Burnside just reached the crossroads community ahead of the Confederates, but he was forced to abandon a number of supply wagons. Longstreet launched an attack to distract Burnside while he attempted to cut the road in the Union rear, but the

Starving in a Land of Plenty

Once the war was underway, Confederate officials in Virginia moved to secure an adequate source of foodstuffs from one of the South's most productive agricultural areas: Tennessee. Beginning in the fall of 1861, food production in Tennessee was reserved for troops fighting in the East. Before the loss of Forts Henry and Donelson, Albert Sidney Johnston's troops were not allowed to draw rations from Nashville, which they were defending.

When Braxton Bragg returned from his unsuccessful invasion of Kentucky in the fall of 1862, he found Middle Tennessee stripped for the Army of Northern Virginia. A partial list of the provisions procured from Tennessee included two million pounds of bacon and 100,000 hogs. Bragg was forced to buy corn as far south as Columbus, Georgia, 400 miles away.

The problem intensified during the winter and spring of 1863, as Tennessee's produce continued to be funneled east. In a two-week period, the Army of Tennessee was short 400,000 rations. Bragg and

(Continued on page 115)

Union general Ambrose Burnside, for whom sideburns are named, wasted his troops at Fredericksburg, Virginia, while commander of the Army of the Potomac. Burnside partially redeemed himself by capturing and holding Knoxville. [HARPER'S WEEKLY]

plan miscarried. On November 17 Burnside was safely within Knoxville's defenses.

The Holston River shielded Knoxville on one side, and heavy earthworks protected the other three approaches. One primary strongpoint was Fort Sanders, a twelve-gun redoubt with eight-foot-high earthen walls and a nine-foot-deep ditch on the outside. However, only 120 yards away was a sheltering creek bed where Longstreet planned to mass his troops for an assault.

The Confederate attack was postponed while Longstreet waited for reinforcements, then bad weather caused another delay. The besieged Federal troops grew hungry, but the shoeless Confederates were hungrier still and, literally, freezing.

Longstreet's assault, launched at daybreak on November 29, was a disaster from the start. A planned bombardment of the fort had been canceled and, as the advancing troops were stunned by the first volley of Union fire, they found themselves entangled in telegraph wire that had been cleverly strung knee high among a forest of stumps. Brave men who gained the deep ditch were enfiladed by triple-shot cannon fire. As the Confederates attempted to scale the wall sixteen feet above their heads, the defenders lit fifty cannon shells and tossed them among the Rebels. After a twenty-

(Continued from page 114)

Joseph Johnston, the theatre commander, protested vigorously, but their concerns were ignored.

In March 1863 the Atlanta depot contained eight million pounds of salt pork and 3,000 head of cattle. It shipped 500,000 pounds of salt meat each week to Virginia, and graciously sent Bragg a three-day supply of meat. Bragg's wagons regularly labored on a 300-mile round trip journey to northern Alabama for supplies.

Bragg's men sickened and died for want of proper food, and many a hungry man deserted rather than starve. When maneuver and battle came, the performance of the soldiers suffered. Draft animals were exhausted, and wagons fell apart under the strain of transporting food from distant places.

Much of the Army of Northern Virginia's success can be attributed to soldiers and supplies provided by the Heartland, men and materiel which could have been used closer to home. ■

The Last Surviving Confederate General ■ Simon Bolivar Buckner

Buckner was born near Munfordville, Kentucky, in 1823 and graduated from the U.S. Military Academy in 1844. After being twice brevetted in the war with Mexico, he left the military in 1855 to enter business in Chicago.

As war clouds gathered, Buckner accepted an offer to command the Kentucky militia. Twice he rejected the rank of brigadier general in the U.S. Army (once by General Winfield Scott, the second at the insistence of Abraham Lincoln), but he accepted a similar rank from the Confederacy in September 1861. Buckner was the only professional soldier among the three generals at Fort Donelson in February 1862. After piercing Grant's lines, Buckner strenuously objected to reentering the fort. He seems to have lost his spirit later in the night by arguing that the Confederate troops could

not fight their way out of Fort Donelson for a second time. Having advised surrender, he was left to do so by Floyd and Pillow.

After being exchanged, Buckner fought at Perryville later in 1862; attended to the defenses of Mobile, Alabama; commanded the Department of East Tennessee when Ambrose Burnside poured over the mountains and forced the evacuation of Knoxville; led a corps at Chickamauga; and finished his long service as Kirby Smith's chief-of-staff in the Trans-Mississippi. Buckner was vilified and persecuted in his native Kentucky. In an extremely unusual case, the Louisville & Nashville Railroad sued Buckner for damage caused to the line while Buckner was in Confederate service and won a decision of $62,000.

Following the war, Buckner became editor of the Louisville

Courier, served a term as governor, and was nominated to run for vice president by the Gold Democrats in 1887. He died near Munfordville in 1914 at the age of ninety-one, the last surviving Confederate general. ■

[LIBRARY OF CONGRESS]

The citizens of Knoxville rejoiced when Union troops under Burnside finally entered town in fall 1863. [HARPER'S WEEKLY]

minute battle, the Confederates staggered back to their lines. They had lost 813 out of 3,000 attacking soldiers, compared to 13 Union casualties from the 500-man garrison of the fort.

After Bragg was driven back from Chattanooga at Missionary Ridge, Grant was ordered to relieve Burnside. In late November Sherman, with the Army of the Tennessee and another corps, executed a quick march. There were rumors that Burnside was starving and would be out of rations by December 3. Sherman was infuriated to find Longstreet gone and Burnside well fed.

Burnside half-heartedly chased the Confederates into East Tennessee, then returned to Knoxville. Longstreet spent a miserable winter in the mountains around Russellville, then entered western Virginia in the spring of 1864 to rejoin Lee. East Tennessee was now a secure Union bastion. ∎

Another Bragg Story

After Braxton Bragg evacuated Chattanooga and ordered Simon B. Buckner to abandon Knoxville, citizens of the Confederacy became very critical of his leadership. According to legend, one little old lady said to another, "I wish, as General Bragg is a Christian man, that he were dead and in heaven; I think that would be a godsend to the Confederacy."

"Why, my dear," her friend replied, "if the general were near the gates of heaven and invited in, at that moment he would fall back." ∎

The Bride of John Hunt Morgan

While Murfreesboro, Tennessee, was under Union rule during the summer of 1862, seventeen-year-old Martha ("Mattie") Ready overheard Federal soldiers ridiculing John Hunt Morgan, the flamboyant cavalry raider. The young lady rose to his defense, and when asked her name, she replied, "It's Mattie Ready now, but by the grace of God one day I hope to call myself the wife of John Morgan."

Morgan, a thirty-seven-year-old widower, heard the story after Confederate forces had recaptured the town. He visited the pretty and patriotic Miss Mattie and was soon courting her. Their marriage on December 14, 1862, was the social event of the Christmas season. The service, performed by Bishop–General Leonidas Polk, was attended by many luminaries of the Army of Tennessee, including Braxton Bragg, William J. Hardee, John C. Breckinridge, and Benjamin F. Cheatham. Fine wines and foods were served at a series of parties, receptions, banquets, and fancy balls attended by the couple.

Just days earlier, Morgan had captured 2,000 Union prisoners in a raid at Hartsville. For that feat, Jefferson Davis brought Morgan a commission as brigadier general as a wedding and Christmas present. A week after the nuptials, Morgan and 3,000 troopers left on the celebrated Christmas raid, which covered 400 miles and resulted in the capture of 2,000 prisoners and the destruction of four important railroad bridges, twenty miles of rail, and two million dollars' worth of supplies.

After Stone's River, Morgan was stationed in McMinnville, picketing the right of Bragg's Duck River line. In April a Union cavalry raid that descended on the town barely missed capturing Morgan, but Mattie was seized and held for a short while.

When William Rosecrans forced Bragg out of Middle Tennessee, Morgan was off on an ill-advised raid across the Ohio River, which resulted in the destruction of his command and his capture. Morgan daringly escaped from prison in Ohio, made his way through occupied Kentucky and Tennessee, and reached South Carolina, where he wired his wife, who was waiting in Danville, Virginia: "Just arrived—will make no stop until I reach you."

Mattie was waiting when Morgan arrived on January 9, 1864. The couple continued to Richmond where the dashing cavalier and his lady were met by cheering crowds and feted at numerous receptions.

Morgan was assigned to the Department of Southwest Virginia, where he worked tirelessly to raise a raiding force that might redeem his reputation, which had been sullied by his unauthorized and unsuccessful raid across the Ohio River. Confederate cavalry strength was at low ebb, and his new troopers were poorly trained and disciplined. A raid into Kentucky resulted in an investigation by Confederate officials into charges of arson, looting, and bank robbing for personal gain. During this difficult period, Morgan became emotionally dependent on young Mattie, not wanting her to be out of his sight when he was home.

At dawn on September 4, 1864, Morgan was surprised by Federal cavalry and killed at Greeneville, Tennessee. Mattie, now pregnant, received a message which read: "With deep sorrow I have to announce the sad intelligence of your husband's death. He fell by the hands of the enemy. . . ."

Mattie was at Abingdon, Virginia, when Morgan's body arrived on September 6. He was buried the following day. ∎

"Stonewall of the West" ■ Patrick Ronayne Cleburne

Cleburne was born in County Cork, Ireland, on Saint Patrick's Day 1828. He was expected to follow in his doctor father's footsteps, but at the age of seventeen he failed the entrance exam for Trinity College in Dublin. Believing he had disgraced the family, Cleburne ran away and joined the Forty-first Regiment of Foot, rising to the rank of corporal in three years of service. When his family immigrated to America in 1849, Cleburne bought his discharge from the British Army and accompanied them, settling in Helena, Arkansas, where he became a pharmacist, merchant, lawyer, and local politician.

In May 1861, Cleburne was elected colonel of the Fifteenth Arkansas. He served under William J. Hardee, commanding a regiment, brigade, and division. Despite Cleburne's native military talent, likened to Nathan Bedford Forrest's instinctive grasp of tactics, many less capable officers were promoted over him, probably because he was not a native, he had not attended West Point, and he had advised arming slaves in exchange for their emancipation.

The enemy feared encountering Cleburne's men, who, thanks to their leader's British training, were the most disciplined and fastest shooting in the Confederate army. Soldiers were proud to serve under Cleburne.

Wounded twice, at Richmond and Perryville, Kentucky, Cleburne received two resolutions from the Confederate congress expressing the gratitude of the nation for saving the Army of Tennessee after the disaster at Missionary Ridge. His division had repulsed William Sherman's determined attacks, then stood fast when the army disintegrated. For sturdy service in nearly every battle fought in the West, Cleburne became known as the "Stonewall of the West."

Before a battle in Mississippi, Cleburne had said, "If this cause which is so dear to my heart is doomed to fail, I pray heaven may let me fall with it, while my face is turned to the enemy and my arm battling for that which I know to be right."

Cleburne's request was granted near the end of the war. As Hardee later said, "When Cleburne's division defended, no odds broke its lines; when it attacked, no numbers resisted its onslaught, save only once, and there is the grave of Cleburne." He died leading his men into battle at Franklin, November 30, 1864. ■

A DRIVING TOUR
■ The Knoxville Campaign ■

This tour begins at Chickamauga Creek in Chattanooga. Chattanooga can be reached on Interstate 24, south from Nashville, or north from Birmingham, or on Interstate 75 south from Knoxville or north from Atlanta. Take Exit 7 off I–75 and drive north on Bonny Oaks, then left onto Lightfoot Road to the creek.

On the morning of November 11, 1861, Union sympathizers burned two railroad bridges over Chickamauga Creek in an attempt to sever communications between Atlanta and Knoxville. They hoped this would encourage a Union invasion from Kentucky through Cumberland Gap, but the effort failed.

Note the railroad bridges to the west. One rests on the original stone piers that were built before the Civil War. Nearby was Chickamauga Station, where Longstreet's corps embarked for transportation to Knoxville during the siege of Chattanooga. Bragg loaded an additional division of his army onto trains for transportation east to reinforce Longstreet, and Cleburne waited here until recalled just before Sherman's attack against Missionary Ridge. When Bragg was driven off Missionary Ridge, this was his only route of escape, as McFarlan Gap and Rossville Gap had been captured

This Confederate cemetery in Chattanooga contains 155 graves of soldiers who died while Confederate general Braxton Bragg was organizing his 1862 invasion of Kentucky.

by Hooker who moved from Lookout Mountain to the west. Cleburne's division fought a stubborn rearguard action to allow the remainder of the shattered Army of Tennessee to escape. Soldiers retreating past the station, which had been an important supply depot, reported scooping up as much food as they could carry from the stores, which had been abandoned.

From the bridge over Chickamauga Creek drive east on Lightfoot Mill Road for .9, then turn right onto Bonny Oaks Drive. At the four-way stop after 4.3 turn left onto U.S. 11–U.S. 64–Lee Highway for .1, then turn right through the stone arch which proclaims "Confederate Cemetery." To the right at .1 down the one-lane road is a large cemetery where 155 Southern soldiers who died while Bragg was organizing his incursion of Kentucky were buried.

Wooden boards inscribed with name, rank, and unit once identified individual graves, but they rotted away before stone replacements could be made. The graves are now all unidentified. A stone wall surrounds the plot, and the entrance is through a second stone arch.

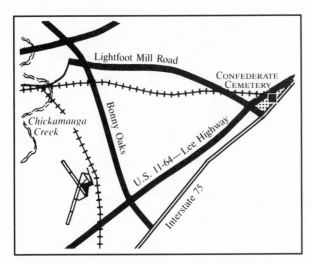

Map 30: The Confederate cemetery area of Chattanooga.

We will follow the route of Longstreet's corps as it advanced on Knoxville. The troops rode trains to Sweetwater, although they had to walk up hills because of the poor condition of the locomotives, and marched from there to Knoxville. This route passes through the beautiful Sweetwater Valley, with the Tennessee River about ten miles to the northwest. This scenic land is fertile farm country. The Cumberland Mountains form a blue-tinted wall to the northwest, and to the southeast are the Chilhowie and Unaka mountains.

From the cemetery turn left back to the four-way stop and turn left. U.S. 11–U.S. 64 hitch a short ride on Interstate 75, so after .2 turn right onto I–75. After 4.2, at Ooltewah, take Exit 11, turn right off the highway and follow U.S. 11–Lee Highway (ignore U.S. 64 when it turns right).

The interstate has taken us through Ooltewah Gap, believed to be where de Soto camped in June 1540, before continuing south toward the site of Chattanooga. When Simon B. Buckner was ordered to abandon Knoxville, he was stationed here briefly, watching for a Union crossing of Walden's Ridge and the Tennessee River in this area of wooded, rolling hills.

After 12.9 miles go straight on U.S. Business 11. At .5 turn left onto North Ocoee. After .1 the Bradley County Courthouse in Cleveland and the beautifully landscaped Johnston Park appear to the left.

The park has a gazebo, ponds, and the Cherokee Chieftain, a gift from sculptor Peter Toth, who is placing unique wooden Indian pieces in each state. A Confederate monument features a soldier atop a high pedestal. In Fort Hill Cemetery is a Union monument, dedicated on May 30, 1914.

In southern Bradley County, just above the Georgia line, is Red Clay State Historic Area, situated in an interesting region of valleys separated by 200-foot-high ridges. This was the last Cherokee council grounds before the removal to Oklahoma. The Indians had adopted American ways, including the language, dress, and culture, and formed a system of government based on the U.S. Constitution. They organized a nation and established their capital at New Echota, Georgia, fifty miles to the south. There Sequoyah (George Gist) developed a syllabary that allowed the Cherokee language to be written. The Cherokees published a newspaper and books in their language and

set up a legislative and court system. In 1832 Georgia stripped them of their political sovereignty and banned any meeting unless it was to surrender their land. Because of these restrictions, the Cherokees moved to Red Clay and remained here until they were forcibly moved in 1838.

At Red Clay the Cherokee held eleven general councils, which were attended by up to 5,000 people. Principal Chief John Ross fought to protect Cherokee rights, but controversial treaties stole their beautiful mountain home. After President Andrew Jackson ignored a Supreme Court decision that favored the Cherokees, the Trail of Tears began here. This route, over which the Indians walked to Oklahoma in the dead of winter, resulting in the deaths of thousands, can now be followed with an automobile tour that can be obtained in the park office.

Red Clay contains the Blue Hole, a spring that was sacred to the Cherokees. The sapphire blue pool is eleven feet deep and issues 400,000 gallons of water daily. A Cherokee farmstead and typical houses have been reconstructed on the grounds. A new feature is a stone fireplace that contains the Eternal Flame of the Cherokee Nation. Coals from the last council fire here were carried to Oklahoma in 1838. The fire was rekindled in North Carolina in the 1950s, and in 1984 ten Cherokee runners carried a torch lit by the fire to Red Clay. It is a memorial to those who suffered and died

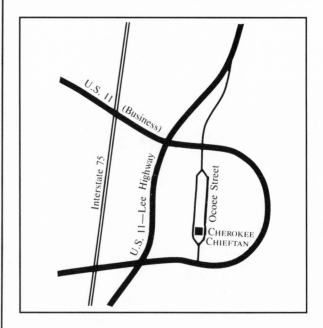

Map 31: The Cleveland area.

This unique sculpture of a Cherokee Indian, by Peter Toth, is in a Cleveland, Tennessee, park.

on the Trail of Tears. A 500-seat amphitheater, a picnic pavilion, and a two-mile loop trail where beautiful limestone outcroppings can be seen are also available. In the James F. Corn Interpretive Center are a theater, exhibits, and artifacts that illustrate the history of the Cherokees, and a resource reading room featuring material about American Indians.

After the Union victory at Missionary Ridge, Red Clay, which is located along the railroad, became an assembly point and supply depot for operations in Georgia. When Sherman moved on Atlanta in May 1864, Schofield's Army of the Ohio advanced from camp here.

East of Cleveland is the Primitive Settlement, a collection of restored log cabins gathered from the area. Each house is authentically furnished with a different style or age of antiques. The rich appointments include furniture, pianos, spinning wheels, and kitchens. Each cabin is at least 100 years old, and some are 150 years old.

Also to the east is the Cherokee National Forest, a 625,000-acre preserve that spreads across ten coun-

ties and includes Lake Ocoee and Sugarloaf Mountain. Atop Chilhowee Mountain is a seven-acre lake with a beach, camping, picnicking, and a hiking trail that leads to Benton Falls and a Confederate campsite. There are wonderful views of the Tennessee Valley and the Cumberland Mountains. The wild and scenic Ocoee River, famed for its white water, is in the forest. There are many opportunities to raft, hike, fish and camp.

Continue straight on North Ocoee past the Bradley County Courthouse, and after .4 a Confederate monument is to the left. Continue north on U.S. 11.

A bronze tablet set in a stone on the northern outskirts of Cleveland designates the graves of Chief John Walker, Jr., known as "Chief Jack," and his wife, Emily Meigs, and the site of their home, Cherokee Farm. Because Walker advocated a peaceful resettlement, he was considered a traitor by some Indians and was assassinated by James Foreman in 1834. The resulting sensational trial was followed throughout the nation.

On the south bank of the scenic Hiwassee River is Charleston. During the summer and fall of 1838, 13,000 Cherokees gathered at Rattlesnake Springs, two miles to the east, for removal to Oklahoma. The last tribal council meeting of the Cherokees held in the East occurred there. In October soldiers herded the Indians along the Trail of Tears. Near the river was the Cherokee Indian Agency, which operated between 1821 and 1838. Two well-known Indian agents were Colonel Return Meigs, father of Chief Walker's wife, and three-time Tennessee governor Joseph McMinn. A Quaker from Pennsylvania, McMinn is buried a few miles north in Calhoun. East of this site was Fort Cass, headquarters of the troops responsible for evicting the Cherokees. Buckner remained here a week in September 1863 watching for Rosecrans.

On the north bank of the Hiwassee is the tiny community of Calhoun, founded in 1819 and named for John C. Calhoun. According to a Cherokee treaty, the Indians were allowed to keep islands in the Hiwassee, Chestatee, and Tennessee rivers. An early settler, John McGhee, desired one of the islands in the Hiwassee but did not know how he could possess it. One day Cherokee chief John Walker, who wanted McGhee's gun, told him, "The chief has dream. He dreamed that White Chief had given him fine gun." This was Walker's introduction to a Cherokee tradition that things asked for in such a fashion were expected to be given as a gift. After a decent interval, Walker told the chief, "White man dream Indian chief give him fine island." Chief Walker pondered this for a while, then responded, "Big Chief give you island, but Indian no dream against white man no more."

After 18.7 turn right onto Business 11. After 7.5 miles of hilly road the McMinn County Courthouse in Athens is on the left.

Athens is a nice, tree-shaded town. At the courthouse is a Grand Army of the Republic monument that honors local Union men who fought during the Civil War. This was the birthplace of Confederate general John T. Morgan, who later served as a U.S. senator from Alabama.

In 1835 abolition was an inflamatory issue in this area. After the proslavery citizens of Athens learned that a number of abolitionist newspapers had arrived at the post office, an angry crowd gathered and demanded the papers, which became fuel for a large bonfire in the streets. The editor of the local paper urged the outlawing of "these filthy and wicked productions."

Athens is home to Tennessee Wesleyan College, founded in 1867 and now called by its fourth name. On the campus is the McMinn County Living Heritage Museum, housed in the Old College Building (1855), which is listed on the National Register of Historic Places. Twenty-six exhibit rooms are crammed with a

diverse collection of 2,000 historical items that illustrate the daily life of this area beginning with the Cherokee Indians and including pioneer settlers, the Civil War, the Victorian era, and the Depression. It has a particularly good collection of nineteenth- and twentieth-century quilts, and Victorian articles. Rooms are dedicated to antique toys, business machines, and the age of spinning wheels and quilting bees. Other items of interest are an 1820 grandfather clock, made locally, and a square grand piano (1875).

Several miles southeast of Athens is the Louisville & Nashville depot in Etowah. This grand building was a primary stop when a new route from Chicago to Atlanta, via Cincinnati and Knoxville, was initiated in 1906. There were originally a turntable, roundhouse, power plant, and engine and car repair sheds. Etowah, which in the Cherokee language means "muddy waters," grew up around the station. When the depot closed in 1974, the community, led by the Etowah Historical Society, restored the depot, which is on the National Register.

Continue straight from the courthouse. At the light after .2, follow U.S. 11 to the left, then make an immediate right. After 2.9 turn right back onto U.S. 11.

This route takes us through Sweetwater, where Longstreet had expected to find stores of food, military supplies, and warm clothing. The supplies were not here, and the Confederates were forced to leave their train cars to march to Knoxville. The Sweetwater Flouring Mill was the first in the South. Fifty employees worked shifts around the clock to produce 900 barrels daily. It was replaced by a large, four-story factory that produced chenille bedspreads, once common items for sale along the route of I–75 through Tennessee and Georgia. When the Civil War began, Sweetwater had a population of 700. Downtown is a gazebo and Pullman car on display beside the railroad.

To the east of Sweetwater is the Lost Sea, which became a Registered Natural Landmark in 1976. The *Guinness Book of World Records* has proclaimed this four-and-one-half-acre body of water the "World's Largest Underground Lake." In prehistoric times a giant jaguar entered the cave, became lost, and died. Its bones are displayed in the Museum of Natural History in New York City. A three-quarter-mile-long tour winds past the remains of a Confederate saltpeter enterprise and down to the lake. Visitors motor quietly around the fascinating lake while some of the largest rainbow trout in the country circle around the boat.

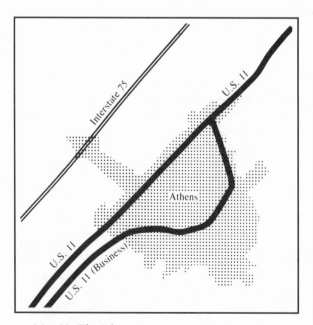

Map 32: The Athens area.

The fish are regularly introduced into the water because it is too cool (58 degrees) for them to reproduce. Cave features include 50 percent of the world's known anthodites, which are rare cave flowers (crystals), large rooms, and cascade formations. The boat ride is soothing, but the climb back to the entrance is strenuous. Above ground, in log cabins that are at least 100 years old, are a general store, restaurant, sweet shop, and blacksmith shop. There are also picnic grounds and a nature trail.

Between Sweetwater and Loudon is the tiny community of Philadelphia, scene of a cavalry skirmish on October 20, 1863. Two Confederate regiments that attacked one Federal brigade captured 700 prisoners, 6 guns, 50 wagons loaded with goods, and many horses and mules. The surviving Federals fled to Loudon.

The Tennessee River in Loudon is reached at 23.7. The railroad bridge is on the left.

The rail span was burned on September 2, 1863, by Buckner after he abandoned Knoxville to Burnside. His 5,000 troops camped here a week before moving closer to Chattanooga as the Chickamauga campaign developed. On October 25 the crew of a Union train, finding themselves trapped between Longstreet's advancing Confederates and the ruined bridge, ran the locomotive and cars off the south end of the trestle to avoid its capture. On December 2, as Sherman advanced from Chattanooga, the Confederates did the same to their remaining train.

Arriving at Loudon on November 13, 1863, Longstreet was delighted to find Burnside on the opposite side of the Tennessee River at Lenoir City. The bridges and ferry boats on the river had been burned, and Burnside hoped to impede Longstreet's crossing of the wide stream. Discovering Huff's Ferry a half-mile downstream, Longstreet sent his army there to cross on a pontoon bridge, hoping to circle around Burnside's flank and trap him.

There are a number of renovated buildings in the downtown area of Loudon, including the depot (1900); the Carpenter's Gothic Cumberland Presbyterian Church (1883); the Mulberry Building, built as a Methodist Episcopal Church and now a business; the Colony Building, which was a Civil War hospital; the Grove Building (1922), built as the European Hotel; and the 1872 Loudon County Courthouse. The Carmichael Inn (1810), beside the river bridge, was built for stagecoach passengers. The Blair Storehouse (pre-1834) belonged to James Blair, who operated it as

a store. Loudon has two historic bed and breakfast inns. The Mason Place (1861) was the center of a plantation where Civil War soldiers camped, and the River Road Inn (1857), a Federal-style structure, is on the National Register.

Continue north on U.S. 11. Across the bridge is Lenoir City, at the junction of the Tennessee River and the Little Tennessee River.

Here is preserved the Lenoir Cotton Mill (1834), one of several mills owned by William B. Lenoir, who manufactured cotton yarn using water power. It was one of the first industrial buildings in Tennessee, and one of the few remaining factories from such an early period. In 1890 it operated 1,000 spindles. During the Civil War Federal troops burned surrounding structures and planned to destroy the mill, but, according to a legend of the kind heard hundreds of times across the South, Dr. Benjamin Lenoir showed the officer in charge a Masonic handshake, and the factory was spared.

Longstreet, arriving at Lenoir City from Loudon via Huff's Ferry and the Hotchkiss Valley Road, attacked Burnside at dusk on November 4, 1863. Burnside managed to hold off the assaults and retreated through Concord to Campbell's Station (modern Farragut) on the following morning.

Southeast of Lenoir City, on the Tennessee River,

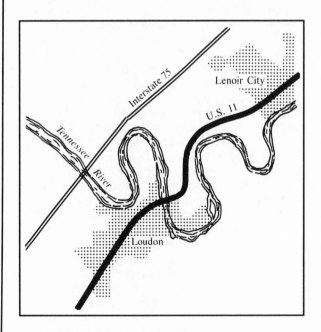

Map 33: The Loudon area.

is the Fort Loudoun Dam. It offers tours of the power house, observation points for viewing the landscape, and a lock. The nearby Tellico Dam forms the 16,500-acre Tellico Lake, with 373 miles of shore line.

On the shore of Lake Tellico is located the 500-acre Fort Loudoun State Historic Area. Built in 1756–57 near the Little Tennessee River by the colony of North Carolina, which had requested a fort here since 1746, this was the first British fort constructed in the area which became Tennessee. The fort had two missions: to stop the French who were expanding their territory east from the Mississippi Valley, and to demonstrate British friendship to the Cherokee Indians. When the Cherokee men were away and hostile tribes threatened the area, their women and children took refuge in the fort. The installation was garrisoned by 90 British regulars and 120 militia, led by Paul Demere. Only two years after the fort was completed, the relationship between the Indians and the British had deteriorated due to repercussions from incidents that happened in Virginia, culminating with the execution of twenty-three Cherokees in North Carolina, and because of the growing French influence. During the winter of 1760 the Cherokees laid siege to the garrison. By late summer the British food supply was exhausted, forcing them to surrender on August 8. The Cherokees were supposed to safely escort the captives, 180 soldiers and 60 women and children, to Charleston, but only fifteen miles away from the fort the Indians turned on the soldiers, killing 20. The remainder became slaves until they were ransomed.

The fort, named for John Campbell, the English Earl of Loudoun who was the British commander in chief in North America, was unlike frontier forts traditionally built by American pioneers. Constructed in the European style of the age, it was diamond shaped. Bastions containing three cannon projected from each corner. The fort was designed by James William Gerald deBrahm, who had an interesting idea. Outside the fort walls was a breastwork twenty-one feet thick. DeBrahm wanted to fill a ditch beyond that with live thorn trees. The twenty cannon, which fired sixteen-ounce projectiles, were brought over the mountains from North Carolina on horseback. With this heavy load, they made six miles a day. The backs of some horses were broken when their load shifted.

Evidence from archaeological excavation and historical research has been used to erect an exact duplicate of the original fort. The palisade consists of large pointed logs, with gaps between filled with smaller logs. Cannon are mounted on wooden carriages in each bastion, and period cabins have been reconstructed inside the walls. A museum displays artifacts taken from the site and exhibits of local history. There are picnic areas and nature trails. The fort hosts "Living History Weekends," when reenactors from the North Carolina Company of Foot and their families recreate life in a garrison of the 1750s.

Across the lake is the excavated foundation of the Tellico Blockhouse, a typical example of a frontier fort of the late 1700s, built on the border of the Cherokee lands. The fort was proposed by Secretary of War Henry Knox, who wanted to avoid disputes between the Cherokees and the settlers, which usually ended with punitive raids in which Cherokee villages were destroyed. John Sevier oversaw construction after the Indian village of Taliguona was burned. The fort became a government trading post, serving the twelve Cherokee tribes that lived in the Tellico Valley. With the Treaty of Tellico, signed here in 1798, the Cherokees surrendered all lands between the Little Tennessee River and the Clinch River. In 1805 they gave up all land that constitutes Middle Tennessee. The garrison was disbanded two years later. President James Monroe and the young duke of Orleans, later King Louis Philippe of France, who traveled across America following an itinerary planned by George Washington, visited the fort, which was on the stagecoach route from Knoxville to Huntsville, Alabama.

In the same area, just south of Venore, is the Sequoyah Birthplace Museum. At the town of Tuskegee, in the Little Tennessee River Valley, which was heavily populated with Indian villages, was born George Gist, a half-Cherokee known best by his Indian name, Sequoyah. He was intrigued by the settlers' ability to communicate with written symbols. Determined to work out a similar system for use with the spoken Cherokee language, Sequoyah labored for twelve years on a syllabary. He endured ridicule from other Cherokees and the fear of his wife, who burned a nearly completed system because she thought it was evil. In 1821 he and his daughter Ayoka introduced the system of eighty-five characters. The Cherokee Nation paid him $500 for the syllabary, which was so simple that within months thousands of Cherokees were able to read and write their language. A newspaper, the Bible, and other books were printed in Cherokee as these Indians created a nation in the image of the United States.

This museum honors Sequoyah, a soldier, silversmith, and statesman, and also the history and culture of the Cherokee people through a number of audio-visual displays. Recordings relate myths and legends of the Cherokees, and many artifacts, which reflect 8,000 years of Indian life, are on display. These were excavated in the valley by the University of Tennessee and the National Park Service before Tellico Dam inundated much of the area. This enterprise is owned and operated by the Cherokee Indians, who returned in 1986 for the first time since the Removal, 150 years earlier. A gift shop offers Cherokee arts, crafts, and books for sale. Near the museum is the Cherokee Memorial, built over a mass grave of eighteenth-century Indians whose graves were disturbed during excavation for Tellico Lake.

In what is now the Cherokee National Forest near Madisonville, the duke of Orleans was hurt in a fall from his horse. The duke's condition improved after he had himself bled. An old Cherokee chief, impressed by this routine, asked to be bled himself. Feeling much better afterwards, the chief invited the young man to a great feast at his lodge. That night the duke slept between two Cherokee women. After he became king of France, he often asked American visitors, "Do they still sleep three in a bed in Tennessee?" He enjoyed the trip, but found the shelter and food in America a little primitive for his tastes.

Madisonville is the birthplace of Confederate general John C. Vaughn, commander of the Third Tennessee Infantry. He was captured at Vicksburg and later commanded the cavalry that escorted Jefferson Davis from Richmond at the end of the war. He is buried here.

West of Lenoir City is Kingston, which was considered for the site of the state capital. The legislature met here for one day—September 21, 1807—before moving back to Knoxville. Here was the home of Colonel Robert King Byrd, who in 1864 raised a Union regiment in East Tennessee. This was once the Cherokee frontier, guarded by Fort Westport, which was built on the Tennessee River in 1792 by John Sevier on the orders of the territorial governor, William Blount. It protected the settlers, who were encroaching on Indian land, and prevented the Cherokees from raiding into territory they had ceded previously. In May 1797 the duke of Orleans passed through on his way to Nashville.

A ludicrous matter of honor occurred near Kingston in 1803. Andrew Jackson and Governor John Sevier, political enemies, had met at the courthouse in Knoxville in October. Sevier made a remark that Jackson interpreted as an insult to his wife. Friends intervened, but on the following day Jackson challenged Sevier to a duel. The governor declined on the basis that he had sworn to uphold the Tennessee constitution, which forbade dueling. Jackson offered to fight in

Georgia, Virginia, North Carolina, or the Indian Territory, and threatened to denounce Sevier in the newspapers as a coward if he failed to fight.

Jackson camped several days on the Cherokee border near Kingston to await developments. When Sevier arrived, the two men stood twenty feet apart with drawn pistols while verbally abusing each other. After they put their firearms aside, Jackson charged Sevier with a cane. Sevier drew his sword, which frightened his horse and caused it to run off with his pistol. Sevier hid behind a tree and berated Jackson for fighting him when he did not have a pistol. Then the antagonists went their separate ways, and Sevier entered Knoxville to a sixteen-gun salute.

Continue north on U.S. 11.

This route takes us through Concord and Farragut (called Campbell's Station during the Civil War). Its name was changed to honor its native son, the legendary Union naval officer David Farragut, the first American to earn the rank of admiral. As commander of the West Gulf Blockading Squadron, he captured the important Confederate ports of New Orleans and Mobile. On November 15 Longstreet pursued Burnside to Campbell's Station. The Federals managed to elude a second trap set by Longstreet, who had sent a division under General Lafayette McLaws via the Kingston Road to cut Burnside off at the junction of the Concord and Kingston roads. Burnside won the race and repulsed three attacks on November 16. That night he retreated into Knoxville.

After 28.6 Bleak House, named for the popular novel by Charles Dickens, is on the right.

It was built by Robert Houston Armstrong in 1858. Made of slave-baked bricks, the house has fifteen large rooms. Longstreet and McLaws made their headquarters here during the ill-advised siege and battle of Knoxville. It has Civil War relics, antique furniture and costumes, and an archives relating to the Confederacy. Southern sharpshooters who occupied the tower of the house fatally wounded Union general William Sanders at a spot now occupied by the Second Presbyterian Church down the street. Sanders is buried in the Chattanooga National Cemetery. The house suffered slight damage from Union artillery, and a number of bullets are embedded in the walls.

Longstreet's headquarters before the siege was Beardon (1848), home of Major Robert B. Reynolds, a Mexican War veteran. Many Confederate troops camped on the grounds. Melrose, a Classical Revival

Bleak House, built in 1858, was Confederate general James Longstreet's headquarters during the siege of Knoxville.

house built in 1850, stood between the lines and absorbed many bullets. A number of men died inside when it was used as a hospital.

Sixteen hundred soldiers, including Longstreet's dead, other Southern soldiers who died in the area, fifty Union prisoners, and twenty Southern veterans who died after the war, are buried in a Confederate cemetery in east Knoxville. A monument, the figure of a Confederate soldier at guard atop a tall stone shaft, was dedicated on May 19, 1892, by the Ladies Memorial Association. Union dead from actions in East Tennessee are buried in the Knoxville National Cemetery, organized in 1863. Adjacent to it is the Old Gray Cemetery, established in 1850, which has many Victorian monuments. William G. Brownlow, the influential Unionist editor of the *Whig,* is buried here.

The once extensive fortification system of Knoxville, much of it on the University of Tennessee campus, has vanished beneath the city's growth. The university was closed when the war began, and most of the students and faculty chose sides and joined the army. The buildings were used for barracks. When Longstreet approached, the city's protection consisted of: Fort Sanders, at Seventeenth Street and Laurel Avenue, where the Confederate attack by four brigades was repulsed; Fort Dickerson, a hilltop position that threw back Wheeler's attempt to capture the high ground before Longstreet arrived; the extensive earthworks of Fort Huntingdon Smith, which mounted eight Jones rifles and four brass six-pounders; Forts

Hill, Higley, Byington, and Stanley; and Batteries Wiltsie and Fearns. Ten hilltop forts, connected by infantry trenches, ringed the city during the siege which lasted between November 17 and December 4. At Knoxville College, Longstreet placed his artillery to shell the city, which was 1,800 yards distant. Thousands of his troops camped there. Another Confederate artillery position was established on Cherokee Heights, across the Tennessee River from the present Neyland Stadium, to shell Fort Sanders before the assault. The Confederate gunnery was ineffective due to old powder, and the pre-assault bombardment was canceled.

As defense against a cavalry raid, Summit Hill was occupied on June 21, 1863, by Confederate artillery batteries, troops, and citizens. A brief artillery duel favored the Federals, who had better guns, but they soon withdrew.

The city hall was used as both a Confederate and a Federal hospital. The courthouse, which stood from 1842 until 1886, was also a hospital for both armies during the fall of 1863. Twelve of Andrews' Raiders were held there and tried for sabotage. They were removed to Atlanta because of Union threats from Cumberland Gap.

Soon after Burnside arrived, in September 1863, the pastor of the First Presbyterian Church, the Reverend W. A. Harrison, was arrested after preaching a sermon, on charges of sedition, treasonable utterances, and inciting rebellion against Union authority. He was exiled to Confederate territory. Until 1866 the church was used as a barracks and hospital for Union soldiers and refugees, and as a school for newly freed slaves.

From Bleak House, turn right onto U.S. 11–U.S. 70. After 2.4 turn right onto Gay for .1, then turn left and the Blount Mansion is on the immediate right.

The Blount Mansion (1792), a two-story frame house, was built by William Blount, a signer of the U.S. Constitution, pioneer, author, public official, and the only governor of the Territory South of the Ohio River, also known as the Southwest Territory, a Federal entity. This structure served as the political, military, and social capitol from 1792 until 1796. On June 1, 1796, fifty-five delegates gathered to draft a constitution which led to the establishment of Tennessee as the sixteenth state. The house, a National Historic Landmark, is furnished with pre-1800 furniture, including a four poster bed, a trundle bed, eighteenth-century

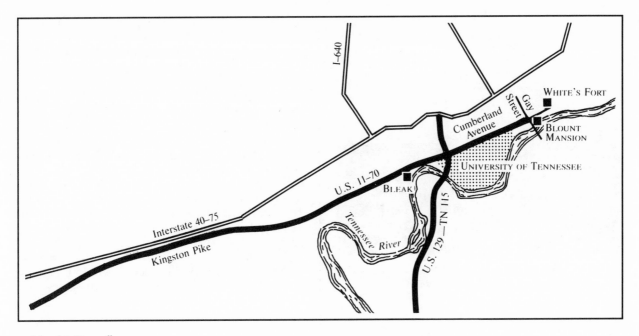

Map 34: Knoxville.

dolls, and wigs. Behind the house is a period garden, a detached kitchen, and Blount's office.

Across the street from the Blount Mansion is the Craghead–Jackson House (1818), a brick two-story Federal structure on the National Register. Inside is the Blount House Visitors Center, with an introductory audio-visual presentation, exhibits, and a gift shop.

Turn right from the Blount Mansion, and after .2 White's Fort is on the left.

In 1786 Captain James White brought his family across the mountains from North Carolina to claim land granted him for service in the Revolutionary War. He marched along the Holston and French Broad rivers until they merged to form the Tennessee River, then followed a large creek that flows into the river a short distance downstream, where he built a home atop a wooded hill. It was elaborate for a pioneer structure— one and one-half stories of hand-hewn square logs. It measured twenty by thirty feet, with three rooms on the ground floor and a sleeping loft. This was truly the frontier then, for Cherokee territory was just across the river, and many Indian settlements were situated nearby in the valley of the Little Tennessee River.

Other settlers soon followed. While they found land for themselves and prepared shelters, many stayed with the White family. The hospitable White built three additional cabins and linked them with a stockade of pointed log posts for protection against the Indians. The cabins formed a two-story strongpoint at each corner. One large gate led to a nearby spring. White also constructed a mill on the creek near his home to grind corn into meal, which was a pioneer staple.

In 1791 William Blount arrived from North Carolina with a commission from President George Washington to assume the newly created position of governor of the territory. Blount naturally selected White's Fort as his headquarters. There he met with forty-one Cherokee chieftains who signed the Treaty of the Holston on July 2, 1791, which ceded some Cherokee lands to the United States.

White agreed to sell some of his property to the government for the establishment of a town. White's son-in-law, Charles McClung, surveyed the town, dividing it into sixteen blocks with sixty-four lots. White retained eight lots, and in 1792 donated the best, which had been cleared and planted for crops, for a church, which is currently the First Presbyterian Church.

The Tennessee River, a vital Civil War transportation route, flows through Knoxville near its source.

coln wanted the rails cut and the mostly pro-Union inhabitants of this area freed from Southern control, but Federal forces were unable to accomplish those goals until midway through 1863. East Tennessee was the only area where troops had to be stationed to prevent the populace from openly revolting, a mission assigned to Felix Zollicoffer. Over 1,500 Unionists were arrested in East Tennessee, and those convicted of crimes or sympathy against the Confederacy were sent to prisons in the deep South. Thousands more fled to sanctuary in Kentucky.

The Federals controlled the city from September 1863 until the end of the war. Considerable destruction was done by retreating Confederate troops and by shelling during the siege. A number of private homes were damaged by occupying Union soldiers. Many of the Northerners were so enchanted with the scenery and climate that they later moved here to live.

The First Presbyterian Church (1901) is the third

The fort was dismantled long ago, but White's original home remained. It was to be destroyed when a new building was constructed, but Isaiah Ford bought the house and moved it. In 1960 the house was purchased by the City Association of Women's Clubs and moved to a site near the original fort. The restored White House, furnished with furniture, tools, and artifacts of the late eighteenth century, serves as the anchor for a recreated White's Fort. The cabins represent a guest house, blacksmith shop, loom house, smoke house, and contain a museum. The fort is now an important teaching tool to show children how pioneers settled the land and lived.

This area was first explored in 1761, when three men made a goodwill visit to the Cherokees. The site was strategically important because four miles to the east the Holston and French Broad rivers merge to form the broad, shallow, navigable Tennessee River. Since the earliest days there has been a great deal of traffic on the river. The East Tennessee & Georgia Railroad was the first line to reach Knoxville, via Chattanooga, in 1855. A branch line connected the city with Nashville the following year, and in 1858 the East Tennessee & Virginia led to Bristol, Virginia.

These rail connections made the city an important military target when the Civil War began. Goods from Tennessee, Georgia, Alabama, Mississippi, and states west of the Mississippi River could be funneled to Confederate armies in Virginia along this route. Lin-

This impressive monument honoring East Tennesseans who fought for the Union guards the Knoxville National Cemetery.

on the site. In the graveyard are the marked graves of William Blount, James White, and many other pioneers.

A number of interesting historical homes are found near Knoxville. The Ramsey House (1797), six miles east of the city, was the first stone house in the area. It was built by Francis Alexander Ramsey, a pioneer and surveyor who arrived with James White. He brought noted architect Thomas Hope from Charleston to design his home. Built in the Gothic style with red granite walls, it is two stories tall, with a basement and attic. The census of 1800 proved this to be the most expensive house in Tennessee. The Ramsey House is a transitional type, between frontier log homes and finer plantation houses. It is open to the public and administered by the Association for the Preservation of Tennessee Antiquities.

Marble Springs, named for the ample springs and marble deposits discovered on the land, was the summer home and farm of John Sevier. This simple, two-story cabin of hewn logs has a stone chimney and wooden shingles. Sevier, a famed Indian fighter known as "Nolichucky Jack," led several expeditions against the Cherokees and fought the British during the Revolution.

Crescent Bend, the Armstrong–Lockett House (1834), was built by Drury Paine Armstrong on his 600-acre farm on a bend in the Tennessee River. It is richly furnished with the Toms Collection of American and English furniture which dates from 1750 to 1820. An outstanding collection of English silver (1640–1720), is also preserved in the house.

Speedway Manor (1830) is a museum that displays English furniture and silver and Oriental porcelain from the eighteenth and nineteenth centuries. Originally built near Tazewell, not far from Cumberland Gap, it survived a Civil War battle and was later moved here.

South of Knoxville, near Maryville, is the Sam Houston Schoolhouse. It was built in 1794 of logs fastened with hand-wrought nails. The site, in a quiet cove, is shaded by large stands of oak, maple, and sycamore trees. The building is twenty feet long, eighteen feet wide, and ten feet high. Light was provided by omitting one log in the wall. This is the oldest preserved school building in Tennessee and one of the last standing structures which has an association with Sam Houston, who taught here in 1812 when he was eighteen years old.

Wheeler approached Knoxville via Sweetwater and Maryville in his unsuccessful attempt to capture high ground outside the city. During the Civil War, when most of the local men had joined the Union or Confederate armies, defense of the community was left to the Blount County Women Home Guards, which consisted of women and elderly men. While approaching Maryville on December 5, 1863, to relieve Burnside with his 25,000-man force, Sherman learned that an enemy skirmish line had been contacted. Riding to the front of this column, he discovered the ladies waiting for him, led by Captain Cynthia Dunn. Their flag, with thirty-two stars on a blue field, is preserved in Lamar Library at Maryville College. Sherman was quartered in the Pride Mansion, home of Dr. Samuel Pride. His three corps camped in Maryville, Louisville, and Morgantown. Outside Maryville is the Brick Mill, used as Union headquarters by O. O. Howard during this period.

A number of fortified positions were built in Blount County during the early years as protection from the Indians. From Houston's Station, erected in 1785, John Sevier led 160 horsemen on a punitive raid in 1786 to attack Cherokee towns. In 1788 a family and thirty-one soldiers from the fort were killed in the area. The Cherokees then attacked the fort but were defeated. At Gamble's Station, built on the Little River in 1790 by Josias Gamble, William Blount arrived to pacify the Indians and disperse settlers who had gathered for battle. When 300 Indians attacked James Gillespy's Fort, the soldiers fought until their ammunition was exhausted. Twenty-eight were captured and seventeen killed, their bodies burned with the fort. Afterwards the site was called the Burnt Station.

Montvale Springs near Maryville was known as the "Saratoga of the South" during the nineteenth century. A log hotel built in 1837 was replaced by the Seven Gables Hotel in 1853. Noted southern poet Sidney Lanier spent much of his boyhood here. After that hotel burned in 1896, it was rebuilt, only to burn again in 1933. ■

Hood's Tennessee Invasion

D uring the winter of 1864, U. S. Grant was promoted to lieutenant general, the first with that rank since George Washington, and made supreme commander of all Union forces. He planned coordinated attacks against the Confederate armies in Virginia, Georgia, and Louisiana for the spring, then left the western theatre to command the massive Army of the Potomac. In May he would assault Robert E. Lee's legendary Army of Northern Virginia.

Sherman was left in charge of Federal troops in Chattanooga. In late spring 1864 he set out to capture Atlanta, Georgia, with the Army of the Cumberland, still led by George Thomas; the Army of the Tennessee, now commanded by General James McPherson; and the Army of the Ohio, under General John M. Schofield, a force which totaled 120,000 men. Opposing him was the Army of Tennessee, commanded by Joseph E. Johnston, who had replaced Bragg in late December 1863. After retreating to the outskirts of Atlanta without initiating a major battle, Johnston was replaced by one of his corps commanders, John B. Hood, who had been Lee's most aggressive divisional general in Virginia. At age thirty-three, Hood became a full general, but unfortunately the war had cost him a leg and the use of an arm. An opiate he took for pain apparently clouded his judgment.

While commanding the Army of Tennessee in Georgia, Hood lost 21,000 men killed and wounded after launching four disastrous attacks against Sherman in an attempt to protect Atlanta, which he was forced to abandon in early September 1864. Sherman occupied the city, and Hood camped nearby to keep an eye on future Union movements.

Late in the month, Hood devised a plan to recoup his losses. He would move north to destroy the Federal rail supply lines, capture isolated garrisons, and force Sherman to leave Atlanta to come after him. Hood intended to defeat Sherman in northern Georgia, regain Atlanta, then strike north. He would recapture Nashville, then advance to the Ohio River and add Kentucky to the Confederacy. That accomplished, he would march east to assist Lee.

The plan would have been grandiose had the Confederate army been in good shape, but the men were exhausted. They lacked clothing and equipment and had lost their faith in Hood, who blamed them for his own short-

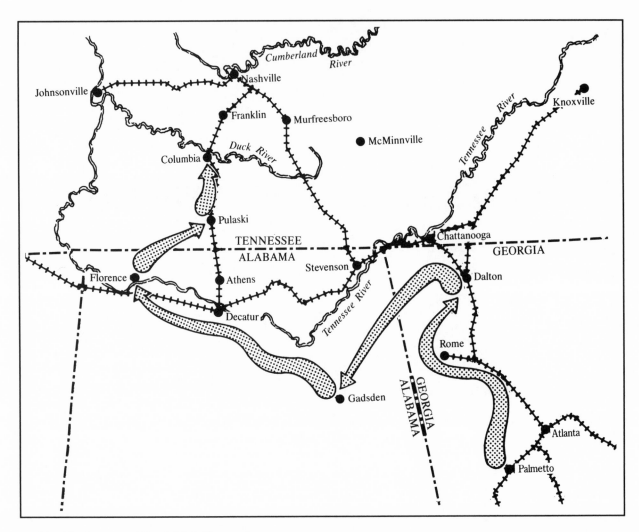

Map 35: Overview of Hood's Nashville campaign.

comings. Despite these serious handicaps, Hood started north in early October.

Having been warned of Hood's plan by the speeches of Jefferson Davis, which were freely published in Southern newspapers, Sherman sent Thomas to Nashville, with many troops following to protect Tennessee. On October 3 Sherman left Atlanta to follow Hood with 55,000 men.

Hood temporarily disrupted the railroad and captured several garrisons but refused to give Sherman battle at La Fayette, Georgia. The Confederates soon crossed into Alabama and approached Gadsden, where Hood hoped to cross the Tennessee River, but the presence of a Union force caused him to continue west.

Grant urged Sherman to destroy Hood, but Sherman believed it was impossible to catch the fast-moving Confederate. Sherman's own plans, to

Sherman's trains labor through the north Georgia mountains during the pursuit of Hood in October 1864. [LESLIE'S ILLUSTRATED]

"The Yellow Rose of Texas" ■ Army of Tennessee Version

The valiant Confederate Army of Tennessee was abused by its commanders through most of the Civil War. Braxton Bragg's brutal discipline was exacerbated by his inability to achieve a battlefield victory. John B. Hood slaughtered his soldiers in useless battles, then blamed the men for his failures. The only commander the soldiers truly loved was Joseph E. Johnston, who led the army through the early part of the Atlanta campaign. Johnston was also unable to win, but he cared for his men and refused to throw away their lives. Reflecting their feelings on the dismal retreat from Nashville, soldiers of the Army of Tennessee revised the popular song "The Yellow Rose of Texas," which had become Hood's theme as he led a division of Texans in Virginia and Georgia:

> And now I'm going
>   southward
> For my heart is full of woe;
> I'm going back to Georgia
> To find my Uncle Joe.

> "You may talk about your
>   Beauregard
> and sing of General Lee,
> But the gallant Hood of
>   Texas
> Played hell in Tennessee. ■

march to the Atlantic Ocean, were being delayed, so he returned to Atlanta. Sherman dispatched Schofield to Tennessee with 15,000 men from the Fourteenth Corps and 12,000 men from the Twenty-third Corps. After another 13,000 men were dispatched to Nashville from Missouri, Thomas had an army of 70,000 men. That was more than enough to handle Hood, believed Sherman, who promptly left for Savannah.

Hood moved west. Finding Decatur, Alabama, strongly held, he marched to Tuscumbia, where he waited for Nathan Bedford Forrest to return from a raid and lead his advance. Although P. G. T. Beauregard, who commanded the Confederate Military District of the West, had given Hood permission for this campaign only if it was launched quickly, more time passed. It was November 21 before Hood finally started for Tennessee. Despite being barefooted, tattered, and hungry as winter settled in, his men were happy when the campaign began. After all, they were the Army of Tennessee, and many were returning home after a long absence.

Hood's army, consisting of 38,000 men and 108 field pieces, was divided

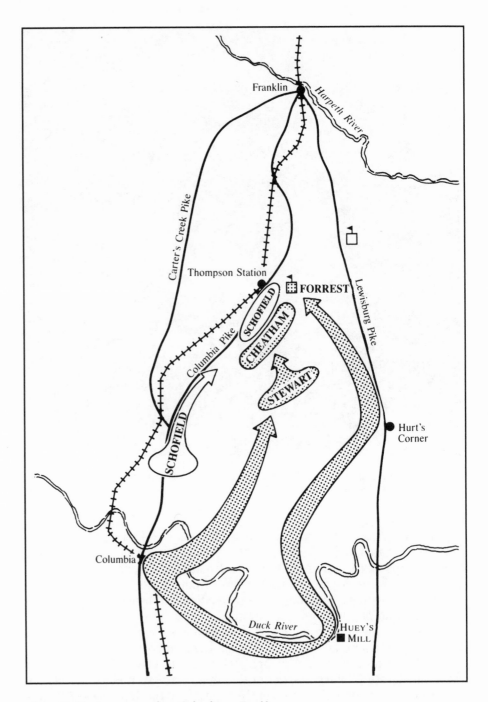

Map 36: Troop movement from Columbia to Franklin.

After Sherman called off the chase of Hood into northern Alabama, his troops marched across the Coosa River on a pontoon bridge as herds of cattle swam alongside. [LESLIE'S ILLUSTRATED]

into three corps. They were led by General Benjamin F. Cheatham, General Alexander Stewart, and General Stephen D. Lee.

The Confederates marched through Waynesboro, Lawrenceburg, and Mount Pleasant on the way to Columbia, where the Franklin and Columbia Turnpike to Nashville crossed the Duck River. Discovering that Schofield's 30,000 men were thirty miles to the south at Pulaski guarding the Decatur & Nashville Railroad, Hood planned to isolate the Union force from Nashville and destroy it. Stewart, closest to Columbia, quickly moved his corps forward, led by Forrest's cavalry.

Schofield realized his perilous situation in time to win the race, reaching Columbia on November 24 just hours ahead of Forrest. The Federals entrenched, but their backs were against the river and their flanks were dangerously exposed. On November 27 Schofield crossed the Duck River and established a position on the northern bank.

Frustrated once in trying to trap Schofield, Hood formulated another plan. On November 28 Forrest crossed the river to Schofield's left at Davis's Ford, and Cheatham and Stewart followed on pontoon bridges. They raced for Spring Hill to cut off Schofield while Lee and the Confederate artillery remained at Columbia to demonstrate. The ruse nearly worked. Schofield ignored reports of Confederates passing around his flank, but luckily a single Federal division reached Spring Hill moments before Forrest arrived on

November 29. The Rebel cavalry was driven off, and an attack by Cheatham was also repulsed. Another Confederate assault was planned, but it failed to materialize due to a lack of coordination between Hood and his generals. However, Hood was north of Spring Hill, seemingly planted squarely across Schofield's route of retreat to Nashville. The Rebel general expected to overwhelm Schofield in the morning. What Hood failed to realize was that his men were camped along the pike, not astride it in a blocking position.

That night one of the greatest maneuvers of the Civil War occurred. While Hood slept, Schofield raced his entire Union army to Spring Hill. Two Union corps and a five-mile-long train of wagons stole past Confederate campfires. Rebel sentries twice aroused Hood after seeing their movement. Hood told them to tell Cheatham, and Cheatham ordered a divisional commander to check out the reports. He reported that nothing was there.

By morning Schofield was eight miles north, entrenching at Franklin, situated in a bend of the Harpeth River. A wagon bridge and a railroad bridge had been previously destroyed, and Schofield had been forced to leave his pontoons at Columbia. Fearing that he would be unable to cross before Hood arrived, Schofield set his men to digging an arc of trenches across the river bend. Headquarters for the two divisions left to stop Hood was the Carter

The Fiercest Fighter in the Army ■ John B. Hood

If ever a soldier was promoted beyond his capabilities, it was John Bell Hood. What made his career a greater tragedy is the fact that he was one of the most ferocious fighters in the Confederate army. Had he remained in divisional command, history would have recorded him as an excellent subordinate officer.

Born in Kentucky in 1831, Hood graduated near the bottom of his West Point class in 1853 and was sent to the western frontier, where Indians had the first opportunity to wound the unfortunate fellow. He soon began his Confederate service at the Confederate retreat from Yorktown, Virginia, during the Peninsula campaign. Hood gallantly led a Texas brigade during the savage Seven Day's battle, Second Manassas, and Antietam. His conspicuous heroism brought him command of a division which fought at Fred-

ericksburg and Gettysburg, where a severe wound cost him the use of his left arm.

Two months later, Hood accompanied James Longstreet to Georgia. While leading his men into the blood bath that was Chickamauga, Hood suffered a wound which forced the amputation of his right leg. He remained in Georgia and was given a corps under Joseph Johnston. During the Atlanta campaign, Hood undermined Johnston's position with poison letters to President Davis. When the young general was appointed commander of the Army of Tennessee, he lost Atlanta by launching four determined, but unsupervised, strikes against Sherman's superior army.

In the fall of 1864 Hood decided that a bold strike north would force Sherman to abandon Atlanta and follow him into the mountains for a decisive

battle. His meandering course frustrated Sherman, but when the Confederate refused to stop for battle, the Union commander sent reinforcements to Tennessee and marched gloriously to the sea.

Hood next determined to recapture Tennessee, and perhaps continue into Kentucky and beyond the Ohio River, but his slow pace allowed the Federals ample time to arrange a defense. Hood missed opportunities for quick victories at Columbia and Spring Hill, then crippled the Army of Tennessee with a suicidal attack at Franklin. After Hood's charade of besieging Nashville, George Thomas destroyed the Confederate army. Hood resigned after the remnant of his force limped across the Tennessee River.

Following the war, Hood entered business in New Orleans, but ill fortune followed him even

there. The business failed, and in 1879 Hood and his wife died from yellow fever, leaving a large family of small children to be divided among various foster homes. ■

[LIBRARY OF CONGRESS]

farmhouse, on a high point of land that commanded a two-mile-wide open plain stretching to the south. While engineers hurried to rebuild the bridges, Schofield accompanied twelve cannon across the river to anchor the Federal left flank at Fort Granger, a previously prepared defensive position.

Hood was furious when he awoke on the morning of November 30 to find Schofield gone. He ordered his generals to a breakfast where there was much recrimination. Accepting no blame for the situation, Hood accused the Army of Tennessee of losing its courage and no longer wanting to attack. The soldiers he blamed were disgusted that their commander had allowed this opportunity for victory to vanish.

The Confederates raced after Schofield to Franklin, where Forrest suggested a flank attack. No, Hood decided, we will strike the center of the Union line immediately, despite the fact that Lee and the Confederate artillery had not arrived. Of eighteen brigades available for the assault, Hood would use only seven. To the left of the road, the attack would be made by two lines with two brigades in each; to the right three brigades advanced in a single line. Forrest would strike Union general James Wilson's cavalry on the extreme right. Other infantry and cavalry units would demonstrate on the left.

Although he was ignorant of the fact, Hood would be attacking the only weakness in the Union line. In the center, where the road passed through the fortifications, a gap had been left for the passage of wagons. The open-

The Intellectual General ■ John McAllister Schofield

Schofield, born in New York in 1831, graduated from West Point in 1853, then served in Florida and taught at his alma mater. Early in the Civil War he served in strife-ridden Missouri, winning a Medal of Honor after the Union defeat at Wilson's Creek. Schofield was given command of the tiny Army of Ohio, which under Ambrose Burnside had captured Knoxville and held it against the Confederate siege by James Longstreet. He performed well during the successful campaign to capture Atlanta, after which his force was dispatched to help deal with John Hood's invasion of Tennessee.

Initially positioned at Pulaski, astride the railroad from northern Alabama to Nashville, Schofield was almost cut off when Hood marched quickly from the southwest. The Federals barely beat the Confederates to Columbia. Several days later Hood skillfully slipped around the Union flank to block their route to Nashville at Spring Hill. Schofield should have been destroyed, but in one of the Civil War's greatest maneuvers, the Northern force escaped past the sleeping Confederates. Enraged, Hood launched a foolish assault against a strong Union position at Franklin which left six Rebel generals dead and the Confederate army crippled. Schofield helped Thomas destroy the Army of Tennessee at Nashville, then rejoined Sherman in North Carolina before the war ended.

Schofield's real talents lay in the academic and administrative fields. Before the Civil War he had taught physics at Washington University in St. Louis. Following the war, he became Andrew Johnson's secretary of war, served as commandant of the military academy, and became commander of the U.S. Army. He died in 1906 in Florida. ■

[LIBRARY OF CONGRESS]

The Carter House, built in 1830, was an important landmark during the Battle of Franklin.

The Controversial Trooper ■ Nathan Bedford Forrest

Forrest, undoubtedly the greatest cavalry commander in American history, was born in Tennessee in 1821. He had little formal education, but considerable native intelligence. By the time of the Civil War, Forrest had made a fortune as a planter (contrary to a widely held belief, he was a slave trader for only a short period of time). He enlisted in the Confederate army as a private, but soon raised a battalion with his own money and was elected its lieutenant colonel.

Forrest's military fame started at Fort Donelson, where, disgusted with the generals who were surrendering the fort, he led his cavalry and a number of infantrymen in escape. In July 1862, he used tactics, courage, and guile to capture Murfreesboro, an important Union supply base. For that exploit he was promoted to brigadier. Through late 1862 and the spring of 1863, Forrest effectively raided Grant's supply lines in West Tennessee. His men fought well at Chickamauga and raided Federal supply lines during the siege of Chattanooga. After quarreling bitterly with Braxton Bragg, Forrest was given an independent command in western Tennessee, with the rank of major general.

His men were charged with murdering black prisoners after overrunning Fort Pillow, Tennessee, in April 1864, an incident which remains controversial to this day. It seems that atrocities did occur, but Forrest attempted to halt them. In June, Forrest routed a vastly superior force at Brice's Crossroads, then stood his own at Tupelo, Mississippi. His activities so disrupted Union supply lines that William Sherman ordered Forrest stopped if it took the lives of 10,000 Union soldiers and bankrupted the treasury. No one could apprehend the elusive Forrest.

After destroying a large Union base at Johnsonville, Tennessee, Forrest led Hood to Nashville in late 1864, then protected his rear on the bitter retreat. At the end of the war, outnumbered and commanding green youths, Forrest was finally defeated, by James Wilson's cavalry, at Selma, Alabama.

Forrest returned to his life as a planter in Memphis. Again, contrary to popular belief, he did not found the Ku Klux Klan. He did become its grand wizard, but disbanded the organization when it turned violent. He died in 1877 and is buried in Memphis. ■

[ARTIST'S PAINTING]

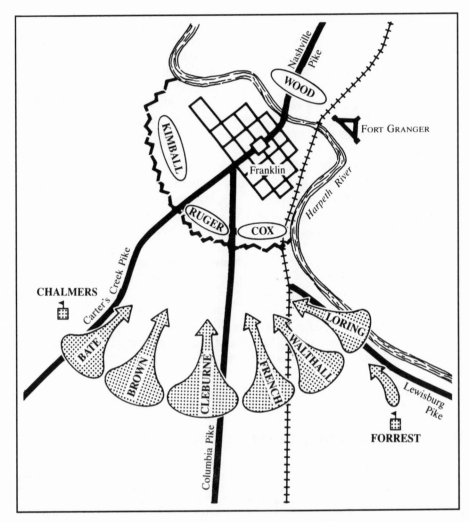

Map 37: The Battle of Franklin.

The Carter Family of Franklin

Fountain Branch Carter, age sixty-seven at the time of the battle, had arrived from Virginia thirty years earlier. He was a merchant, farmer, and surveyor. The 1860 census indicated he owned twenty-eight slaves, and his property was worth $37,000. All on the same day in May 1861, three of his sons joined Company H, Twentieth Tennessee Infantry. At the time of the battle of Franklin, Moscow Carter, a lieutenant colonel when he was captured in 1862, had returned home to serve out his parole. Francis Carter had been terribly wounded at Shiloh. After spending months in hospitals, he was discharged in 1862. Theodrick ("Tod") Carter was a captain in the Army of Tennessee when the war arrived at his family's doorstep.

Home on November 30, 1864, was the patriarch, Moscow, four daughters, one daughter-in-law, and three sets of grandchildren. Including servants, there were seventeen people in the house. Early in the morning Union general Jacob Cox awoke Mr. Carter and announced that the structure would be his temporary headquarters. Cox and Moscow both believed Hood would do the intelligent thing and move around the Federal flank, so the family remained in the house.

The battle of Franklin swirled around the house while the Carters huddled in their basement. They awoke to find their fields covered with the carnage of war. Informed that Tod had fallen several hundred yards away, the family searched among the wounded and dead soldiers. Fountain Branch Carter found his son, who was carried back to the house where he had been born and raised. He died a short time later. ∎

ing was protected by four cannon and a second line of works 200 feet to the rear, with additional artillery positioned behind that. Two Federal brigades had also been unwisely ordered to remain on the road outside Union lines.

At 4:00 P.M. Confederates formed up as bands played "Dixie" and "The Bonnie Blue Flag." The magnificent advance, clearly visible from Union lines, flushed warrens of rabbits and coveys of quail. A mile from the Union line the Confederates paused to reform, then advanced with the distinctive piercing yell of Rebel armies. The two isolated Union brigades broke, leaving 700 captured, and the Federals in Franklin could not fire for fear of hitting their own men. When three Confederate divisions followed the fleeing Federals through the gap, the four cannon were abandoned and a Union regiment stationed at the gap fled.

For a brief moment a smashing Confederate victory seemed imminent. Then a brigade of Union reinforcements threw itself into the breach. The clash resulted in some of the bloodiest hand-to-hand fighting seen in the Civil War. The Confederates were driven back to the opposite side of the Union works, where they were unable to retreat. Union cannon and repeating rifle fire slaughtered the trapped Rebels, forcing many to surrender. Hood, positioned far behind the lines, could not see the action and issued no additional orders. On the right, Forrest and his two cavalry divisions had crossed the river and hit the Union flank, but Wilson drove them back, one of the few reverses Forrest suffered during the war.

Union general Jacob Cox, who directed the battle, urged Schofield to counterattack and destroy Hood, but Schofield refused. At 11:00 P.M. the Federals began to withdraw. By 3:00 A.M. the army had crossed the Harpeth and burned the bridges. The Union wounded were abandoned to Confederate care, and Schofield slipped safely into Nashville's defenses without further combat.

With 18,000 Confederates participating in the assault, this had been a larger attack than Pickett's famed charge at Gettysburg. It was just as devastating for the South. Hood found his dead piled in heaps at the Union works. There were 7,000 Rebel casualties, with 1,750 killed, including 6 generals who died leading their men. Five other generals were wounded, and another captured. Of 100 regimental commanders, 54 became casualties. One general, the gifted Patrick Cleburne, had muttered before the

The Deaths of Five Confederate Generals at Franklin

Because of the military tactics in use during the Civil War and the primitive means of communication, generals led their troops from the front, a fact made clear by the number of high-ranking officers killed and wounded during battle. The decimation of Confederate leaders at Franklin was the greatest loss of general officers during the war.

Patrick Cleburne, a naturally gifted and immensely popular general, was gloomy as he surveyed the Union defenses of Franklin from Winstead Hill. "They have three lines of works. And they are all finished," he muttered to a friend, General D. C. Gowan. Cleburne believed they were all doomed, but concluded, "If we are to die, let us die like men." As he led his men into battle, Cleburne's horse was wounded by a can-

non shot. He mounted a second horse, which was quickly killed by artillery fire. Cleburne disappeared into the smoke of battle, leading his division on foot, waving his hat. He was found dead with a single rifle shot in the side.

General John Adams inspected his battle line, then led his men in the attack. He leaped his horse over a defensive ditch and reached the top of the Union parapets, a feat so daring that Union colonel W. Scott Stewart called for his men to hold their fire. "We hoped he would not be killed," said one Federal. "He was too brave to be killed." When Adams tried to snatch a regimental flag, he was shot and fell dead into the ditch.

General Otho Strahl found himself trapped in the ditch with his men. Standing atop the

dead and wounded, he loaded rifles and passed them up to his soldiers before dying from three wounds.

General Hiram Granbury was also killed in the Union ditch.

General States Rights Gist continued the attack on foot when his horse was killed, then fell with a bullet to the heart. He was carried to a field hospital, where he died during the night.

The bodies of Cleburne, Adams, Strahl, Granbury, and Gist were placed on the rear porch of the Carnton Mansion. Many of Cleburne's men, survivors of the fierce, senseless battle, came to pay their last respects.

The remains of the generals were taken to Columbia on December 1, 1864, and buried the following day. ∎

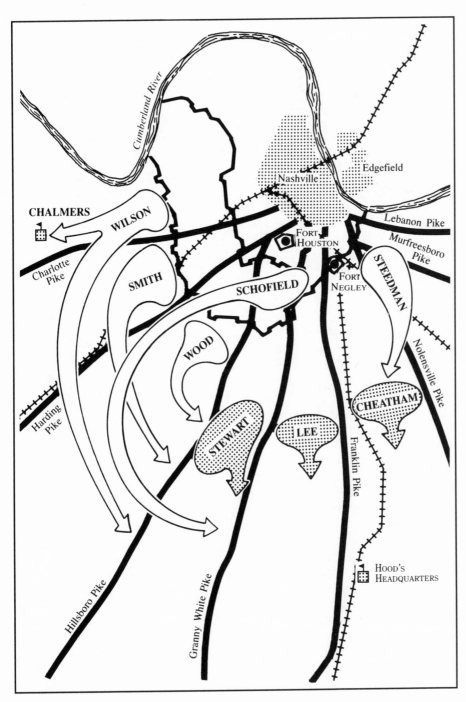

Map 38: The Battle of Nashville.

The Second Battle of Franklin

In September 1923 Metro Pictures Corporation of Hollywood, later Metro-Goldwyn-Mayer, came to Franklin to reenact the Civil War battle for the climax of a movie titled *The Human Mill.* Movie crews spent days digging trenches and planting hundreds of mines to imitate the explosions of artillery shells. Four thousand men, including many World War I veterans, arrived to act as soldiers.

The reenactment is said to have been the most exciting ever staged. Mines exploded, rifles fired blanks, smoke wreathed the field, and hundreds of soldiers grappled in hand-to-hand combat. An old Confederate veteran was seen in the spectator area trying to break free of a security guard and yelling, "Let me at 'em boy! I fit 'em here in '64, and I ain't afeared to fite 'em now!"

The movie was never completed, and the battle footage was reportedly destroyed in a fire. ∎

The Cumberland River at Nashville during the Civil War. [BATTLES AND LEADERS]

battle, "If we are to die, let us die like men." The angry soldiers felt betrayed by Hood's attack. To them, it was nothing short of murder. Despite this staggering casualty list, Hood reported a victory to his superior, General P. G. T. Beauregard, but the ranks knew better. Schofield had suffered 1,222 soldiers killed and wounded and 1,100 missing.

Nashville, which Hood reached on the morning of December 1, was one of the most heavily fortified cities in America. Since occupying the city in early 1862, the Yankees had spent nearly three years strengthening its defenses. Two lines of infantry trenches, which connected artillery forts, stretched from east to west between the banks of the Cumberland River. Within the city, Thomas's 60,000 well-equipped soliders were warm and adequately fed. Outside, on the frozen, snow-covered ground, were 23,000 cold, hungry Confederates. Incredibly, Hood set about besieging Thomas.

The Union line was ten miles in length, protecting eight roads that led south. Hood's men could only form a four-mile-long line in the Brentwood hills, covering four roads. The Confederate line was thin, and both flanks were hanging precariously in the air. Hood planned to repulse any Union attack, then follow Thomas's defeated troops into the city.

Thomas intended to crush Hood, but he demanded time to remount his cavalry. Schofield, having been pushed into Nashville by Hood after refusing to attack the Confederates at Franklin, now criticized Thomas for his slow movements. He had designs on Thomas's position. Grant, Halleck, Stanton, and Lincoln also urged Thomas to attack, but winter storms, which only added to the Confederate misery, further delayed an assault. Grant, besieging Lee at Petersburg, was boarding a train for the West to personally relieve Thomas when the methodical general acted.

Cheatham held the Confederate right, Lee the center, and Stewart the left. The extreme left was bolstered by five redoubts, each equipped with four cannon and 100 infantry, which were designed to operate independently. In spite of the redoubts, the Union right far overlapped Hood's left.

Fort Negley, the primary Union stronghold in Nashville, as seen in January 1863. The stout work was built of stone, railroad iron, logs, and earth. Thomas launched his assault against Hood from this position in December 1864. [HARPER'S WEEKLY]

On December 7 Hood sent Forrest to attack Murfreesboro, thirty miles to the southeast, in the hope that Thomas would weaken Nashville to reinforce the Union garrison there. Thomas did not, and Hood had deprived himself of his reconnaissance force and the hard-fighting cavalry. With Forrest's 6,500 men gone, Hood had only 15,000 soldiers.

Thomas planned to feint on the Confederate right with one division, then attack the left with one army corps, another infantry division, and a cavalry division. Wilson's cavalry would range far around the left, with Schofield held in reserve.

At 4:00 A.M. on December 15, 7,600 Union troops, supported by two batteries, made a good start on Hood's right, but the attack bogged down. A second Union assault fixed the Confederate right and center in place.

While Wilson led 12,000 cavalry around the Rebel flank, 12,000 infantry under General Andrew J. Smith attacked the left, with another 12,000 men under General Thomas J. Wood extended to his left. They drove the Confederates off Montgomery Hill, a forward position, and back to the main Southern line. On their own initiative, the Union troops continued the attack, breaking Stewart's line and capturing four guns. On the left, only the five redoubts remained. The Confederate gunners and infantry resisted heroically, but one by one they were smothered by masses of Federal infantry and dismounted cavalry.

By 1:30 P.M. Wilson was in the Confederate rear. Schofield threw his men into the battle with Smith and Wood in a renewed attack that broke the Rebel line beyond repair. The Confederates, whose fighting was generally described as listless, managed to withdraw in good order to form a line two miles south. The new position was two miles long and covered two roads. Cheatham, who was in reasonably good shape, crossed from the right to the left, his flank resting on what later would be called Shy's Hill. The center was commanded by Stewart, and Lee had the right flank on Overton Hill. Despite their exhaustion from the nine-hour battle, the Rebels built works throughout the night.

Thomas's report of success to Washington was greeted with joy by Grant, Lincoln, and Stanton. But they cautioned "Old Slow Trot" that Hood must not be allowed to escape. There was little chance of that happening.

Union general James B. Steedman faced Overton Hill, then from the Union left to right were Wood, Smith in the center, and Schofield at Shy's Hill, with Wilson overlapping the Confederate left. The same plan would be followed in the morning: feint to the Confederate right, crush the left.

December 16 dawned with a long, heavy, and devastatingly accurate Union bombardment of the Confederate line. At 3:00 P.M. the Federal feint at Overton Hill was driven back by a storm of fire. As Thomas had hoped, Hood reinforced Overton Hill with men from Shy's Hill. Wilson circled around Shy's Hill, disrupting the Rebel rear, and more Confederates were sent to deal with the cavalry threat. Shy's Hill was not only left thinly defended, but the works were poorly built and had no protecting abatis.

Hood, "Victory," and Defeat in Tennessee

On the day after the fearful slaughter of the Army of Tennessee at Franklin, Hood congratulated his men on the great "victory" they had won. He apparently wanted to keep the fruits of this engagement secret, for on December 3 he informed his superior, P.G.T. Beauregard, of his loss in officers, but made no mention of enlisted casualties. Two days later, in a message to Richmond, Hood again elected to omit his casualty count, but offered that the loss of officers "was excessively large in proportion to the loss of men." He also mentioned that there was "a very large proportion of slightly wounded men." Hood would not admit the truth to Richmond until January.

The Confederate government was also left ignorant of the results of Nashville. Officials only learned of Hood's retreat to Mississippi indirectly. On Christmas Day, Beauregard was informed that General Stephen Lee, of Hood's command, had sent a telegram from Florence, Alabama. A week later Beauregard heard that the army had crossed the Tennessee River on December 26–27.

On January 1 Beauregard ordered Hood by telegraph to report on his situation. Hood ignored the demand, prompting Beauregard to leave Charleston, South Carolina, for Tupelo, Mississippi, for a personal inspection. He had Jefferson Davis' authorization to relieve Hood if that proved necessary. Richmond was expecting Hood to reinforce the command that would oppose William Sherman's move into South Carolina, and they had been led to believe that Hood had a large force available.

At a stop in Macon, Georgia, Beauregard discovered that Hood had lost fifty cannon in the retreat from Tennessee, although on January 3 Hood reported that he had withdrawn "without materiel loss." His later messages reported small losses at Franklin and Nashville.

At Tupelo Beauregard received the staggering news that the Army of Tennessee was reduced to 15,000 men, only half of them combat effective. The troops had abandoned 13,000 rifles during the campaign, and they had little food, clothing, or blankets. Hood admitted the truth of his disastrous campaign on January 8 when he offered his resignation to Richmond. ∎

Union cannon protected the Tennessee State Capitol in Nashville. [BATTLES AND LEADERS]

Late in the afternoon Wilson begged Schofield to attack, but there was no response. Wilson angrily galloped off to see Thomas. While Thomas was ordering Schofield to advance, a division under John McArthur, to Schofield's left, surged forward without orders. Schofield and Smith joined in and broke the Confederate line, capturing many prisoners as Shy's Hill was enveloped from three sides. Only sixty-five men on the hill escaped as the Army of Tennessee collapsed. Some of the toughest veterans in the Confederacy threw away their weapons and ran headlong for the rear. The Rebels abandoned fifty-four cannon in the rout.

Inspired by the action at Shy's Hill, Steedman renewed his attack against Overton Hill and drove Lee back. Lee was seen organizing a new line, shouting, "Rally, men, rally! For God's sake rally! This is the place for brave men to die." Lee managed to organize a rearguard that halted Union pursuit for the night.

Hood had lost 6,400 men, Thomas 3,000. Those figures fail to tell the true story of the battle of Nashville. For the only time in the history of the Confederacy, a Southern army had been destroyed. The survivors limped south toward the Tennessee River. Forrest rejoined Hood at Columbia on December 19 and protected the Rebel column as it retreated through Pulaski and crossed the Tennessee River at Bainbridge, Alabama, on December 28. Wilson slashed at the column until Thomas called off the chase. Just 18,000 men, only half of them in fighting shape, remained with Hood when he camped at Tupelo, Mississippi. On January 1, 1865, Hood asked Davis to relieve him of command. His request was granted on January 23.

The war in Tennessee, and the West, was over. The shattered remnants of the Army of Tennessee would be returned to Joseph Johnston, who raced into North Carolina in the spring of 1865 in an attempt to stop Sherman's march. The thin ranks fought well at Bentonville on March 19 but lost to vastly superior numbers. On April 26, 21,000 men surrendered and began the long walk back to their homes. The Civil War was over. ■

A DRIVING TOUR
■ Hood's Tennessee Invasion ■

This tour begins at the Sam Davis Monument on the southern edge of the Giles County Courthouse in Pulaski. Pulaski can be reached on Interstate 65 south from Nashville or north from Birmingham, or on U.S. 64 east from Chattanooga or west from Memphis.

Here Schofield waited for Hood to approach along the line of the Nashville & Decatur Railroad. Instead, Hood left Florence, Alabama, and advanced in three columns through Columbia. The left wing passed through Lawrenceburg to Mount Pleasant, led by Forrest on November 19 and followed by Stevenson's corps on November 22. The center passed through West Point and Henryville to Mount Pleasant, and the right went through Waynesboro to Mount Pleasant. Realizing his mistake, Schofield raced for Columbia, barely beating Hood there. After the disastrous Confederate defeat at Nashville, Hood retreated through Pulaski into Alabama.

The Western & Atlantic Railroad bridge over Chickamauga Creek was supported by this stone pier just south of Missionary Ridge. Chickamauga Station was nearby.

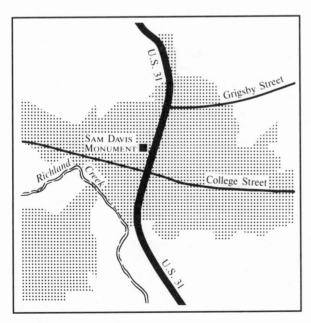

Map 39: The Pulaski area.

At Buford, Forrest, supported by General Edward C. Walthall's infantry, checked Wilson's cavalry on December 24 and 25. While the slow Rebel wagon train lumbered through Pulaski on December 26, the Confederate rearguard launched a fierce counterattack against its pursuers at Cool Springs Church on TN 11, capturing prisoners, a cannon, and several hundred horses. On the following day, near Sugar Creek, Forrest established a position in a ridgetop gap. When the Federals entered it, his two regiments opened fire, then charged and drove them back two miles. When Forrest crossed the Tennessee River, the Civil War in Tennessee was over. Thomas called off the pursuit.

The Ku Klux Klan was born in Pulaski on Christmas Eve 1865. The Klan, the idea of Judge T. M. Jones and his son Calvin, was meant to be an organization that would help normalize social life disrupted by the Civil War. The club soon developed exotic initiation rites, spooky ceremonies, and the traditional Klan regalia: long, flowing white robes and conical hats topped with horns. The organization spread rapidly throughout the South, but it soon outgrew its social club roots and became a terrorist organization that at-

"Boy hero of the Confederacy" Sam Davis is honored in Pulaski, near the site of his hanging.

tempted to run carpetbaggers back north and intimidate the newly freed slaves. In 1869 Nathan Bedford Forrest, then the grand wizard, officially disbanded the Klan because of the violence.

The Sam Davis Monument was erected by the U.D.C. in 1906. On East Hill Street is the Sam Davis Museum, which presents a general view of the Civil War and has exhibits concerning the young martyr. It is at the spot where Davis was hanged on November 27, 1863. A monument also marks the spot. In southern Giles County near the Alabama line is yet another monument, unveiled on July 22, 1925, at the site where the soldier was captured. It is preserved in a small park along TN 11.

John Adams, one of the Confederate generals killed at Franklin on November 30, 1864, is buried in a cemetery just south of East College Street. The statue of a Confederate soldier guards the courthouse grounds.

Pulaski is a historic community where life still revolves around the courthouse, which is surrounded by thriving stores, offices, and banks. The Giles County Courthouse, built in 1909 at a cost of $131,000, has an interesting dome and clock on the exterior. The doors have solid brass pulls, which are incised with "Giles." Inside, on the arched vault of the skylight, are sixteen beautiful caryatids.

Pulaski has two historic districts: the Sam Davis Avenue Historic District and the South Pulaski Historic District. The Giles County Historical Society sponsors a Christmas tour of homes with the proceeds used to purchase historical markers for homes. They have placed an impressive forty markers so far.

A few of the interesting homes in Pulaski are Colonial Hall, home of Confederate general John C. Brown; the two-story Federal-style Wilkinson–Martin–Sims House (1835), owned by one family for over a century; the Greek Revival Hewitt House (1830s), built to house the Pulaski Female Academy and noted for its monumental columns and cupola; the Federal-Greek Revival-style Wilkinson Place (1820), on the National Register; the two-story brick Federal-style Elisha White House (1811), scene of Indian battles and Civil War skirmishes, and used as a hospital by both armies; the Flournoy–Ballentine–Mackey House (1836), which grew from a simple four-room Federal-style house to an Italianate mansion with a grand staircase; the Knox–Dunavant House (1850), a log structure with a dog trot; the Burch–Enghlim–Overs House (1890), a Tennessee country Victorian; the Sumpter–Sordeson House (1880); the Victorian Abernathy–Rose House (1905), featuring much gingerbread woodwork; and the home of the president of Martin College (1906), a Colonial Revival house.

The historical society maintains a museum in the city library. The Old First Street Cemetery, used between 1817 and 1885, is now a historical park. Martin College, established in 1870, has a beautifully shaded campus just two blocks from downtown. Information about Pulaski's historical attractions may be obtained from the chamber of commerce.

On September 27, 1864, Forrest rode from northern Alabama to cut Sherman's supply lines. He fought a Federal force near Pulaski, then withdrew to damage the Nashville & Chattanooga Railroad. Casualties from a skirmish at Tarpley's Store, south of Pulaski on U.S. 31, are buried in a nearby cemetery. The graves are marked by a monument erected after the war by Confederate colonel V. Y. Cook.

Elkton, near the Alabama line on U.S. 31, was the birthplace of Confederate general John C. Brown, a twice-wounded divisional commander who became governor of Tennessee in the 1870s. He is buried in

Pulaski.

On the courthouse square in Lawrenceburg, to the west, is a Confederate memorial, a monument that honors the men of the town who died at Monterey, during the war with Mexico, and a statue of Davy Crockett with his rifle, "Old Betsy," in one hand and waving a coonskin cap with the other. Near Lawrenceburg is David Crockett State Park, on the site of Crockett's home from 1817–1827. Crockett operated a powder mill, grist mill, and distillery on the rapids of Shoal Creek and served in the Tennessee legislature. The grist mill has been recreated.

From the Sam Davis Monument, proceed east to the corner of the courthouse square and turn left onto U.S. 31 North–First Avenue. After 30.8 turn right onto West 7th Street. The Maury County Courthouse is directly ahead.

Maury County is one of the most historic in Tennessee. Founded in 1807, its county seat, Columbia, was established the following year. The Duck River, lined with beautiful limestone bluffs, runs through the region. The land is extremely fertile, dotted with bluegrass meadows and rolling, forested hills. The county quickly became the agricultural center of Tennessee,

The beautiful Athenaeum is a Gothic Revival house built in 1835 in Columbia.

a fact demonstrated by the several hundred fine plantation homes that remain. The county abounds in Greek Revival, Victorian, Plantation Plain, and even Italianate homes.

Early settlers, including over 100 Revolutionary War veterans whose service was rewarded with land grants in the West, crossed the mountains from the Carolinas and Virginia. General Nathaniel Greene received 25,000 acres and, although he died before taking advantage of the land, his daughter came and built a home which still stands. The remainder of the property was sold to other settlers. The grinding stone of the first mill in the county, built in 1808, can be seen at the Camp Ground Cemetery in Culleaka.

Two early paths, the Natchez Trace, connecting Nashville with Natchez, Mississippi, and the McCutchan Trace, an old Indian trail, led through this area. In 1815 Andrew Jackson's men blazed the Military Path as they moved south to fight Indians in Alabama and Florida.

During the Civil War many skirmishes were fought in Maury County. Homes and churches occupied by Union forces suffered some damage and vandalism, but, fortunately, few buildings were destroyed. During a skirmish in 1863, three of John Hunt Morgan's men were killed on the lawn of the Hurt House.

A walking tour of downtown Columbia, which boasts ninety-one surviving buildings from the 1820s or earlier, is available from the Maury County Chamber of Commerce. In the fall several guided tours of homes are offered. Of Civil War interest is the Elk's

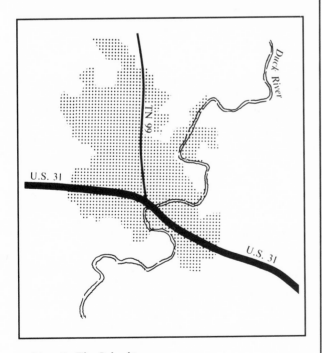

Map 40: The Columbia area.

Club, which was a private home when General Patrick Cleburne's body was brought here after the battle of Franklin. St. Peter's Church, organized in 1860, was only partially completed when it became headquarters for a Union provost marshal. In the church were held the funerals of Earl Van Dorn, after his murder at nearby Spring Hill in 1863, and of Generals Cleburne, Otho F. Strahl, and Hiram B. Granbury, three of the Confederate generals killed at Franklin. Halcyon Hall (1845) was struck by a cannonball that pierced an upstairs door. The scar is still visible.

The Greek Revival State Bank of Tennessee Building, now a private home, was the scene of impassioned secession speeches before the Civil War began. The bank closed during the war. The present courthouse, Maury County's fourth, was built in 1904. It replaced the Civil War structure, which was fortified by Union and Confederate forces as the town changed hands several times. Official records were removed for fear the courthouse would be burned. Federals used the building for a guardhouse. The building suffered so much damage that after the war it was declared the shabbiest in Tennessee. Troops drilled on the town square.

While Forrest was stationed in Columbia in 1863, he fought a duel of honor with Lieutenant Wills Gould at a downtown corner. Both men were wounded, but Gould died of a stab wound in June 1863 at the Nelson Green Tavern.

In Rose Hill Cemetery's Confederate Square is a monument honoring the Confederate dead. On top is the figure of a soldier leaning on his musket.

Zion Presbyterian Church (1849) has a small table made of wood from the first church pulpit, which pioneers brought over the mountains from South Carolina. Over 1,500 people are buried in the graveyard, including eleven Revolutionary War veterans, three soldiers from the War of 1812, and forty-seven who fought in the Civil War.

On Athenaeum Street is the Columbia Athenaeum, one of the most unusual homes in Tennessee. Built in 1837 by the Reverend Frank G. Smith, it served as the rectory of two girls' schools. The style of the house is a Moorish version of Gothic Revival. Although Smith was from Vermont, he and the school outfitted a Confederate company, the Maury Rifles. In 1973 the home was donated to the Association for the Preservation of Tennessee Antiquities and now serves as headquarters for the organization. It is open for public tours.

During the 1820s a poor young tailor opened a shop on the public square. Andrew Johnson would become

The home of James K. Polk, the eleventh president of the United States, is preserved in Columbia.

president of the United States upon Abraham Lincoln's death in 1865. Martin Van Buren spoke to the citizens of Columbia at the square when he stopped there in 1842.

An unusual monument, honoring Edward F. ("Pop") Green, a noted trainer of pacing horses, is found in a downtown park. Maury County was once the center of harness racing in Tennessee.

Columbia was the home of James K. Polk, the eleventh president of the United States, who was born in North Carolina in 1795 and moved to Maury County in 1806. While Polk was attending the University of North Carolina, his parents built this Federal-style house which he inherited.

After completing his education, Polk returned to Columbia to open a law office. He served a term in the Tennessee legislature, then was elected to seven terms in the U.S. House of Representatives. Polk was the only Speaker of the House to be elected president. He returned to Tennessee to serve as governor and was a successful dark horse presidential candidate in 1845.

The James K. Polk Home, listed on the National Register, is furnished with pieces used in the White House and also items from his law office. In the collection is the Bible used at Polk's inauguration, china and silver used at state dinners in the White House, Mrs. Polk's Parisian ball gown, and a collection of portraits.

The historic site also includes the Sisters' House next door, where two of Polk's sisters lived. It houses a museum that traces Polk's career. A detached kitchen, a fountain, and boxwood gardens are on the grounds.

Polk is also honored with a stained glass window that displays his likeness at the First Methodist Church.

Maury County was the home of four cousins of James K. Polk, the sons of Colonel William Polk, who arrived in the county in 1807. At his death, Polk's extensive property was divided equally between Leonidas, Lucius, Rufus, and George. Each built a fine plantation home, two of which survive: Lucius's Hamilton Place (1832) and George's Rattle and Snap (1845), which is considered to be one of the finest examples of Greek Revival architecture in the country.

At the point where the four properties joined, Leonidas Polk, who was the minister of St. Peter's Episcopal Church in Columbia and later was the bishop of Louisiana, built St. John's Church (1842), for the use of his brothers and their neighbors. This Gothic building is thought to be one of the last surviving plantation churches in the country. Leonidas was a West Point graduate who left the military to follow a religious calling. He was a close friend of Jefferson Davis, who made him a general in the Confederate army when the Civil War began. Polk's military legacy with the Army of Tennessee was not distinguished. He argued endlessly over orders and refused to attack or did so late on many occasions. Polk was killed by an artillery shell at Lost Mountain, near Kennesaw Mountain, during the Atlanta compaign in 1864 and is buried in Louisiana, after nearly a century's emtombment in Augusta, Georgia.

Ashwood Hall, built in 1836 by Leonidas Polk and destroyed by fire in 1874, was purchased by Andrew Polk, a brother of William Polk. Andrew had a lovely daughter, Antoinette, and the home became a social gathering place for Confederate officers. When Federals occupied the home, Antoinette overheard their plans for capturing a nearby Confederate garrison and jumped on a horse to warn them. The Federals followed in hot pursuit, but they were only able to grab a feather from her hat. Her father was severely wounded during the Civil War and, after Antoinette married into French royalty, Andrew went to Europe to live with her.

In November 1864, as the Army of Tennessee chased after Schofield, Confederate general Patrick Cleburne was impressed by the St. John's Church and its quiet cemetery. "It is almost worth dying for to be buried in such a beautiful spot," he murmured, perhaps foretelling his own death. Cleburne was killed at Franklin two days later. After a funeral in Columbia, Cleburne was indeed buried in the St. John's cemetery

but his body was later moved. Several Episcopal bishops remain buried here.

Union general Schofield made a stand in Columbia, then crossed the Duck river and decided to hold Hood there. Most of the Confederate army, minus Lee and the artillery, marched around Schofield's left flank by crossing to the east on a pontoon bridge at Davis's Ford, near Fountain Creek on TN 50, forcing Schofield to race for Spring Hill.

Beechlawn (1852) was Schofield's headquarters during his retreat to Nashville, then became Hood's command post when he and Forrest discussed isolating Schofield at Spring Hill. While he was there, Schofield promised the mistress of the house, Mrs. Cornelia Francis Warfield, that if her husband, Confederate major A. W. W. Warfield, were captured, Schofield would treat him well. Schofield escaped Hood's trap, but Major Warfield was later captured in Alabama. Schofield kept his word.

In the cemetery beside the Zion Presbyterian Church is buried Sam Watkins, a Confederate enlisted man whose memoirs, *Co. Aytch,* is one of the funniest and most honest of all Civil War books. He left Shelby County with 120 men; 12 returned. Watkins died at his nearby farm in 1901 at age sixty-seven.

Mount Pleasant has a nice Confederate monument on its public square, a statue of a soldier on guard, dedicated September 27, 1907. There are several beautiful homes, including the Lawrence–Smith House (1858), which has ruby glass in the front entrance; and Manor Hill (1855), where slave quarters and a smokehouse still stand. Nearby Arlington Cemetery marks the site of Confederate Camp Lee during the Civil War.

At Cross Bridges is Vine Hill, an enormous frame home that is one of the great American mansions. Twin staircases from two sixty-foot-long halls give access to the second floor. A unique feature is that no room in the house can be entered from another. Donated to the Maury County Historical Society in 1972 and restored, the house is listed on the National Register and has a view of five counties.

Federal soldiers guarded the railroad and vital trestles at Calleoka, where Rebel guerrillas burned the depot. Sante Fe saw a great deal of guerrilla activity. The community sponsored the Maury Light Artillery, which fought well for the Confederates at Fort Donelson.

Just east of Columbia, in Chapel Hill, is the birthplace of Nathan Bedford Forrest. A monument marks the site of the cabin where the gifted cavalry commander was born on June 13, 1821.

Return to U.S. 31 and turn right. This was the Franklin Pike on which Schofield and Hood raced to Nashville and later Hood retreated from Nashville. It passes through Spring Hill and Thompson's Station.

Spring Hill has much Civil War history. This is where Forrest maintained his headquarters, in an 1846 Greek Revival home, while recovering from his dueling wounds in 1863. Here is Oaklawn, the home of Absalom Thompson and Hood's headquarters the night Schofield marched past his sleeping army. Here is also the Martin Cheairs home, which was the headquarters of Confederate cavalry general Earl Van Dorn. On July 5, 1863, Van Dorn was killed by Dr. George Peters for allegedly having an affair with Peters's wife, Jessie. It is now part of the Tennessee Orphans Home. Hood camped here for the night of November 29, 1864.

The Saturn Corporation bought a large tract of land around Spring Hill in the mid-1980s for a massive automobile plant. They purchased the Haynes House for use as a corporate guest house, and the home of Nathaniel Cheairs, built in the 1850s, is being restored as a meeting center for the corporation and local citizens. In 1862 it was the headquarters of Union general William ("Bull") Nelson and the site of Hood's acrimonious breakfast meeting the morning after Schofield's escape. A spirited skirmish had been fought on the property the previous day. After the war ended, Richard S. Ewell, a noted general under Lee in Virginia, retired here to his final home when he married the Widow Brown (after their marriage he continued to introduce her as "my wife, the Widow Brown"). Grace Episcopal Church (1877) is a simple Gothic structure with walnut finishings and an English bell made in 1839.

The twin mysteries of Spring Hill—Van Dorn's murder and Schofield's escape—are covered in Volume VII, Issue 2, of *Blue and Gray,* now available in a commemorative issue. It has extensive driving tour information for the area.

In March 1863 two foraging Federal infantry columns from Nashville were ordered to meet at Spring Hill. One column, led by John Coburn, was hit from the front by Confederate cavalry under General Earl Van Dorn, while Forrest raced into the Union rear, capturing 1,200 men and considerable supplies at Thompson's Station. Forrest's favorite horse, Roderick, was killed in the action.

In northern Williamson County on December 17, 1864, Forrest and Lee's corps established a position along the Little Harpeth River to fight off the Federal pursuit. They drove off one Union attack; but when Federal cavalry flanked the position, the Confederates withdrew south through Franklin. Later in the day, they established a second position south of Franklin and beat off another Union assault. When Lee was wounded, General Carter Stevenson took command of the rearguard. They camped at Spring Hill that night.

After 21.8 miles from the courthouse in Columbia, turn left into the parking area at Winstead Hill, two miles south of Franklin.

Follow the stairs to the pavilion on top of the hill. An excellent metal topographical map of the area directs visitors to important features to the north. This was the view Hood had when he watched the battle of Franklin through field glasses. There were open fields and few houses between here and Franklin. More Confederate soldiers than participated in Pickett's charge at Gettysburg formed their lines at the base of the hill and stoically marched to destruction in Franklin.

Turn left onto U.S. 31 and after two miles turn left into the Carter House in Franklin.

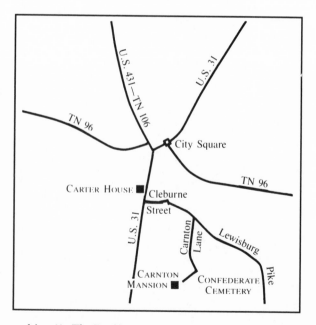

Map 41: The Franklin area.

The bodies of five Confederate generals were laid out on the back porch of Carnton following the bloody Battle of Franklin.

Fountain Branch Carter built the house in 1830. His slaves cut timber on the property and sunbaked the bricks. Note the stone caps on the ends of the gables and the beautiful double front door.

Federal general Jacob Cox, who directed the Federal defense, used the house as his headquarters. The savage fighting at Franklin erupted suddenly, leaving local inhabitants little time to flee. The Carter family and their neighbors huddled in the basement as fierce combat raged above them. The portion of the Union line that was overrun was only ninety yards south of the Carter House. Soldiers fought from the porch as bullets regularly pelted against the walls and a cannonball crashed through the house. The scars left by bullets and shells are still visible. When the battle ceased, the Carter family went out to look for a son, Tad, who was in the Army of Tennessee. Tad had fought in battles all across the West, but he was found mortally wounded fifty yards beyond the Union line on his own farmland, which he had not seen in three years. The family brought Tad into the house, where he died forty-eight hours later.

The Carter House was bought by the state of Tennessee in 1953 and preserved as a memorial to the battle of Franklin. The house and several outbuildings have been restored. Carter's wooden office building was riddled by holes, and it is said to be the most battle-scarred structure surviving from the Civil War. The bricks of the smokehouse are pitted from bullets. A twenty-five-minute narrated slide program and di-

orama in the Visitors Center–Museum illustrates the battle. Among other Civil War displays is an exhibition of medical instruments, including a saw purportedly used to amputate John Hood's leg after Chickamauga. Artifacts that belonged to the Carters illustrate the life of a farm family in the nineteenth century.

An interesting exhibit in the museum is an iron coffin, seven feet long and weighing 300 pounds, in which Colonel William Shy was buried. Shy's Hill, also a street and subdivision in suburban Nashville, commemorates the defensive position where this local officer was killed in the battle of Nashville. Shy was buried in the family cemetery nearby. After looters unearthed the grave in 1977, the police thought it was the body of a recently deceased man. Murder was suspected until tests proved that the remains were those of a very well preserved Colonel Shy, who was reburied, with appropriate ceremonies, in a new coffin.

From the Carter House turn right to retrace your steps on U.S. 31 for .1, then left onto Cleburne Street. After .3 turn right onto Lewisburg for .3, then right onto Carnton Lane. After .6 the Confederate Cemetery is immediately ahead, and the Carnton Mansion .4 down the road to the right.

Carnton (1826–28) was built by Randal McGavock, who served a term as mayor of Nashville. Mrs. Andrew Jackson helped his wife, Sarah, plan the flower garden. The house, one of the grandest in the area, was the center of McGavock's 1,000-acre plantation. His passions were breeding Thoroughbred horses and politics. Visitors to his home included two U.S. presidents—Jackson and Polk—and the first president of the independent nation of Texas—Sam Houston. The house boasts carved water tables, limestone lintels, and twenty-eight light windows. It is being restored by the Carnton Association, which welcomes visitors.

On the night of November 30, 1864, this was the rear area of Stewart's corps. Throughout the night an appalling number of wounded Southern soldiers were brought into the house, leaving the floors soaked with blood. Every inch of space in all but one room was filled with groaning, screaming men. Five dead Confederate generals were laid out on the long back porch.

The Confederate Cemetery is thought to be the only privately owned one in the nation. McGavock donated two acres adjoining his family cemetery for the burial of the Rebel dead at Franklin. At his own expense, in April 1866 the bodies of 1,481 men were

A stone Confederate soldier guards the square in historic downtown Franklin.

moved from graves on the battlefield. Following the Civil War, Confederate general Johnston L. Duncan was buried here.

Williamson County was one of the richest areas in Tennessee before the Civil War. It was the center of extensive plantations and magnificent estates established amid the beautiful hills and fields along the Harpeth River. Franklin is one of the prettiest towns in the state. It boasts of having the first three-story building in Tennessee, the first Masonic Lodge, the first Protestant Episcopal Church, and the first Methodist Conference west of the Alleghenies. Fifteen blocks of revitalized downtown buildings are listed on the National Register. Williamson County Tourism offers several useful guides.

Notable structures in town include the McPhail Office (1839), owned by Dr. Daniel McPhail and used as Federal headquarters during the battle of Franklin; the Old Factory Store (1821), which manufactured cloth and was a hospital following the battle; and the Gothic-style Hiram Masonic Lodge (1823), Tennessee's first three-story building, which suffered extensive damage during Union occupation. A claim filed with the U.S. government was paid fifty years later, the money arriving just in time to help remodel the structure.

The Williamson County Courthouse (1859) has four columns of cast iron that were mined and smelted locally. In the center of the square is a Confederate monument erected by the United Daughters of the Confederacy in 1899. Cannon are placed at each corner. The statue, a soldier at parade rest, is made of Italian marble. It is six feet, six inches tall and rests atop a tall, granite base. When the monument was unveiled on November 30, 1899, the thirty-fifth anniversary of the Battle of Franklin, 10,000 people attended the ceremonies. Among the many Confederate veterans present was General George W. Gordon, the main speaker, who had been wounded in the battle. Union soldiers saved his life by dragging him by the hair into their works.

The Maney House (1829) was the home of Mrs. Sallie Gout, an unwavering supporter of the Confederacy. While Federals occupied the town, she climbed onto her roof via a secret trap door to spy on the Yankees, then passed the information on to the Rebels. The first Confederate flag in town flew here. Following the war, Mrs. Gout organized the local U.D.C. chapter.

Scars are still visible on St. Paul's Episcopal Church (1831), which suffered heavy damage during the war. Church records and silver were buried for safe keeping across the street. While the church was being used as a Union hospital, pews and pulpits were used as firewood and horse troughs. Fires were set on the floor, and the tower became a smoke stack. Organ pipes were found scattered throughout the streets.

John Bell, presidential candidate for the Constitutional Union party in 1860, started his law practice in Franklin. This city was also home to Matthew F. Maury, remembered as the father of oceanography and the Pathfinder of the Seas. After extensive service in the U.S. Navy, he developed deadly torpedoes for the Confederacy.

The Harrison House, near Winstead Hill, was the scene of skirmishes during the summer of 1864. It was the headquarters of Federal general James D. Brownlow. John Herbert Kelly, the youngest general in the Confederacy, was wounded at the battle of Perry Station on September 7, 1864, and died in the house. Initially buried in the Harrison's garden, Kelly was reinterred in Mobile two years later. On November 30 Hood drew up his battle plans in the library, then argued bitterly with Forrest over strategy. After the battle of Franklin, wounded Confederate general John C. Carter was brought to the house. He died on December 10 and is buried in Columbia.

Fort Granger, occupied by Schofield during the battle of Franklin with 8,500 men and twenty-four guns, is on an inaccessible hill east of town. Schofield has been criticized for not being present on the battlefield, but he expected a flank attack in this area, like the one proposed by Forrest and other Confederate officers.

Along the road to Brentwood is Creekside. The

floors were so saturated with blood after it was used as a hospital that the stains could not be removed when the house was later remodeled. Forrest and his cavalry camped the night before the battle of Nashville at Green Pastures (1840). Federal troops also camped in the yard, and legend claims that a Union soldier who verbally abused the lady of the house, Mrs. Eli Hadley, was ordered shot by his commanding officer. Another home, Mooreland, was used by Federals and Confederates as a hospital.

Midway (1829), an elegant brick home, was headquarters to both armies. Several skirmishes were fought on the grounds. In 1954 the house and land became part of the Brentwood Country Club. Trenches and breastworks were found during construction of the golf course.

In the same area is Myler Manor (1840), an elaborate frame house. "E. M. Frazier, February 25, 1867," is scratched on an upstairs window. The home was used as a hospital by both armies, and it is believed that Frazier was a Federal soldier who was nursed by the women of the house. When Frazier returned after the war to marry one of the women, he etched his name on the window with her diamond engagement ring.

The Truett Place (1846) suffered some damage when Schofield rushed through on his way to Nashville, pursued by Hood. Fifty-one years later the family received a government claim check for $39.50.

East of Franklin is Century Oak (1840s). When Federal troops arrived, Samuel and Lucy Ann Wilson guided their blindfolded horses up a circular stairway to the third floor ballroom to prevent their being stolen. James Hazard Wilson II, owner of Ravenwood (1825), spent $10,000 outfitting a Confederate company.

In Brentwood on March 24, 1863, Forrest enveloped a Union garrison with a pincers movement and captured 785 men and their stores, while suffering only one killed and two wounded. Forrest was again in action on December 16, 1864, when he and Lee's corps formed a rearguard late in the evening to protect Hood's withdrawal from Nashville.

Return to the Carter House to restart the mileage, heading north on U.S. 31. After 13.6 turn left onto Battery–Harding Place in Nashville. After 2.1 turn left onto Benton Smith, and at .1, beside the historical marker to the right, is a set of stairs overgrown with vegetation.

The stairs lead to the summit of Shy's Hill, the most important spot on the thin Confederate line on the

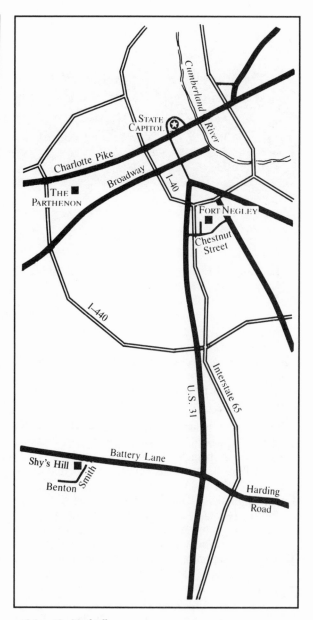

Map 42: *Nashville.*

second day of fighting at Nashville. The top of the hill has been purchased by the Tennessee Historical Society. There are trenches on the north and west sides, as well as a good view of the surrounding countryside. In the 1950s when homes were being built in this area, contractors unearthed many minié balls buried in this area.

The ruins of Union Fort Negley, which protected Nashville during the Civil War, are overgrown with trees and brush.

Return to U. S. 31 and turn left. After 3.9 turn right onto Chestnut, and after .1 turn left onto Ridley Boulevard, then right to the gates that guard the ruins of Union Fort Negley on St. Clair Hill. This is now the grounds of the Cumberland Museum and Science Center.

When Thomas began his attack against Hood on the first day of the battle of Nashville, batteries of cannon emplaced here pounded the Confederate line. On top of the hill are the remains of a reconstruction of the fort, which the WPA built during the 1930s. The position, named for Union general James S. Negley of Pennsylvania, was designed by General James St. Clair to command three pikes leading south. This European-style fort was polygonal in form and had two large bombproofs. It was constructed with logs, stone, earth, and railroad iron. The Ku Klux Klan held meetings in the fort during Reconstruction.

To the west, at Linden and Eighteenth avenues, is a hill that was an important Union defensive position. From there Thomas watched the opening battle. In Sevier Park, on Twelfth Avenue South, is Sunnyside, an outstanding example of antebellum architecture built in 1840 by Mrs. Jesse Benton. It stood between Union and Confederate lines on December 15, 1864. Struck by forty-two bullets, the house became a hospital after the battle. Near the intersection of Hillsboro Road and Hobbs Road is the site of Redoubt No. 5. Across the road is the Compton House (1849), which was also utilized as a hospital. Portions of the other four redoubts are preserved on private property. Farther out, Twelfth Avenue South becomes the old Granny White Pike. A self-guided driving tour of the battle of Nashville, prepared by the Tennessee Historical Society, is available from the Convention & Visitors Division of the Nashville Area Chamber of Commerce.

Part of the extensive Union fortifications of Nashville can be seen on the Vanderbilt University campus near the entrance on Twenty-first Avenue South. Other earthworks can be found near the historical marker at the intersection of Twenty-first Avenue South and Bernard Avenue.

Nashville is a great southern city, the home of seventeen colleges and universities and many museums and galleries. Literally dozens of tour services are available for visitors. Listings can be found in the phone book, various visitors centers scattered across the city, or from the chamber of commerce. Better yet, get a map, examine the promotional literature, and decide what *you* want to see.

The first European settlement here was made by the French, who established a trading post in 1710. During the fall of 1779 two groups of pioneers began a long journey to the salt and sulphur springs at Cedar Bluffs, which longhunters had located along the banks of the Cumberland River. One group, led by James Robertson and consisting of 300 men and boys, marched overland from the Carolinas. They crossed the frozen river on January 1, 1780, and built Fort

Along the Cumberland River near the re-created Fort Nashborough is a monument honoring city founders James Robertson and John Donelson.

During the Civil War, a stockade surrounded the Tennessee State Capitol in Nashville.

Nashborough for protection. A week later they drew up the Cumberland Compact, which organized the first civil government in the region.

The second group—250 men, women, and children led by John Donelson—built forty flatboats in East Tennessee to transport heavy supplies and floated down the Tennessee River to the Ohio River, then made their way upstream on the Cumberland. They were frozen in a river for six weeks, attacked by Indians, nearly killed by a whirlpool at what is now Chattanooga, survived thirty-five miles of rapids at Muscle Shoals, and strenuously poled their way up the Cumberland. They arrived in April 1780, after a four-month journey. With the group was Donelson's thirteen-year-old daughter Rachel, who became the wife of Andrew Jackson. In addition to Fort Nashborough, these settlers established seven other fortified stations. Indian attacks were common for several years, but the community survived and soon became a flourishing town. Fort Nashborough, occupied until 1792, was left to decay. However, it has

now been reconstructed on a smaller scale close to the original site on the riverbank. The original enclosed two acres and was four times as large as this replica. Visitors today can examine two-story cabin-blockhouses built at two corners as defensive strong points and three other cabins that illustrate different aspects of pioneer living. Costumed staff explain the life and chores of pioneers. In a park beside the fort are statues of two pioneers, with the names of the 256 settlers who signed the Cumberland Compact engraved on the side of the monument.

Nashville's growth was astonishing. By 1790 it was a manufacturing center. Development was stimulated by the arrival of the first steamboat in 1818. By 1850 a suspension bridge spanned the Cumberland River, and the Nashville, Chattanooga, & St. Louis Railroad reached the city in 1854. Because of its manufacturing and transportation facilities, Nashville was one of the most important cities in the Confederacy, but after Fort Donelson fell many families fled with the Confederate army. The state legislature relocated to Memphis with the state archives and money. On February 18, 1862, General Floyd, one of the two incompetent generals at Fort Donelson, destroyed all bridges over the river despite protests from the citizens. On February 24 Buell's army arrived.

The city remained occupied for the next three years, despite Hood's disastrous attempt to recapture it in December 1864. In March 1862 Tennessee senator Andrew Johnson, a Unionist from the eastern mountains, became its military governor and imme-

This statue group near the capitol honors Tennessee men and women who served the Confederacy.

These statues honor Tennessee veterans of a later war: Vietnam.

diately declared martial law. The city became a vital link in the North's campaigns against the Confederate West and was headquarters for many Civil War notables, including Buell, Rosecrans, Thomas, and Grant. By the end of the war, Nashville was practically denuded of trees, which had been cut for firewood, fortifications, and barracks.

Dominating the skyline of Nashville is the magnificent Tennessee state capitol on the highest hill in the city. Built by noted architect William Strickland, who designed the striking tower at Independence Hall in Philadelphia, it is considered one of the best examples of Greek Revival architecture in the United States. The locally quarried limestone blocks are four-and-one-half to seven-and-one-half feet thick. The marble in the building came from East Tennessee. Construction started in 1845 and continued until 1858. Exquisite details are found on the interior and exterior, and there is an abundance of wrought iron work. An eighty-foot tower caps the structure, and Ionic columns grace each side of the building. Interior features include a grand stairway and murals in the gubernatorial suite, on the ceilings of halls, the library, and supreme court chambers. In the library is an intricate cast iron railing and spiral staircase. The capitol, which is 236 feet long, 107 feet wide, and 206 feet tall, cost one and one-half million dollars. It is the second oldest working capitol in the country.

In accordance with his request, Strickland, who died before the building was completed in 1853, was buried in the walls. His tomb is near the north en-

trance. Buried beneath a grand monument on the grounds are President and Mrs. James K. Polk. The Polks were originally interred near their Nashville residence, but, when the house was destroyed, they were moved to this place of honor. An equestrian statue of President Andrew Jackson, by Clark Mills, is on the grounds. Two duplicates of this work are displayed at New Orleans and Washington, D.C. Another statue honors Alvin York, the humble American hero of World War I. There is also a bronze statue by Julian Zolnay of Sam Davis, the "Boy Hero of the Confederacy," erected April 30, 1909. Contributions for the statue were raised in every state, and a donation was made by former Union general G. M. Dodge, whose duty it was to sentence Davis to death.

The Legislative Plaza, directly in front of the capitol, provides a grand view of the downtown area. Here is the War Memorial Building (1925), built to honor Tennessee's World War I dead. In front of this neo-Classical structure is a bronze statue of a young man called *Victory,* which symbolizes the strength and valor of America's soldiers. The artists were Leopold Scholz, an Italian, and Nashville native Belle Kinney, who was also responsible for the Women of the Confederacy Monument. Depicting women ministering to a soldier, it was dedicated on October 10, 1921, at the nearby Memorial Plaza. In the same area is the Tennessee Vietnam Veterans Monument, designed by Nashvillian Alan LeQuire.

The War Memorial Building houses the Tennessee State Museum Military Branch, which preserves the state's military history from post-Civil War times through World War II.

Across the street in the James K. Polk Building is the Tennessee State Museum. Its collection originated with the Tennessee Historical Society (established 1849), which succeeded the Antiquarian Society (1819). The museum concentrates on Tennessee from prehistory through 1900. An extensive collection (the museum holds 6,000 historical objects) is displayed in 50,000 square feet of exhibit space. Presented here is one of the most extensive collections of Indian artifacts in the nation and outstanding displays describe the antebellum South. The Civil War in Tennessee is told in exquisite detail with an excellent assembly of relics. Other collections include paintings, furniture, silver, and quilts. Also housed here are replicas of a log cabin, tobacco barn, and grist mill. The lives of Davy Crockett, Andrew Jackson, James K. Polk, and other acclaimed Tennesseans are also explored. Daniel Boone's pocket knife, Crockett's musket, the hat Jackson wore to his inauguration, and P.G.T. Beau-

This monument commemorates Nashville men who fought for the Confederacy.

regard's hand-drawn map of Shiloh are displayed.

Nashville's Civil War monuments include the Battle of Nashville Monument, a bronze sculpture by G. Maretti. It consists of two charging horses, symbolizing the North and South, held in check by a young soldier of World War I. It was unveiled on November 11, 1927. The Frank Cheatham Bivouac Monument, depicting a weary, seated soldier, was dedicated in Centennial Park on June 19, 1908. In Confederate Circle at Mount Olivet Cemetery, the statue of a soldier, erected in 1892, stands guard atop a high base.

On Fifth Avenue South was the home of William Driver, a sea captain who retired to Nashville in 1837. He possessed a flag that had been given to him in 1831 by his mother and neighbors in Salem, Massachusetts, to fly over his ship. Touched by their gesture, Driver announced, "I will call her Old Glory." To thwart the Confederates who repeatedly searched his home for the flag, Driver sewed it inside a quilt. When the Federals occupied the city in 1862, "Old Glory" was flown at the capitol. As the story spread across the country, "Old Glory" became a popular name for the American flag.

On Eighth Avenue was the home of Hetty McEver, a staunch Unionist who flew the U.S. flag on a pole outside her house throughout the war. However, she also cared for Confederate casualties and made clothing for the soldiers. In Nashville following the Civil War, Caroline Meriwether Goodlett organized the National Daughters of the Confederacy, which became the United Daughters of the Confederacy a year later. On Sixth Avenue North is the site of a house which quartered various Union Civil War commanders, including Buell, Rosecrans, Thomas, and Grant.

In the City Cemetery (established 1820), at Fourth Avenue South and Oak Street, are buried General Richard S. Ewell, who earned his reputation with Lee in Virginia and spent his final years in Spring Hill; General Felix K. Zollicoffer, the Nashville newspaper editor whose nearsightedness caused his death at Mill Springs, Kentucky; and William Driver. James Robertson, one of Nashville's founders, eight Revolutionary War soldiers, and fourteen city mayors are among those buried here. In Mount Olivet Cemetery are buried Confederate general William B. Bate, Supreme Court Justice John Catron, and John Bell, U.S. Speaker of the House, secretary of war, senator, and presidential candidate.

Fighting during the battle of Nashville raged in a peach orchard on the property of Traveller's Rest, which was Hood's headquarters. Construction of the magnificent home was started in 1799 by one of Nashville's early settlers, John Overton, who was Andrew Jackson's law partner and campaign manager and the first U.S. Supreme Court justice from Tennessee. The original structure was expanded in 1812 and again in 1828 to a two-and-one-half-story, L-shaped mansion with sixteen rooms. Among the distinguished visitors to Traveller's Rest were Jackson, Lafayette, Sam Houston, and Nathan Bedford Forrest. Changes made in the house are illustrated in a museum that includes Indian artifacts, Civil War relics, and displays of the Victorian era. Overton's law offices have been recreated, and exhibits and audio-visual presentations laud the public service of Overton, who was a pioneer, statesman, educator, farmer, politician, and jurist. On the grounds are a number of outbuildings, including a functioning weaving house, a smokehouse, and a formal garden. Bricks made on the grounds were used in building the Maxwell House hotel in Nashville, after which the well-known brand of coffee was named. It was Theodore Roosevelt who is thought to have said, "It's good to the last drop."

The world's only full-scale replica of the Parthenon is found in Nashville's Centennial Park.

Belle Meade (1853), a plantation house built by William J. Harding, is considered one of the grandest in Tennessee. It was the center of a 5,300-acre working plantation, with one of the nation's first stables for Thoroughbred horses, complete with a racetrack. A deer park, also stocked with buffalo, was on the grounds. When the Civil War started, Tennessee governor Isham G. Harris appointed Harding to the Military and Financial Board of the state; he was responsible for distributing five million dollars for the Confederacy. Southern general James R. Chalmers made his headquarters here during the siege, and bullet scars from skirmishing that occurred early on the morning of December 15, 1864, remain on the six limestone columns on the front porch. Union soldiers shot all the deer and buffalo, confiscated tons of grain and hay, and burned miles of fencing. In 1868 Harding's daughter married Confederate cavalry general William H. Jackson, who managed the estate. In 1954 the Association for the Preservation of Tennessee Antiquities acquired the house and twenty-four acres. The organization preserves eight outbuildings, includ-

ing a carriage house that contains twenty carriages, one of the South's largest collections. The children's playhouse is being remodeled, and landscape architects are erecting period fencing. The original paint colors and intricate patterns of wallpaper are being reproduced inside the house.

The Belmont Mansion (1850s) is a magnificent Italian Renaissance villa built by Adelicia Acklen, one of the richest women in the antebellum United States. Her home was the center of Nashville social life for fifty years. Mrs. Acklen is said to have charmed officers of both armies in order to profit during the Civil War. Cotton from her plantations in Louisiana (she stocked a lake on her property in Nashville with alligators from Louisiana) was protected by Confederate soldiers and taken to market in Federal wagons, ultimately being sold in Liverpool. In 1890 the estate became a women's college and is today on the campus of Belmont College. The Grand Salon is considered the most elaborate room from antebellum Tennessee, and there are extensive collections of original marble statues and paintings. The house has a huge double staircase and thirty-two rooms. Several outbuildings, including a playhouse and bowling alley, remain; and on the impressive grounds is the largest collection of garden ornaments in the nation. The house is open to visitors.

In Centennial Park stands a unique attraction, the massive Parthenon. Because Nashville was already known as the "Athens of the South," the city built a wood and stucco replica of the fifth century B.C. Greek temple for the Tennessee Centennial Exposition in 1897. The exhibit proved so popular that a full-scale concrete replica, the only one in the world, was constructed. It is 228 feet long, 101 feet wide, and 65 feet high. This Parthenon is identical in every detail to the original. Among the many outstanding details are fifty-four classical statues by Scholz and Belle. Also displayed are plaster cast replicas of the Elgin Marbles, fragments of statuary which adorned the Greek Parthenon that are now in the British Museum.

Just completed is a statue of Athena Parthenas, goddess of wisdom, like the one which stood in the original Parthenon. This forty-two-foot-high work of art, the largest indoor statue in the Western world, was created by Alan LeQuire during an eight-year effort. In the statue's left hand is a shield seventeen feet in diameter, and in the outstretched right hand is a six-foot-high statue of the goddess Nike.

On display in the western part of Centennial Park are a pair of solid iron rollers, three feet in diameter and one foot thick, that were used to grind gunpowder. These once produced powder at the Augusta, Georgia, Confederate Powder Works, the largest facility in the nation. In 1868 all the machinery was moved to Sycamore, Tennessee, where the factory supplied one hundred families with jobs until 1906. Nearby is a bronze sculpture group by Julian Zolany with two tablets engraved with the names of Nashville's World War I dead.

Near the ruins of Fort Negley is the Cumberland Science Museum, with its many hands-on displays for children and the Sudekum Planetarium, where laser light and sound presentations transport viewers into the universe.

Other interesting places to visit in Nashville include the Oscar Farris Agricultural Museum at the Ellington Agricultural Center, which has an extensive collection of home and farm artifacts that illustrate the self-sufficient rural life of the 1800s and early 1900s; the Nashville Toy Museum, which includes an entire room of rare toy trains; the Museum of the Americas, which displays Indian artifacts and a collection of rare firearms; the Upper Room, which features a wood carv-ing depicting Leonardo da Vinci's mural, *The Last Supper*; and Cheekwood, a three-story, fifty-room Georgian mansion built as an elegant private estate by Leslie Cheek, founder of Maxwell House Coffee. On fifty-five surrounding acres are the Tennessee Botanical Gardens; and in Botanical Hall are a tropical atrium and sculpture fountains.

The Metropolitan Historical Commission has prepared an excellent tour of the art and architecture to be found in downtown Nashville. It includes William Strickland's Downtown Presbyterian Church (1851), one of the few Egyptian Revival structures in the United States; St. Mary's Roman Catholic Church (1845–47), the first permanent Catholic church in the state and Nashville's oldest surviving church building; Christ Church Episcopal, a pure Victorian Gothic; the castle-like Customs House (1877), its cornerstone laid by President Rutherford B. Hayes; the Victorian Romanesque Union Station (1900), built for the Louisville & Nashville Railroad, a National Historic Landmark recently opened as a 125-room luxury hotel; and the wonderful Victorian Gothic Ryman Auditorium. Built with money raised by riverboat captain Tom Ryman, who despite his best intentions was saved at a tent meeting, this was originally a non-denominational revival hall called the Union Gospel Tabernacle. Famed evangelist Billy Sunday, pioneer black educator Booker T. Washington, feminist Carrie Nation, and inspirational Helen Keller spoke in the Ryman; and Caruso, Sarah Bernhardt, Helen Hayes, and Isadora Duncan performed here. For thirty years, from 1943 until 1974, the Grand Ole Opry was broadcast live from the auditorium, which became known as the "Mother Church of Country Music."

One cannot write of Nashville without mentioning its role as Music City. This is the home of country music and the Grand Ole Opry, which originated in 1925. Through war and peace, prosperity and depression, the Grand Ole Opry has never missed a Saturday night broadcast. The Ryman Auditorium closed in 1974 (though it is open for tours) when the Opry moved to Opryland USA, a 120-acre theme park just east of the city. At its new home, visitors can watch live musical shows, view the taping of The Nashville Network television programs, enjoy over twenty state-of-the-art rides, and take journeys on two riverboats.

Nashville and the Middle Tennessee area are filled with interesting places to visit and things to do. Promotional literature is widely available in hotels, motels, restaurants, and tourist locations area-wide. ■

Conclusion

Popular study of the Civil War focuses on Virginia. There the mighty Army of Northern Virginia, led by the resourceful Robert E. Lee, fought valiantly against the superior numbers of the Army of the Potomac, which was ineptly led by an odd assortment of incompetent commanders. Those eastern battles—Manassas, the Seven Days, Antietam, Fredericksburg, Chancellorsville, Gettysburg, the Wilderness, and Petersburg—were titanic affairs. Some of them were classic examples of warfare long studied in military colleges around the world. Examined in the full context of the Civil War, however, those were mere holding actions, vicious sideshows to the dramatic campaigns that were waged west of the Appalachian Mountains.

In the East, successive attempts to destroy the Southern army and capture the Confederate capital at Richmond were always parried, but Lee never had the strength to threaten the North seriously. His was a savage, four-year-long stalemate that only ended when factors from the western theater came into play. U. S. Grant, after honing his bloody skills in the West, came east to bludgeon the Confederacy into submission. Accompanying him was Philip Sheridan, another man unfettered by any romantic notion of war. While Grant battered enemy forces, Sheridan destroyed the Shenandoah Valley and made Virginians, military and civilians, hungry.

The Army of Northern Virginia received the bulk of its food from the West. While the Army of Tennessee starved in a land of plenty, government agents stripped Tennessee and the deep South states of provisions. When Tennessee was secured for the Union, Lee's troops began to grow hungry. When Georgia fell to William Sherman, soldiers in the East began to starve.

Richmond was an important industrial city, but much of Lee's munitions, clothing, and other essential materiel was manufactured in western cities, such as Nashville, Chattanooga, Atlanta, Columbus, Augusta, and Selma. When these cities were overrun and the railroads that transported their products were destroyed, the Army of Northern Virginia lost the means it needed to continue the struggle.

Many soldiers in the East came from beyond the Appalachians. Georgians, Texans, Alabamians, Mississippians, and others fought bravely for Lee. When their homes were destroyed and their families placed in harm's way, the Westerners left the army to protect their hearths.

In March 1865 Richmond was in Confederate hands and the Army of

Northern Virginia, although substantially reduced in strength, was intact. But to the west, Kentucky and Tennessee had long been subdued, the Mississippi River was open to Federal commerce, portions of Mississippi and Louisiana were in Union hands, the produce of Alabama was rendered useless for lack of transportation, Georgia and South Carolina still smoldered, and William Sherman was ripping through North Carolina. This almost complete destruction of the Confederate West is what brought about the end of the war; Lee's surrender at Appomattox was a practical recognition of the futility of continuing the war.

Those hallowed eastern battlefields have their place in history, but the western campaigns deserve more attention than they usually receive in the study of Civil War history. While the Confederate West functioned, it fed and armed the Virginia armies. When the West finally collapsed, the Confederacy died. ■

Appendix A ■ Chronology

1862

October 30. Union general William Rosecrans is given command of the Army of the Ohio, following the relief of General Don Carlos Buell for failure to pursue the Confederate Army of the Mississippi after the battle of Perryville, Kentucky.

November 24. Confederate president Jefferson Davis appoints General Joseph E. Johnston commander of the western theater and renames General Braxton Bragg's force the Army of Tennessee.

December 10. Davis visits the Confederate camp at Murfreesboro, Tennessee. He orders Johnston to send a quarter of Bragg's troops to reinforce Vicksburg.

December 26. Rosecrans advances the newly renamed Army of the Cumberland from Nashville.

December 29. Rosecrans finds Bragg drawn up along Stone's River. Confederate cavalry general Joseph Wheeler destroys 500 wagons in Rosecrans's rear.

December 31. Bragg's fierce attack almost breaks Rosecrans's line at Stone's River, but at great cost.

1863

January 2. An ill-advised Confederate attack against the Union left flank at Stone's River is thrown back with terrible losses.

January 3. Bragg evacuates Murfreesboro and withdraws to establish a line of defense along the Duck River from Manchester to Shelbyville.

May 23. Rosecrans launches a complex offensive against Bragg's Duck River line which completely bewilders the Confederates.

May 27. Union general George Thomas occupies Manchester as Bragg withdraws to the south.

July 1. Bragg establishes a line along the Elk River near Winchester.

August 4. Union secretary of war Edwin Stanton orders Buell to continue the pursuit.

August 9. Confederate general James Longstreet's first units leave Virginia for Chattanooga.

August 15. Union general Ambrose Burnside moves against the Confederates at Cumberland Gap and East Tennessee.

August 16. Rosecrans renews his advance against Chattanooga, a vital railroad center.

August 21. While Rosecrans flanks Chattanooga to the southwest, a small Federal unit shells Chattanooga.

August 29–September 4. Rosecrans's army crosses the Tennessee River at Shellmound, Bridgeport, and Caperton's Ferry.

September 2. Burnside occupies Knoxville.

September 4. Bragg retreats across the Tennessee River and enters Chattanooga.

September 7. The Confederates surrender Cumberland Gap.

September 8. Bragg abandons Chattanooga and retreats further south.

September 9. Union general Thomas Crittenden occupies Chattanooga while Bragg concentrates his forces at La Fayette, Georgia.

September 10. Confederate generals D. H. Hill and Leonidas Polk fail to attack Thomas in McLemore's Cove.

September 12. Polk fails to attack Crittenden near Lee and Gordon's Mill.

September 13–17. Rosecrans orders his army to assemble at Lee and Gordon's Mill.

September 18. Confederates cross Chickamauga Creek and take up position to attack Rosecrans. General John Hood's division of Longstreet's corps arrives from Virginia.

September 19. A savage, day-long battle erupts along the La Fayette Road near Chickamauga Creek as units are thrown piecemeal into the fray. Rosecrans's line is threatened several times, but the attacks are beaten off.

September 20. During the night, Longstreet arrives after a long journey from Virginia. In the morning, Polk's corps is decimated in attacks against Union log breastworks, but in the early afternoon three divisions led by Longstreet break through a hole accidentally left in the Union line. Half the Federal army flees to Chattanooga, but Thomas prevents its total destruction with a valiant stand at Snodgrass Hill.

September 22. After rejecting his officers' advice to move immediately on Chattanooga, Bragg slowly advances to besiege the city, which Rosecrans has heavily fortified. The Confederates take position on Lookout Mountain and Missionary Ridge, overlooking the city.

September 24. Union general Joseph Hooker begins a long trip from the Army of the Potomac in Virginia to reinforce Rosecrans.

September 28. Rosecrans brings charges against two corps commanders, Alexander McCook and Crittenden, for their actions at Chickamauga.

September 29. General-in-chief Henry Halleck orders General U. S. Grant, in Mississippi, to reinforce Chattanooga.

October 2. Hooker's troops begin arriving at Bridgeport, Alabama.

October 9. Jefferson Davis arrives at Confederate headquarters in an attempt to make peace among Bragg's nearly mutinous generals.

October 10. Davis meets with Bragg and his officers, who voice the opinion that their commander should be removed from command.

October 11. Longstreet's offer to resign is declined by Davis; Union general William T. Sherman's men leave Memphis for Chattanooga.

October 17. Grant is appointed commander of all Union forces in the West.

October 19. Grant relieves Rosecrans of command of the Army of the Cumberland, replacing him with Thomas.

October 23. After traveling from Nashville via Stevenson and Bridgeport, Grant suffers the arduous trek over Walden's Ridge, to enter besieged Chattanooga; Polk is reassigned to Mississippi.

October 27. By capturing Brown's Ferry with a combination land–amphibious force, the Federals open a supply line across Moccasin Bend to Bridgeport.

October 29. In the early morning hours, John W. Geary's divisions repulse Longstreet's attack at Wauhatchie.

October 31. The "Cracker Line" is open.

November 4. In an ill-advised, politically motivated move, Longstreet's corps, with Wheeler's cavalry, is sent to recapture Knoxville.

November 14. Sherman's vanguard reaches Bridgeport.

November 15. Longstreet arrives at the Tennessee River and attempts to cut Burnside off from his refuge in Knoxville.

November 16. Burnside wins the race to Lenoir's Station and just reaches Campbell's Station before the Confederates arrive in a second attempt to isolate him.

November 17. Burnside safely enters the fortifications of Knoxville.

November 20. After a long march from Vicksburg and Memphis, Sherman arrives in Chattanooga with additional reinforcements.

November 23. To determine if Bragg has withdrawn from Missionary Ridge, Grant sends Thomas to capture Orchard Knob. The successful attack alarms Bragg, who recalls General Patrick Cleburne's division from the railroad depot.

November 24. Hooker attacks the thinly held Confederate lines on Lookout Mountain in the legendary "Battle above the Clouds." After severe fighting at the Cravens' House, Bragg decides he cannot hold Lookout. The position is abandoned during the night. Sherman bridges the Tennessee River and positions his troops to attack Missionary Ridge.

November 25. When Sherman's fierce attacks against the northern end of Missionary Ridge are defeated by Cleburne, Grant orders Thomas to capture Confederate rifle pits at the base of the mountain. The Federals continue up Missionary Ridge and shatter Bragg's line, forcing the Confederates to retreat thirty miles to Dalton, Georgia.

November 26. Cleburne's fierce rearguard action at Ringgold, Georgia, halts the Union pursuit. Grant sends Sherman to reinforce Burnside in Knoxville.

November 29. Following an ineffective siege, Longstreet attacks Fort Sanders at Knoxville, but is repulsed with heavy losses.

December 1. At his own request, Bragg is relieved of duty. Davis brings the controversial general to Richmond to serve as his military adviser. General William J. Hardee assumes temporary command of the Army of Tennessee.

December 4. Sherman's Army of the Tennessee approaches Knoxville. Unable to capture the city, and realizing his force is no match for Sherman, Longstreet withdraws into East Tennessee for the winter.

December 6. Sherman enters Knoxville.

December 9. Burnside asks to be relieved of duty.

December 27. Joseph E. Johnston arrives in Dalton to lead the Army of Tennessee.

1864

March 2. Grant is promoted to the rank of lieutenant general and placed in charge of all Union armies.

March 17. Grant announces he will accompany the Army of the Potomac in Virginia to destroy General Robert E. Lee's Army of Northern Virginia. He places his trusted subordinate, Sherman, in command of all armies in the West.

April to October. Sherman invades Georgia with three armies: the Army of the Cumberland, the Army of the Tennessee, and the Army of the Ohio, some 120,000 men. After a series of battles in a campaign known for its classic maneuvering, Sherman arrives outside Atlanta in early July. Davis removes Johnston from command, replacing him with General John B.

Hood. After four disastrous attacks, Hood evacuates Atlanta on September 1. In October the Confederates march north to disrupt Sherman's supply lines.

October 3. Sherman leaves Atlanta in pursuit of Hood. Thomas arrives in Nashville to defend against a Confederate invasion of Tennessee.

October 22. Hood reaches Gadsden, Alabama, planning to cross the Tennessee River at Guntersville. Sherman arrives at Gaylesburg, near the Georgia border.

October 26. Finding Guntersville and Decatur strongly held by Federal garrisons, Hood continues farther west.

October 27. Sherman abandons the chase and returns to Georgia to organize his March to the Sea.

October 30. At Tuscumbia, Hood finally crosses the Tennessee River to Florence, where he waits for Confederate cavalry general Nathan Bedford Forrest to return from a raid in West Tennessee. The Confederates are idle until November 19. Sherman dispatches General John Schofield to reinforce Thomas at Nashville.

November 1. Troops under Union general Alfred Smith arrive from Missouri to reinforce Thomas in Nashville.

November 14. Schofield arrives to command 18,000 soldiers in Pulaski, where Thomas expects Hood will begin his invasion of Tennessee.

November 22. Hood marches quickly from the southeast toward Columbia, hoping to cut Schofield off from Nashville. Schofield discovers Hood's movement and races toward Columbia.

November 24. Schofield's advance guard occupies Columbia minutes before Forrest arrives.

November 28. During the night Schofield abandons Columbia and occupies a position north of the Duck River. Hood decides to cross the Duck River north of Schofield and occupy Spring Hill to trap the Federals to the south.

November 29. Deceived by a demonstration south of Columbia, Schofield barely reaches Spring Hill before Confederate forces close their trap. During the night he sneaks past Hood's sleeping army.

November 30. Hood, infuriated to find Schofield gone, attacks stout defenses at Franklin. He loses almost 7,000 men and 6 generals. Schofield reaches Nashville that night.

December 1. Hood arrives outside Nashville and establishes a short, thin siege line.

December 4. Hood orders Forrest's cavalry to Murfreesboro, hoping Thomas will weaken his army to reinforce the city.

December 14. After extensive preparations, delayed by ice storms and a lack of mounts for his cavalry, Thomas issues orders to attack Hood on the following day.

December 15. Thomas crushes Hood and throws the Confederate army back several miles.

December 16. When Thomas renews his attack, Hood's line is shattered and the Confederates begin a hasty retreat.

December 17–24. Protected by Forrest's fierce rearguard actions, Hood retreats from Tennessee, hounded by a large force of Union troopers.

December 25–29. Hood crosses the Tennessee River. Thomas cancels the pursuit.

1865

January 10. The Army of Tennessee limps into Tupelo, Mississippi, at the end of the Nashville campaign.

January 13. Hood asks to be relieved of duty.

January 23. Davis relieves Hood of command.

March 19–21. After Hood's resignation, Joseph Johnston is returned to command the Army of Tennessee. The pitiful remnants rush to the Carolinas to oppose Sherman. The last battle of the western armies occurs at Bentonville, North Carolina. After Sherman blunts Johnston's attack, the Confederates withdraw.

April 26. Johnston surrenders to Sherman, and the Army of Tennessee is disbanded.

Appendix B ■ Resources

Basic State Resources

Tennessee

Tennessee Tourist Development, Post Office Box 23170, Nashville, Tennessee 37202-3170. (615) 741-2158. (Ask for these three valuable guides: *Tennessee Historic Places; Tennessee Scenic Parkway System;* and *Tennessee State Parks.*

Alabama

Alabama Bureau of Tourism and Trade, 532 South Perry Street, Montgomery, Alabama 36104. (205) 261-4169; (800) ALABAMA.

Alabama Department of Conservation and National Resources, Alabama State Parks, Division, 64 North Union Street, Montgomery, Alabama 36130. (205) 261-3334.

Georgia

Georgia Department of Industry, Trade, & Tourism, 285 Peachtree Center Avenue, Suite 1000, Atlanta, Georgia 30303. (404) 656-3590.

Georgia Department of Natural Resources, Office of Information, 270 Washington Street, Southwest, Atlanta, Georgia 30334. (404) 656-3530.

Georgia Travel Publications, Inc., 600 West Peachtree Street, Suite 1500, Atlanta, Georgia 30308. (404) 874-5745.

Georgia State Parks & Historic Sites, 205 Butler Street, Southeast, Atlanta, Georgia 30334. (404) 656-2753.

Map Resources

As always, we advise the adventurous traveler to secure county maps from the states. These maps will enable you to keep up with the tour on maps and will be invaluable if you decide to stray off the tour route or accidentally zig when you should have zagged.

County maps for Tennessee are available from the Tennessee Department of Transportation, Map Sales Office, Suite 300, James K. Polk Building, 505 Deaderick Street, Nashville, Tennessee 37243-0345. (615) 741-2195. Tennessee has a wonderful deal. For $25.00 plus $3.00 handling cost, you can have a complete set of all 95 Tennessee counties (specify:

Scale 1" = 2 miles, 18" x 24"). Individual maps are 50 cents each. Maps needed for our tours are Blount, Bradley, Coffee, Davidson, Franklin, Giles, Hamilton, Knox, Loudon, McMinn, Maury, Monroe, Rutherford, and Williamson.

For Alabama county maps write the State of Alabama Highway Department, 1409 Coliseum Boulevard, Room R–109, Montgomery, Alabama 36130. Attention: Map Sales Office. (205) 261-6071. The maps cost $1.10 each (including postage; specify 1" = 2 miles). The single county we travel is Jackson.

County maps are available for the state of Georgia at $1.50 each from the Department of Transportation, 2 Capital Square, Atlanta, Georgia 30334. The counties involved are Catoosa, Dade, and Walker.

Good city maps of Nashville, Knoxville, and Chattanooga are also essential.

Resources for a Driving Tour of Stone's River

Each resource appears in the order in which it is needed on the tour.

Sam Davis Home, 1500 Sam Davis Road, Smyrna, Tennessee 37167. (615) 459-4353.

Stone's River National Battlefield Park, Route 10, Box 495, 3501 Old Nashville Highway, Murfreesboro, Tennessee 37129. (615) 893-9501.

The Rutherford County Chamber of Commerce, Post Office Box 864, South Front Street, Murfreesboro, Tennessee 37133. (615) 893-6565.

Cannonsburg Pioneer Village, South Front Street, Murfreesboro, Tennessee 37133. (615) 893-6565.

Oaklands Mansion, Post Office Box 432, 900 North Maney Avenue, Murfreesboro, Tennessee 37133-0432. (615) 893-6565.

Greater Nashville Regional Council, 7th Floor, Stahlman Building, 211 Union Street, Nashville, Tennessee 37201. (615) 259-5491. (For brochure, *Middle Tennessee Country*).

Resources for a Driving Tour of the Chickamauga Campaign

Each resource appears in the order in which it is needed on the tour.

Greater Nashville Regional Council, 7th Floor, Stahlman Building, 211 Union Street, Nashville, Tennessee 37201. (615) 259-5491. (For brochure, *Middle Tennessee Country*).

Stone's River National Battlefield Park, Route 10, Box 495, Murfreesboro, Tennessee 37129. (615) 893-9501.

The Rutherford County Chamber of Commerce, Post Office Box 864, South Front Street, Murfreesboro, Tennessee 37133. (615) 893-6565.

Old Stone Fort State Park, Stone Fort Drive–Highway 41 North, Route 2, Manchester, Tennessee 37355. (615) 728-0751.

Manchester Chamber of Commerce, 305 Murfreesboro Highway, Manchester, Tennessee 37355. (615) 983-2441.

Franklin County Chamber of Commerce, Post Office Box 280, Winchester, Tennessee 37398. (615) 967-6788.

Old Jail Museum, 400 First Avenue Northeast, Winchester, Tennessee 37398. (615) 967-0528.

Tims Ford State Park, Route 4, Winchester, Tennessee 37398. (615) 967-4457.

The Cowan Connection, Post Office Box 321, Cowan, Tennessee 37318.

Cowan Railroad Museum, off U.S. 64–41A, Cowan, Tennessee 37318. (615) 967-7233.

Scottsboro–Jackson County Chamber of Commerce, Post Office Box 973, 134 East Peachtree Street, Scottsboro, Alabama 35768. (205) 259-5500.

La Fayette Area Chamber of Commerce, 304 North Main Street (Gordon Hall), La Fayette, Georgia 30723.

Gordon–Lee Mansion, 217 Cove Road, Chickamauga, Georgia 30707. (404) 375-4728.

Chickamauga & Chattanooga National Military Park, Post Office Box 2128, Fort Oglethorpe, Georgia 30707. (404) 866-9241.

Resources for a Driving Tour of the Siege of Chattanooga

Each resource appears in the order in which it is needed on the tour.

Chattanooga Convention & Visitors Bureau, 1001 Market Street, Chattanooga, Tennessee 37402. (615) 756-2121. (800) 338-3999 (within Tennessee); (800) 322-3344 (outside Tennessee).

The John Ross House Association, Post Office Box 863, Rossville, Georgia 30741.

Rossville Area Chamber of Commerce, Post Office Box 31, Rossville, Georgia 30741. (404) 866-7404.

Chickamauga & Chattanooga National Military Park, Post Office Box 2128, Fort Oglethorpe, Georgia 30742. (404) 866-9241.

Point Park, 1101 Brow Road, Lookout Mountain, Tennessee 37350. (615) 821-7786.

Cravens' House, Cravens Terrace, Chattanooga, Tennessee 37409. (615) 821-6161.

Chattanooga National Cemetery, 1200 Bailey Avenue, Post Office Box 1111, Chattanooga, Tennessee 37404. (615) 855-6590.

Rock City Gardens, 1400 Patten Road, Lookout Mountain, Georgia 37350. (404) 820-2531.

Ruby Falls, Route 4, Scenic Highway, Chattanooga, Tennessee 37409. (615) 266-3406.

Incline Railway, 827 East Brow Road, Lookout Mountain, Tennessee 37350. (615) 821-9403.

Raccoon Mountain Caverns, Route 4, Cummings Highway, Chattanooga, Tennessee 37409. (615) 821-9403.

Medal of Honor Museum/Hall of Valor, Auditorium, 399 McCallie Avenue, Chattanooga, Tennessee 37402. (615) 267-1737.

Chattanooga Regional History Museum, 400 Chestnut Street, Chattanooga, Tennessee 37402. (615) 265-3247.

Tennessee Valley Railroad Museum, 4119 Cromwell Road, Chattanooga, Tennessee 37421. (615) 894-8028.

Confederama, 3742 Tennessee Avenue, Chattanooga, Tennessee 37409. (615) 821-2812.

Lookout Mountain Museum, Park Place, 1110 East Brow Road, Lookout Mountain, Tennessee 37350. (615) 821-7980.

TVA Energy Center, 1101 Market Street, Chattanooga, Tennessee 37402. (615) 267-7599.

Booker T. Washington State Recreation Park, Route 2, Box 369, Chattanooga, Tennessee 37416. (615) 894-4955.

Harrison Bay State Recreational Park, Route 2, Box 118, Harrison, Tennessee 37341. (615) 344-6214.

Resources for a Driving Tour of the Knoxville Campaign

Each resource appears in the order in which it is needed on the tour.

Chattanooga Convention & Visitors Bureau, 1001 Market Street, Chattanooga, Tennessee 37402. (615) 756-2121. (800) 338-3999 (within Tennessee); (800) 322-3344 (outside Tennessee).

Cleveland–Bradley Tourist & Convention Bureau, Post Office Box 2275, 2100 Keith Street, Cleveland, Tennessee 37320-2275. (615) 472-6587.

Red Clay State Historic Area, Route 6, Box 734, Cleveland, Tennessee 37311. (615) 472-2627; (615) 472-5324.

Primitive Settlement, Route 11, Box 962, Cleveland, Tennessee 37311. (615) 476-5096.

Cherokee National Forest, Post Office Box 2010, 2800 North Ocoee Street, Cleveland, Tennessee 37320. (615) 476-9700.

Athens Area Chamber of Commerce, 13 North Jackson Street, Athens, Tennessee 37303. (615) 745-0334.

Loudon County Visitors Bureau, Route 1, Box 435, 1060 U.S. Highway 321, Lenoir City, Tennessee 37771. (615) 986-6822.

Lost Sea, Route 2, Lost Sea Pike, Sweetwater, Tennessee 37874. (615) 337-6616.

Monroe County Tourism Council, 110 Locust Street, Madisonville, Tennessee 37354. (615) 442-4588.

Fort Loudon State Historical Area, Route 2, Box 565, Venore, Tennessee 37885. (615) 884-6217.

Roane County Chamber of Commerce, Post Office Box 666, 501 North Kentucky Street, Kingston, Tennessee 37763. (615) 376-5572.

Knoxville Convention & Visitors Bureau, 500 Henley Street, Post Office Box 15012, Knoxville, Tennessee 37901. (615) 523-7263.

Middle East Tennessee Tourism Council, Post Office Box 19806, Knoxville, Tennessee 37939-2806.

Confederate Memorial Hall (Bleak House), 3148 Kingston Pike Southwest, Knoxville, Tennessee 37919. (615) 522-2371.

James White's Fort Association, 205 East Hill Avenue, Knoxville, Tennessee 37915. (615) 525-6514.

Blount Mansion, Post Office Box 170, 200 West Hill Street, Knoxville, Tennessee 37901. (615) 525-2378.

Maryville Chamber of Commerce, 309 South Washington Street, Maryville, Tennessee 37801. (615) 983-2241.

Sam Houston Schoolhouse, Sam Houston Schoolhouse Road, Maryville, Tennessee 37801. (615) 983-1550.

Smoky Mountain Visitors Bureau, 1004 Smoky Mountain Highway, Thompson–Brown House, Maryville, Tennessee 37801. (615) 984-6200.

Great Smoky Mountains National Park, U.S. 441, Gatlinburg, Tennessee 37738. (615) 436-1200.

Oak Ridge Convention & Visitors Center, Post Office Box 160, Oak Ridge, Tennessee 37830-0160. (615) 482-7821.

Resources for a Driving Tour of Hood's Tennessee Invasion

Each resource appears in the order it is needed on the tour.

Pulaski–Giles County Chamber of Commerce, Municipal Building, Pulaski, Tennessee 38478. (615) 363-3789.

David Crockett State Park, Post Office Box 398, Lawrenceburg, Tennessee 38464. (615) 762-9408.

Columbia–Maury County Chamber of Commerce, Post Office Box 1076, Columbia, Tennessee 38402-1076. (615) 388-2155.

Columbia Main Street, Post Office Box 1940, 20 Public Square, Columbia, Tennessee 38402-1940. (615) 388-3647.

James K. Polk Home, West Seventh Street, Columbia, Tennessee 38401. (615) 388-2354.

Williamson County Tourism, Post Office Box 156, 109 Second Avenue South, Suite 107, Franklin, Tennessee 37065-0156. (615) 794-1225.

Downtown Franklin Association, Post Office Box 807, Franklin, Tennessee 37064. (615) 790-7094.

Heritage Foundation (Visitors Information Center), East Main Street–U.S. 31), Post Office Box 723, Franklin, Tennessee 37064. (615) 790-0378.

Carter House, Post Office Box 555, 1140 Columbia Avenue, Franklin, Tennessee 37065-0555. (615) 791-1861.

Carnton Mansion, The Carnton Association, Inc., Carnton Lane, Franklin, Tennessee 37064. (615) 794-0903.

Nashville Area Chamber of Commerce, 161 Fourth Avenue North, Nashville, Tennessee 37219. (615) 259-4700.

Tourist Information Center, James Robertson Parkway (Exit off I–65 at Exit No. 85). (615) 259-4747.

Nashville International Airport Welcome Center, One Terminal Drive, Suite 501, Nashville, Tennessee. (615) 275-1674; (615) 275-1675.

Greater Nashville Regional Council, 7th Floor, Stahlman Building, 211 Union Street, Nashville, Tennessee 37201. (615) 259-5491.

Metropolitan Historical Commission, 701 Broadway, Nashville, Tennessee 37203. (615) 259-5029.

Historical Commission of Metropolitan Nashville and Davidson County, 701 Broadway, Nashville 37203. (615) 259-5027.

Tennessee State Museum, Polk Cultural Center, 505 Deaderick Street, Nashville, Tennessee 37243-1120. (615) 741-2692.

Tennessee State Capitol, c/o Tennessee State Museum, Polk Cultural Center, 505 Deaderick Street, Nashville, Tennessee 37243-1120. (615) 741-0830.

Belle Meade Mansion, 110 Leake Avenue, Nashville, Tennessee 37205. (615) 352-7350.

Belmont Mansion, Belmont College, 1900 Belmont Boulevard, Nashville, Tennessee 37212. (615) 268-9537.

Fort Nashborough, 170 First Avenue North, Nashville, Tennessee 37201. (615) 255-8192.

Cumberland Science Museum, 800 Ridley Boulevard, Nashville, Tennessee 37203. (615) 259-6099.

Bibliography

Abbazia, Patrick. *The Chickamauga Campaign: December 1862–November 1863*. Bryn Mawr, Pennsylvania: Combined Books, 1989.

Ambrose, Stephen E. *Halleck: Lincoln's Chief of Staff*. Baton Rouge: Louisiana State University Press, 1962.

Buck, Irving A. *Cleburne and His Command*. Dayton: Morningside Bookshop, 1982.

Catton, Bruce. *Never Call Retreat*. Garden City: Doubleday and Company, 1965.

Cleaves, Freeman. *Rock of Chickamauga: The Life of Major General George H. Thomas*. Norman: University of Oklahoma Press, 1948.

Commager, Henry Steele. *The Blue and the Gray*. New York: The Fairfax Press, 1982.

Connelly, Thomas L. *Autumn of Glory: The Army of Tennessee, 1862–1865*. Baton Rouge: Louisiana State University Press, 1971.

Cox, Jacob D. *The March to the Sea—Franklin and Nashville*. New York: Charles Scribner's Sons, 1906.

Davis, William C. *Breckinridge: Statesman, Soldier, Symbol*. Baton Rouge: Louisiana State University Press, 1974.

———. *The Orphan Brigade*. Baton Rouge: Louisiana State University Press, 1980.

Downey, Fairfax. *Storming the Gateway: Chattanooga 1863*. New York: David McKay Co., Inc., 1960.

DuBose, John W. *General Joseph Wheeler and the Army of Tennessee*. New York: Neale, 1912.

Duke, Basil W. *Morgan's Cavalry*. Bloomington: The University of Indiana Press, 1960.

Foote, Shelby. *The Civil War, a Narrative: Fredericksburg to Meridian*. New York: Random House, 1963.

———. *The Civil War, a Narrative: Red River to Appomattox.* New York: Random House, 1974.

Grant, Ulysses S. *Personal Memoirs of U. S. Grant.* New York: Charles L. Webster and Company, 1885.

Harrison, Lowell H. *The Civil War in Kentucky.* Lexington: The University Press of Kentucky, 1975.

Hood, John B. *Advance and Retreat.* Bloomington: Indiana University Press, 1952.

Horn, Stanley F. *The Army of Tennessee.* Norman: University of Oklahoma Press, 1953.

———. *The Decisive Battle of Nashville.* Baton Rouge: Louisiana State University Press, 1956.

Johnson, Robert U., and Clarence C. Buel, editors. *Battles and Leaders of the Civil War. Volume 3: Retreat from Gettysburg. Volume 6: The Way to Appomattox.* New York: The Century Company, 1884, 1888.

Johnston, Joseph E. *Narrative of Military Operations.* Bloomington: Indiana University Press, 1959.

Kentucky: A Guide to the State. New York: Viking Press, 1939.

Knapp, David. *The Confederate Horsemen.* New York: Vantage Press, 1966.

Lamar, William M. *The Edge of Glory: A Biography of General William S. Rosecrans.* New York: Harcourt, Brace, and World, Inc., 1961.

McDonough, James L. *Chattanooga—A Death Grip on the Confederacy.* Knoxville: The University of Tennessee Press, 1984.

———. *Stone's River: Bloody Winter in Tennessee.* Knoxville: The University of Tennessee Press, 1980.

McDonough, James L., and Thomas L. Connelly. *Five Tragic Hours—The Battle of Franklin.* Knoxville: The University of Tennessee Press, 1983.

McWhiney, Grady. *Braxton Bragg and Confederate Defeat.* New York: Columbia University Press, 1969.

Parks, Joseph H. *General Leonidas Polk, C.S.A.: The Fighting Bishop.* Baton Rouge: Louisiana State University Press, 1962.

Piston, William Garrett. *Lee's Tarnished Lieutenant—James Longstreet and His Place in Southern History.* Athens: University of Georgia Press, 1987.

Polk, William M. *Leonidas Polk: Bishop and General.* New York: Longmans, Green, and Co., 1915.

Rowell, John. *Yankee Artillerymen*. Knoxville: The University of Tennessee Press, 1975.

Sherman, William T. *Memoirs of General William T. Sherman*. Westport, Connecticut: Greenwood Press, 1957.

Starr, Stephen Z. *The Union Cavalry in the Civil War, Vol. 3: The War in the West*. Baton Rouge: Louisiana State University Press, 1985.

Symonds, Craig L. *A Battlefield Atlas of the Civil War*. Baltimore: Nautical and Aviation Publishing Company of America, 1983.

Tennessee: A Guide to the State. New York: Viking Press, 1939.

Tucker, Glenn. *Chickamauga: Bloody Battle in the West*. New York: Bobbs–Merrill, 1961.

Van Horne, Thomas B. *The Life of Major General George H. Thomas*. New York: Charles Scribner's Sons, 1882.

Warner, Ezra J. *Generals in Blue*. Baton Rouge: Louisiana State University Press, 1965.

———. *Generals in Gray*. Baton Rouge: Louisiana State University Press, 1959.

Watkins, Samuel R. *Co. Aytch*. New York: Collier Books, 1962.

Williams, T. Harry. *Beauregard: Napoleon in Gray*. Baton Rouge: Louisiana State University Press, 1955.

Wyeth, John A. *Life of General Nathan Bedford Forrest*. Dayton: Morningside Bookshop, 1975.

Index

Numbers in **boldface** indicate an illustration.